$f\mathbf{P}$

What We Lost

in the Great

Suburban

Migration,

1966–1999

THE FREE PRESS

THE OLD NEIGHBORHOOD

RAY SUAREZ

THE FREE PRESS
A Division of Simon & Schuster Inc.
1230 Avenue of the Americas
New York, NY 10020

THE FREE PRESS and colophon are trademarks
of Simon & Schuster Inc.

Manufactured in the United States of America

10 9 8 7 6 5 4 2 1

Library of Congress Cataloging-in-Publication Data
Suarez, Ray. 1957–
The old neighborhood: what we lost in the great suburban
migration. 1966–1999/Ray Suarez.
p. cm.
1. Cities and towns–United States. 2. Neighborhood–United States.
3. City and town life–United States. I. Title.
HT 121.S83   1999
307.76'0973–dc21   98–53349
CIP

ISBN 0-684-83402-2

Contents

Contents

Acknowledgments

My family paid a lot of the price for the writing of this book. My kids didn't have me around for many weekends. A lot of other weekends, there I was, pounding away at a laptop on the living room couch, but not really available to them. So, Rafael and Eva, I hope when you're old enough to read this book you will realize how much your ability to roll with the punches contributed to it being written.

My wife, Carole, has been along at literally every step of the way since I was a copy boy. This book is a product of her love and faith as sure as it's a product of nights and weekends on the couch. My parents, Rafael Sr. and Gloria, get special thanks for never leaving the city, through thick and thin. They also get my love and gratitude for teaching me how to read and write.

Turning journalists into authors, I imagine, can require daunting alchemy. My editor, Bruce Nichols, must have the philosopher's stone. With good humor, patience, and terrific instincts about turning a vast and rambling manuscript into a coherent piece of work, he helped make this into a book.

My agent, Jonathan Lazear, told me people would want to read this book. And he backed that belief up with skillful steering of the product from a three-page proposal into the book you hold in your hands.

Acknowledgments

One of the parts of being a reporter that is a constant surprise is the willingness of people to open their lives to a curious stranger. During the months of research and interviews, I was struck by the generosity, honesty, and willingness to share of people all around the country. I rang their bells, wandered into their yards, and joined them sitting on the front porch. People dropped what they were doing to give me rides. They took long lunches, skipped mornings at work, and introduced me to other people they felt I should know for my story.

The reminiscences from so many people who loved and lost their old neighborhoods were funny, touching, and sometimes painful. Thanks to the Manelli family, Chip Bromley, Bob Hartley, Bobbi Reichtell, the Wos family, David Shucker, Fr. David Baldwin, Bishop John Manz, Gary Schwab, Gregory Pitts, Jeanette Fields, Daniel Lauber, the Davis family, Tom O'Connell, Regina Lind, Rick Rosenfeld, Veronica Evans, the Petroff family, Art Atkinson, Joe Waters, Ferd Kramer, the Gallagher family, Felix Bartholomew, Auguretto Batiste, Elijah Anderson, Chakah Fattah, Helene Hoffman, the Zielinski family, Arnold Duncan, Dempsey Travis, Tom Bier, and so many others.

Special thanks to the John D. and Catherine T. MacArthur Foundation, the University of Chicago, and the Benton Fellowships for their assistance with my research.

Chapter 1

What We Lost

The fix was in. The whispers rasped over a million dinner tables and the numbers were crunched over a thousand conference tables as another family decided, "That's enough," and cities continued to slide down the population tables. Maybe you've heard of cities as the hole in the doughnut. Or maybe you've heard of chocolate cities and vanilla suburbs. Perhaps you've heard a recent speaker of the House denounce the cities as parasitic bodies living off their hardworking American host.

They now speak with an accent. Their plaster is shot. Their windows rattle in the sash. We eat in their restaurants, wondering if the car is safe. We listen to their symphonies and regret that long drive home. We remember a million years in ten million childhoods. We feel a mixture of sadness, nostalgia, and relief when we take that final turn and swing onto the freeway entrance ramp. We head home: to a place where we can choose our neighbors.

When you talk about the city, the conversation ends with an exasperated litany. In the city, the kids don't learn to read and still want more and more of our taxes to pay for their crumbling buildings, and to pay the salaries of the members of the teacher's unions. Violent young men commit random acts of mayhem. The cities satisfy America's craving for drugs, cheap labor, and expensive entertainment. In front of the late TV news we shake our heads in disgust over their comically corrupt politics, goofball racial agitators, and the parade of black and brown suspects into the back of squad cars.

Starting in 1945, one of the Great Migrations of American history took place, and it continues to shape the country to this day, politically, economically, and socially. Unlike the nineteenth-century flow of Conestoga wagons through the Cumberland Gap and on to the West, and unlike the early-twentieth-century black migration from the Jim Crow South to the urban North, this was a choreographed combination of minimigrations: white migrants left the old neighborhood behind and left the very idea of "neighborhoods" behind. They left the old giants—New York, Philadelphia, Chicago, and Detroit—and the industrial centers—Pittsburgh, Cleveland, Buffalo, and St. Louis. While the settlers a century ago, and blacks earlier this century, left all that was familiar to start again in a strange new world, these modern migrants sometimes headed just a little past the city line. Their old world was not "gone" but now just a car ride away. But the force of each small journey combined to slam the old cities of America like a hurricane. While those earlier migrations survive in family stories and fading photographs, this last one lives vividly in present memory. Maybe you or your parents were part of it. . . .

Nostalgia, mixed with geographic proximity and racial resentment, creates a toxic potion. The pioneers of the postwar urban migration are convinced there was once a better city than the one we see today. We know there was because we used to live there. The old city lives on in the speeches of politicians and in flickering black-and-white reruns on a hundred cable channels. There's Chester Riley. And Ralph Kramden. And Lucy Ricardo. And Lou Costello. And Mrs. Goldberg. Urbanites all. They walk to the grocery store. They know their neighbors. They may have even walked to church (or shul).

It's not hard to get people to tell the stories of that good, gone life. In Cleveland's Buckeye neighborhood. In Philadelphia's Mantua on the west bank of the Schuylkill River. In Miami's Opa-Locka and the Grand Concourse in the Bronx. Back on Ninety-first Street in Chicago. Maybe you lived there. You may even drive by every now and then. Or maybe you find you want to less and less. It doesn't look like the place where you stood after your first Holy Communion, hair slicked into place, smiling through the gaps in your teeth.

> *There was constant talk during those years: Who was going? Who was staying? I think it made me cynical beyond my years. People would say, "We are not moving! We are not going! We are staying here forever!" Then they'd move at night! When the chips were down they would leave.*

> **Bob Hartley, on Chicago's Austin neighborhood in the 1970s**

Everybody's got a story. Some are bathed in sepia, others filled with "be-gats," like an Old Testament book. The alibis are short, starting with, "Well, you know," and ending with "the schools," "the crime," or "the neighbor-hood." Where does folktale stop and reality begin? Now that the damage is done, and the cities are hollowed out, it still matters enough to you to point fingers, though you may not always be sure you're pointing them in the right directions. Can you assign culpability to a crime with ten million accomplices?

The year 1950 was the last full cry of urban America, at least on the surface. It was the year many of the cities visited in this book reached their historic peaks in population. Everybody was working, in folk memory, and in fact. Armies clad in overalls poured out of plants at quitting time or watched as the next shift filed in. Houses cost a couple of thousand bucks, or in high-cost cities some fifteen thousand. The mortgage was often less than a hundred a month. The teeming ethnic ghettos of the early century had given way to a more comfortable life, with religion and ethnicity, race and class still used as organizing principles for the neighborhood. The rough edges of the immigrant "greenhorns" were worn smooth, and a confident younger generation now entered a fuller, richer American life. Grandma and Grandpa had their accents and old ways intact, and still mumbled sayings in the language your parents used when they didn't want you to understand. You could still find *Il Progresso, Freiheit, Norske Tidende,* and *Polish Daily Zgoda* on the newsstands, but the neighborhoods themselves were no longer alien places. It was the ghetto, yes, but made benign by assimilation.

It was this world that the first surge tide into the suburbs left behind. They were people for whom the city had done its work, making Americans out of families from Dublin to Donetsk. America had given the urban young educations, and expectations. For many, those expectations had been nurtured through world war and economic depression. Something better was needed for the baby boomers.

Charles and Anne Marie Manelli both grew up in St. Louis neighborhoods. When they came back to the Midwest from a stint in Denver, young son in tow, they headed right back to Anne Marie's neighborhood on the far north side, not far from the city line, and now found something lacking. "I don't think we would have stayed in the city even if we could have found a big enough house on the same block where we were living," Anne Manelli says. "We wanted change. The neighborhood was getting older, though I guess at that time it wasn't really that old, maybe twenty-five years old or so."

Charles Manelli recalls the spirit of the times. "People our age at that time all wanted to buy houses, and there just weren't any houses available in the city of St. Louis. So they all moved, and bought homes out in the county. The city was really emptying out quickly at that time. So sure, there were houses, but they were not the houses that the young people would have wanted. There was a lot of old real estate in the city, and the new subdivisions was where the young people wanted to go.

"We bought our first home on the GI Bill, that's the way everyone was going then. You had two bathrooms, three bedrooms, it was different. And you could buy these houses for twenty thousand dollars, eighteen thousand dollars. That's what the young people wanted. They didn't want the big brick bungalows."

The Manellis were not alone. Millions moved from central cities to newly created suburbs, and from the northeast quarter of the country to the south and west. In 1950, the populations of New York, Chicago, Philadelphia, Washington, Boston, Cleveland, St. Louis, Buffalo, Pittsburgh, and Baltimore reached their historic highs. Some, like Detroit, Pittsburgh, St. Louis, and Cleveland, would soon enter free fall, shrinking by 50 percent or more. Others, like Boston, Baltimore, and Philadelphia, had simply grown as much as the economic realities of the day would allow, and entered a phase of slow and steady population decline, while the suburbs around them grew.

1.	New York	7,891,957		11.	San Francisco	775,357
2.	Chicago	3,620,962		12.	Pittsburgh	676,806
3.	Philadelphia	2,071,605		13.	Milwaukee	632,392
4.	Los Angeles	1,970,358		14.	Houston	596,163
5.	Detroit	2,000,398		15.	Buffalo	580,132
6.	Baltimore	949,708		16.	New Orleans	570,445
7.	Cleveland	914,808		17.	Minneapolis	521,718
8.	St. Louis	856,796		18.	Cincinnati	503,998
9.	Washington, D.C.	802,178		19.	Seattle	468,000
10.	Boston	800,000		20.	Kansas City, Mo.	457,000

Take a look at the list of America's twenty largest cities in 1950, shown above. With the exception of Los Angeles, every city in the top ten is on, or east of, the Mississippi River. Among the top twenty, only Los Angeles, San Francisco, Houston, and Seattle fall out of the nation's northeast quadrant, running from Minneapolis in the north, along the Mississippi, to St. Louis in the south, east to the Atlantic Coast and north to Boston. Almost half of the top twenty had been sizable cities by the middle of the nineteenth century. Only five cities had populations of over a million, and only one city west of the Mississippi had reached that plateau.

These were the top twenty cities for 1960:

1.	New York	7,781,984		11.	San Francisco	740,316
2.	Chicago	3,550,404		12.	Milwaukee	741,324
3.	Los Angeles	2,479,015		13.	Boston	697,197
4.	Philadelphia	2,002,512		14.	Dallas	679,684
5.	Detroit	1,670,000		15.	New Orleans	627,525
6.	Baltimore	939,024		16.	Pittsburgh	604,332
7.	Houston	938,219		17.	San Antonio	587,718
8.	Cleveland	876,000		18.	San Diego	573,224
9.	Washington, D.C.	763,956		19.	Seattle	557,087
10.	St. Louis	750,026		20.	Buffalo	532,759

By 1960, Los Angeles had surged ahead of Philadelphia, growing by almost a third in size. Houston, through rapid growth and significantly, by annexation (it more than doubled from 160 to 328 square miles in area), jumped seven places. San Antonio and San Diego joined the top twenty, giving Texas and California three cities each on the list. The exodus from "old" urban America to the suburbs and the new cities of the Sun Belt was on.

Cities like Philadelphia and Detroit were shrinking in overall population, but the urban cores of metropolitan areas were still growing. Washington and St. Louis were already showing the early signs of their long, slow declines, while their metropolitan areas grew, and towns once little more than names on a map began to grow with increasing speed. By 1960 it is clear that the axis of growth in the country was moving away from the North and East toward the South and West.

The twenty largest cities in 1970:

1.	New York	7,894,862	11.	Indianapolis	744,624
2.	Chicago	3,366,957	12.	Milwaukee	717,099
3.	Los Angeles	2,816,061	13.	San Francisco	715,674
4.	Philadelphia	1,950,098	14.	San Diego	696,769
5.	Detroit	1,511,482	15.	San Antonio	654,153
6.	Houston	1,232,802	16.	Boston	641,071
7.	Baltimore	905,759	17.	Memphis	623,530
8.	Dallas	844,401	18.	St. Louis	622,236
9.	Washington, D.C.	756,510	19.	New Orleans	593,471
10.	Cleveland	750,903	20.	Phoenix	581,562

By 1970, as your late-night local news weatherman would say, the map is really in motion. Houston nearly doubled in size since 1960, again through annexation, but also through robust population growth. The populations of Philadelphia, Detroit, Washington, Cleveland, St. Louis, and Boston are heading to the new suburbs surrounding those old cities. Los Angeles, Houston, Dallas, San Diego, and San Antonio continue their steady growth. Indianapolis (another product of suburban annexation) jumped from nowhere to eleventh on the list.

Here's 1980:

1.	New York	7,071,639	11.	San Antonio	685,809
2.	Chicago	3,005,078	12.	Indianapolis	700,719
3.	Los Angeles	2,966,848	13.	San Francisco	678,974
4.	Philadelphia	1,688,210	14.	Memphis	646,356
5.	Houston	1,595,167	15.	Washington	638,333
6.	Detroit	1,203,339	16.	Milwaukee	636,212
7.	Dallas	904,074	17.	San Jose	629,442
8.	San Diego	875,538	18.	Cleveland	573,822
9.	Phoenix	789,704	19.	Columbus	564,866
10.	Baltimore	786,775	20.	Boston	562,904

The dynamic we saw at work in 1970 had taken hold more fully by 1980. New York City lost more than eight hundred thousand people in the 1970s. Think of it: a loss larger than the entire city of Phoenix at that time. Factories continued to close. Fortune 500 corporate headquarters continued their steady flight from the city. New Yorkers left for other regions of the country and for the burgeoning suburbs of northern New Jersey, Westchester County, and Nassau and Suffolk counties, which the census bureau would soon classify as a separate metropolitan statistical area—no longer an appendage of the city. The economic decline of New York's bread-and-butter industries, like clothing, printing, and shipping, landed heavily on all New Yorkers. The poor saw themselves as stuck. The rich could surround themselves with physical barriers, continuing to live a charmed life in a declining city. The middle class lacked the cash to insulate themselves from the diminishing quality of services, but they had one thing the poor did not: mobility.

In the 1970s, large-scale population loss continued in Chicago, Philadelphia, Detroit, and Baltimore, while the metropolitan areas of all these shrinking big cities continued to grow. Columbus, its economy built on state government and insurance, was on its way to becoming the largest city in Ohio, while metal-bashing, blue-collar Cleveland continued its decline. In just ten years, Phoenix jumped from twentieth place to ninth on the list. San Jose, a small city of just ninety-five thousand in 1950, living in the shadow of nearby San Francisco, was now nipping at its heels (in part by growing from 17 to 171 square miles). This was Cleveland's last appearance in the top twenty, and St. Louis had already dropped from it, never to be seen again.

By 1990, America's urban future is more clearly visible. The 1990 census is the last time any city with fewer than one million inhabitants will appear on the list of the largest American cities. But at a time when magazine covers and conferences bemoan the "decline of urban America," not all of urban America is in decline. Just the old one. Los Angeles, Houston, San Diego, Dallas, Phoenix, San Jose, and San Antonio continued their rapid growth in the 1980s. Chicago, Philadelphia, Detroit, Baltimore, Milwaukee, Washington, and Boston continued to shrink. From an urban population concentrated in the northeast quadrant of the country in 1950, America's biggest cities have become a far more diverse group, now straddling the coasts and the southern tier of states. The Metropolis of the Prairie—Chicago—will be the only city of the ten largest cities outside the Old South and the coasts in 2000, but it will have lost nearly one million people since 1950. Philadelphia, according to census estimates, will have shrunk by a third. Detroit's population will have dropped in half, that of St. Louis by almost two-thirds. Washington continues its rapid decline and may be down to half a million people by the turn of the century. In other words, the capital of the world's remaining superpower will be home to fewer people than the capital of Ohio. Sparks, smells, the hum of the mill, and the clank of the machine are *out*. "Clean" industry, government employment, retirees, and service industries are *in*.

The twenty largest American cities in 1990:

1.	New York	7,322,564	11.	San Jose	782,248
2.	Los Angeles	3,485,498	12.	Baltimore	736,014
3.	Chicago	2,783,726	13.	Indianapolis	731,327
4.	Houston	1,630,553	14.	San Francisco	723,959
5.	Philadelphia	1,585,577	15.	Jacksonville	635,230
6.	San Diego	1,110,549	16.	Columbus	652,910
7.	Detroit	1,027,974	17.	Milwaukee	628,088
8.	Dallas	1,006,877	18.	Memphis	610,337
9.	Phoenix	983,403	19.	Washington	606,900
10.	San Antonio	935,933	20.	Boston	574,283

Hidden in the raw numbers, there is another math at work dictating the fates and fortunes of the country's big cities: Race. As the cities that have become the home to the largest minority populations are consistently described as places of "blight" and "decay," the largest and fastest-growing cities, with few exceptions, are inhabited by whites in percentages higher than that of white people in the overall national population.

Some cities now face declines in their overall black population as well: In Chicago, Washington, D.C., and Cleveland, for example, middle-class blacks can use the same mobility wielded by their white counterparts twenty and thirty years ago to head for the suburbs.

I felt kind of threatened that my neighborhood was being invaded by these people. It proved difficult for one kid, that moved in that was a new pupil, and his name was Andre Baker. I really made it rough. We had a big fight, it came to blows. I really beat the crap out of him, and that was it. And then, as time went on, we became best friends. We got together, we were friends all the way through high school.

As the neighborhood started to change the first black families moved away just like the white families did, and they started to be replaced by a lower class of black people, and it started to get rough. I really got beat up a lot. Then the reverse happens. They become very aggressive, and I was the little white kid. I was really intimidated. And all my friends were gone. I felt very alone. My only friends were at high school. It was really rough. I had to ride that bus and walk from the bus every day.

Walt Zielinski, Cleveland

American Latinos, too, are a highly urbanized people. Their presence has grown markedly in the obvious places, like Southern California and Florida, and in the not-so-obvious places, like Milwaukee, Chicago, and Washington, D.C. When you compare the gross population data from the census counts, from 1950 to 1990, and break down those figures by racial composition, a striking number of figures emerges. Cities that appear to have maintained their populations end up occupying a very different place in the imaginations of the largest single population group in the country, the white middle class. While population plateaus or gentle decline from historic highs give the appearance of a certain viability, another look at the statistics illustrates a verdict pronounced by the white middle class:

	white	black	Latinos	% white
New York				
1950	7,116,441	747,608	n.a.*	90
1990	3,827,088	2,102,512	1,783,511	52
Chicago				
1950	3,111,525	492,265	n.a.	85
1990	1,263,524	1,087,711	545,852	45
Philadelphia				
1950	1,692,637	376,041	n.a.	81
1990	848,586	631,936	89,193	53
Los Angeles				
1950	1,758,773	171,209	n.a.	89
1990	1,841,182	487,674	1,391,411	52
Washington				
1950	517,865	280,803	n.a.	64
1990	179,667	399,604	32,710	29
Baltimore				
1950	723,655	225,099	n.a.	76
1990	287,753	435,768	7,602	39

*In 1950, the census did not count this group.

Between 1950 and 1990, the population of New York stayed roughly level, the white population halved, and the black population doubled. As Chicago lost almost one million people from the overall count, it lost almost two million whites. As the population of Los Angeles almost doubled, the number of whites living there grew by fewer than ninety thousand. Baltimore went from a city of three times as many whites as blacks in 1950 to a city that will have twice as many blacks as whites in the year 2000. All this has happened while the number of blacks in the United States has stayed a roughly constant percentage, between 11 and 13 percent.

By contrast, here are the breakdowns for some of the fastest-growing cities in the country during those same forty years:

	whites	blacks	Latino	% white
Houston				
1950	470,503	124,766	n.a.*	78
1990	859,069	457,990	450,483	52
San Diego				
1960	528,512	34,435	n.a.	92
1990	745,406	104,261	229,519	67
San Jose				
1960	197,403	1,955	n.a.	96
1990	491,280	36,790	208,388	62

*In 1950, the census did not count this group.

The population of whites declined as these cities moved in the years af-ter the war from small and midsized regional population centers to major national players. Though the overall percentage of white population has declined in all of them, the number of whites has more than doubled in San Jose and grew by almost four hundred thousand in Houston. Latinos in large numbers—almost half a million in Houston—don't yet seem to scare off a growing and stable white middle class.

It's no longer worthwhile to ask, "What do Americans want?" There are too many of them who want too many different things and are simply too different from one another to get an answer that makes any sense. But it is valid to say tens of millions of Americans—tens of millions of white middle-class Americans—don't want to live in cities at all. Millions more don't want to live in cities with large minority populations.

Scott Thomas, author of *The Rating Guide to Life in America's Small Cities*, found that many of the fastest-growing small cities, where the residents report a very high quality of life, are also some of the whitest places in America.

"I was looking at 219 different areas, and only about a quarter of them had the proportion of black population comparable to what you find in the country as a whole. With the Hispanic population, there are very few small towns, most of them near the Mexican border, with anywhere near even the national average."

Thomas says that looking at these "micropolitan" areas demands a wider set of variables when assessing people and the way they live. "Diversity is something that goes beyond some of the simple racial categories. I think adults are generally less educated in the communities I profiled. You're going to find less depth of experience or fewer adults who have gone beyond college degrees, and if that's something that's important to you you're not going to find it except in the college towns like Pullman, Washington, or Ames, Iowa, or Ithaca, New York." Thomas points out that the populations of these small cities, many now enjoying robust growth, are almost entirely native-born. New York and Los Angeles, meanwhile, the two largest cities in the United States, are now home to millions of foreign-born and first-generation Americans.

When discussing their own family's history in America, many people plead "not guilty" to the charge of being an accessory to the postwar meltdown of many older cities. "We just wanted a better life," they say, "and this was the only way to get it." It is easy to forget how many people made their first class adjustment by moving up, but not out: the west side of Cleveland, the neighborhoods along City Line Road in Philadelphia, a string of neighborhoods at the south end of Brooklyn. For hundreds of thousands of families, these neighborhoods became the waiting room for getting out. Getting out didn't have to be the only choice facing a family, since many cities offered a wide range of housing stock and a wide range of lifestyle options. When your family's fortunes began to improve, you could live with people at roughly your own income, without leaving the city.

There was crime in the old neighborhood, but not the kind of crime that's launched ten thousand nightly reports "live, from the scene," on your eleven o'clock news. The unlocked door is a potent symbol in the collective memory of the white-flight generation. As if you've never heard it before, or perhaps knowing you've heard it a million times, as a rhythm of ritual and truth builds during your second decade on the rosary. "We *never* had to lock our doors. Everybody knew everybody. We weren't afraid." Afraid was later. Afraid was coming.

Schools were far from perfect back then. Before 1940, only a minority of the fresh-faced ninth graders who walked in one end walked out as eighteen-year-olds with a high school diploma in their hands. There was teenage pregnancy, but it ended in marriage more often, which helped camouflage its presence in the neighborhood scene.

For all its shortcomings, life worked. Millions in the American middle class stand on the shoulders of urban America and its public institutional life. The parks and their leagues and summer camps. Varsity teams and school bands. Cub Scouts, Boy Scouts, Camp Fire Girls, Girl Scouts, and Brownies, in units sponsored by public schools and PTAs. Public libraries. Public schools. Public universities that extended the privilege of higher education to an academic elite rather than one created by "good" families and fat bank accounts.

Today, at the other end of the migration, the change is palpable. The era of American urban decline tracks nicely with the decline of a consensus culture. There was a time when the broad American masses all "knew" the same things. *Colliers, Life, Look,* and the *Saturday Evening Post* didn't deliver wildly different versions of America in their pages, nor did any of those magazines drop a very different America into the mailbox from the one you heard about on the big radio and television networks. There was a widely shared set of norms in the 1940s, 1950s, and even the wildly oversold "counter culture" 1960s that gave Americans very definite instructions about what to think. These instructions could be a straitjacket, and they could be merciless to those who colored outside the lines; but the broad consensus culture for white, economically active Americans made community life more reassuring than confining.

For all the wild racial mythology that marked these same decades—the deep separation that actually existed between Americans—those outside the white mainstream bought into the same bourgeois dreams as their distant neighbors. Black workforce participation, marriage, divorce, single parenthood, and other rates far more closely resembled that of the national average than they do today.

I've spoken to hundreds of white city residents who see their lives as conditional, temporary, and fragile. "We can only stay until Jenny hits third grade, then we're out of here," says one. "As long as my son is small, and I can keep an eye out, we're fine. Once he starts moving around by himself more, we can't really stay," says another. The examples are legion: we're staying as long as . . . , we can only stay if . . . , we're only here until . . . , if we couldn't afford private school, we'd be gone. Implied in each qualifier is the assumption of mobility, the understanding that the moment a family wants to pull the plug on urban life, it can. It's an option not as easily invoked across the racial divide or lower down the economic scale.

Eventually, goes the story for today's urban sojourners, "compensation fatigue" sets in. The strain of having eyes in the back of your head, higher insurance, rotten local services, and the day-upon-day-upon-day stream of bad news finally carries you across a line you were inclined to cross one day anyway. Your parents are already "out there"; so are your brothers and sisters and your friends from high school. The bragging rights of the hardy urbanite are trumped by the brownie points of "doing the right thing."

Back in the city, choices for thousands of other families were already narrow and kept on narrowing. The white working class could head to the new blue-collar suburbs just over the city line, but those new communities would be effectively closed to black home buyers for years to come. In the cities being abandoned, lower-middle-income and poor city dwellers lost the political clout of their middle-class neighbors, who had held institutions like public schools to an acceptable baseline of quality; at the same time, they were losing the kind of economic opportunities that might have allowed them to choose private or parochial education for their children, as businesses followed their owners and their middle managers to the suburbs.

There was a period early on, when it was mixed half-and-half maybe, and you could see that it was working, and it was fine. Then all of a sudden there was a big rush and it was totally changed. But there were so many things . . . the principal at my old school, at Louella, he was a bastard! He had been kicked out of another school, I think by the community, in a black area. I remember him saying to us at meetings, "There's a monster out there waiting to devour you and you better stick together." He was talking about the changes in the community!

Metta Davis, on the Chicago public schools in the early 1970s

After taking a ferocious pounding in the 1960s, the bottom was dropping out of America's shared assumptions in the 1970s. We no longer "all knew" the same things. The further we moved from each other in distance, in racial segregation, and in class stratification, the more different our various Americas became. By the 1980s, along with the steady erosion of the consensus culture there came a lack of affinity and empathy for all those who couldn't share our assumptions. That lack of affinity for those over the line dovetailed nicely with the fiscal realities of new suburban life. The suburban homeowner could target his spending in a way no urban taxpayer ever could: he could decide to send his money to the things that mattered to him—his own kid's school, his local public park—and deny money to things he wanted no part of—urban school systems and public libraries.

It might have been a comforting illusion to believe there was once an America where we were "all in it together." To the extent that it was ever true, the myth was shattered in the thirty years from 1950 to 1980. By the 1980s, not only was it crystal clear that we weren't "all in it together," nobody even had the desire or the energy to pretend it was true.

A feedback loop was established that destroyed the heart of some of America's great cities: Those Americans given a leg up in the new economy—arbitrageurs and software writers, intellectual property lawyers and plastic surgeons—pulled up stakes from shared institutions, weakening them, and took their presence, influence, and money elsewhere. For each family that decided to stick it out, the decision to stay became harder and harder to make as the quality of common life sagged. The migrants were the Americans most likely to demand solutions for municipal problems, most likely to vote, and most likely to get attention. The more this group left its fellow Clevelanders, Philadelphians, New Yorkers, and St. Louisans behind, the more those left behind needed them.

When we no longer lived and worked in proximity to one another, we no longer knew the same things. Once we no longer knew the same things, we no longer had a need for cultural cohesion. Once we no longer had cultural cohesion, it was easier and easier to draw circles of concern more and more narrowly around one's own doorstep. . . .

Let me explain what was happening in Louisville at the time. Urban renewal had come and torn down half of downtown, and blacks started moving west. The minute that happened you could hear people saying it, adults, children repeating what they had heard at home, "The niggers are coming. The niggers are coming," as if it was the plague or something. The questions people asked revolved around it: "When are they going to get here? What does it mean for me?"

Regina Lind, on Louisville in the 1960s

This latest Great Migration has left deep, unacknowledged scars in the lives of millions of families. They were obeying the American siren call to mobility; they were only doing the best thing for their children; they were spending new money in search of space—but the scars were still there. Not all the changes were for the better; not all the motivations were unsullied.

Millions of us feared, fled, and hated. Today we look back on it all in hurt and wonder. How did this happen? Where did that good life go? When an accidental detour or a missed expressway exit brings us into contact with the world we left behind, we can still place all the blame firmly and squarely elsewhere. The shuttered factories and collapsing row houses, the vacant storefronts and rutted streets are regarded with the same awe reserved for the scenes of natural disasters. We look out on a world that somehow, in the American collective memory, destroyed itself.

When we left in '76 there were still houses there. The grammar school is right down here. . . . I got seven kids through that school, I raised seven kids here . . . we had one more after that. Seven sons and a daughter. The Furmans lived here . . . can't remember all their names . . . Scotty and his brother. One of the things you've got to consider in all this is the upward mobility, the desire to be in a better place than your mom and dad were, to want more for yourself and your kids, too. So the upward mobility might not be hinged on what the racial makeup of a neighborhood is, but the desire to improve themselves.

And then there are the senior citizens, what with the constant barrage from kids who had either moved out early and moved to the suburbs or simply moved into some other white sections, saying all the time, you better get out of there. It's not safe for you to be there.

Tom O'Connell, touring his old block in Chicago

It wasn't all the desire for a bigger kitchen and a parking space for the car the family could finally afford that had families in their tens of thousands loading up the moving vans and heading out. What is quite apparent, and what no one wants to admit, is that the forces behind white flight were in part malign: redliners, panic peddlers, and blockbusters.

Mary Gallagher recalled the struggles she joined with her husband, Phil, during the 1970s and 1980s to shore up a Brooklyn neighborhood targeted by business interests. "One of the battles, there was a plague of real estate people who descended on us, in all these little storefronts there'd be another Realtor moving into this area. One of the fights we had in our street was over a house diagonally across from us which was put up for sale and one of those Century 21 signs went up and people were afraid there would be, suddenly, twenty signs on their street, that property values would plummet because of that. We tried to get the guy to remove that sign, he didn't want to take it down so we went to the Realtor."

Phil Gallagher remembers trying a less confrontational approach at first. "We tried talking to Realtors for about a year, and that turned out to be completely nonproductive I'd say. We began to realize that there was an enormous difference between dealing with bankers, who didn't take what we did, the pressure we were bringing, personally, and dealing with real estate brokers who always took it personally. We chickened out when we started to be threatened with having our legs broken and things like that. We decided to play it more institutionally and we began writing these somewhat amateurish legal briefs; we're not trained as attorneys in any way [but we] started going after the banks."

Real estate agents hoped to contain racial change by writing off marginal neighborhoods, the way crews in the Rockies set new fires to put existing fires out. Banks redlined. Builders didn't build where the demand was and instead set off to create new demand elsewhere. Churches were silent from the pulpit. Industries fled from unions, minorities, work rules, and high wages. First the federal government subsidized "greenfield" housing, then built the highways to get you there. After waving its magic wand to create acres of mind-numbingly banal new towns in rings around the city, the Feds developed the black arts in the core city, with badly conceived and administered loan programs, bringing chaos and destruction to previously stable areas.

Older neighborhoods did not suddenly fill up with black renters and aspiring home buyers by accident. A couple of generations of racial inequality came roaring back to bite us. GIs getting married had to choose between overcrowded urban housing and new suburban construction. Mayors tried to straddle the desires of middle-class whites who were offended by suddenly not winning every argument, and underserved black and Latino residents who were bursting out of the ghettos.

Even good intentions can end up leaving scars. The impulse to start over that once got millions of our families here in the first place, and sent people streaming out of the exhausted farm areas of New England and the stinking tanneries, rendering pits, and sewers of the big cities of the East, has allowed Americans to sever more completely the connection between place and well-being than any other people on earth.

The creation myths of people the world over, not to mention American Indians, feature first-men and -women who are products of the very soil that is still their home. This is potent stuff, the starting point for a narrative that follows the life of a place and the people who live on it from a time before memory until today. Americans are missing that gene. One place, we've told ourselves, is interchangeable with another, and the landscape we've built in the last fifty years seems to bear that out.

If you were to be kidnapped in Southern California, your captors might not even have to blindfold you. You could drive for hours and not think you had gone anywhere. If you were to break away and reach a phone, your surroundings—a 76 gas station, a Taco Bell, a Pep Boys, a used-car lot, and mountains in the smoggy distance—would be of no use at all to the police.

Making a home in America today is nothing more than the exercise of options, a bewildering array of appliances, bathroom towels, sofa sets, local schools, and bus, train, and car routes to work. We choose–pick a life off the shelf. We act on desire and personal decision, consuming our way into little customized worlds, as individual as a thumbprint, yet as interchangeable as shoes in a shoe store.

But that would mean that millions of Americans happily "choose" to sit in crawling traffic, or freely opt to make cathedral ceilings the chic home builders' accessory of 1990, or request a life that forces women to drive their children from place to place to place, since *no place* is within walking distance.

The Manellis, even after thirty-five years in their St. Louis County subdivision, yearn for the closeness, the coherence, that an old urban neighborhood gave their lives.

ANNE: There's no place around here to walk to. Not even a grocery store.
CHUCK: There's an area downtown called Columbus Square, and I'd love to live there, but the surrounding area is just terrible. It would be great for us, we could walk right downtown. It would be nice, but I wouldn't move there because the surrounding area's bad. No way you could walk around there at night. Downtown St. Louis closes up at night. Unless there's a ball game or something down there, but now, after the ball game, everyone leaves.
ANNE: I found out within the last three or four years that I had cataracts, and I couldn't drive. So I was stuck here, in this house, waiting for Chuck to take me any place and every place I wanted to go. That I was not prepared for. I got the eyes operated on, so now I can see and I can drive.
CHUCK: It was just a wonderful place. These kids are missing so much now. I just can't believe . . . I know it will never go back to the way it was, but that's a shame because it was great. It's the reason for a lot of the problems we have now.

Life has increasingly become a string of pearls, incidents and encounters staged in a wide range of almost random physical locations, strung together by the automobile. We get in our cars and watch the passing urban scene, not realizing the ride is poisoning the very landscape we

19

watched through its windows. The automobile, that ultimate isolator, turned life into a TV show, a mediated set of images seen through the "screen" of our windshields. The deadening touch of the automobile created empty, uninviting streets. Those now auto-mobile dictated a world built for their infernal combustion convenience, a bad fit for the chock-a-block life of an old-style city. Then the migrants lit out for the "built to suit" wide-open spaces of Auto Suburbanalia.

The dense space of the city, built for an age of easy economic intercourse, was eventually infected and weakened by the automobile. It couldn't beat 'em, so it joined 'em . . . and lost anyway. The downtowns of city after city—Detroit, Cleveland, Chicago, St. Louis—peter out, ending in a raggedy edge of parking lots. It is a symptom of terrible rot when the space once occupied by offices and stores now becomes yet another lot. Sitting with a few tons of paying customers from nine to five has become the highest and best use for these pieces of land. But the unraveling of urban life, when married with wasteful suburban-style land use, isn't simply confined to the blight of lots.

What does five o'clock look like on Ashland Avenue in Chicago? Flatbush Avenue in Brooklyn? Euclid Avenue in Cleveland? Santa Monica Boulevard in Los Angeles? Five or six lanes of slowly moving traffic and near-empty sidewalks. Try selling furniture with no foot traffic. Or men's clothing. Or kid's shoes. Merchants once courted success by going where the customers lived. To survive they got off the neighborhood streets in search of where the cars go. When neighborhood commercial life erodes, other uses evolve for the space. Into the linear vacuum moves other, less desirable uses. They are often uses that continue to fuel the desire for the holdouts to surrender, and go.

The most serious decline and loss of population has come in the quadrant of the country east of Saint Louis and north of Washington, D.C., the home of America's oldest big cities. But the Sun Belt has not escaped the telltale signs of urban planned obsolescence either.

Crime has gotten worse. The number one concern we get when we're talking to potential buyers up north, or prospects for our communities, their number one concern is security.

Jerry Schwartzwelder develops retirement communities near Tampa, a fast-growing area of Florida far from the white-hot negative publicity of Miami. He told NPR that doesn't make that much difference.

It used to be, go do a seminar up north, which is what I do, and they'd ask you a question, "Well, what about the bugs in Florida?" and all this other stuff, or "What's the weather like?" or "What kind of terrain do you have, et cetera, et cetera, in your part of Florida?"

First question I get today is, "What's the crime like in your area? Is it as bad as they say on television?"

Life in the city, for the millions who lived it, was once something less than the sum of their lifestyle choices: they woke up, they ate, they shoveled coal, loved, hated, prayed, mated, reproduced, died. For most, the home was not a display object but a place to keep the few things they had managed to hold on to from the surpluses produced by their labor. Their material life was made of the things they didn't have to eat, wear, or burn *right this minute*. A concertina maybe? A family Bible? A hunting rifle?

This world, of tiny accumulation, of life lived *very* close to the edge, is not a remote part of our national past. Many people in our midst still remember it. For some it was such a terrifying experience that the rest of their lives has been marked by an odd relationship to money and things. Our *Masterpiece Theatre* social class swoons over the portraits of nineteenth- and early-twentieth-century existence brought to fussy, golden-lit life from the pages of Edith Wharton novels. The real-life mass class of new Americans who lived in New York, Cleveland, Boston, Chicago, St. Louis, Milwaukee, Philadelphia, Newark, and Pittsburgh through the early years of this century would more quickly recognize their own lives in Upton Sinclair's *The Jungle* than in Edith Wharton's *The House of Mirth*, or a TV season's worth of miniseries draped in antimacassars and fringed in bric-a-brac.

The streets and parks and skylines of the early-twentieth-century American city are built on the bones of a worker's army put into harness by the new men of the country's commerce. The moneyed boys made big plans, paid little wages, and built the wonders of their age. Central Park is a beautiful place, but it's also an example of the transformative spirit of American capitalism wrought in boulders and meadows, ponds and promenades. Carnegie's Pittsburgh, Field's Chicago, Busch's St. Louis, Morgan's Manhattan were not yet the mature machines for living they would eventually become for millions of Americans in the new middle class. They were still home to desperate families living by piecework, child laborer's photographed by Lewis Hine and Jacob Riis.

After World War II, the bosses were making so much money that even the workers were in for a taste. Unions, growing along with the employment options created by the enormous concentration of productive capital in the fast-growing cities, made peace for the price of a fatter paycheck. Labor peace created more prosperity, and sowed the seeds for destruction later. The high cost of urban labor became the justification when manufacturing fled the cities. Not just labor's cost, but the inflexibility of work rules, the costs of shedding and hiring workers—all the humanizing guarantees hammered out with management to buy peace—now had a greater cost than anyone had contemplated.

The urban interplay between home and workplace, conceived and nurtured for its efficiencies and unquestioned economic benefits, was now, we were told by the 1950s and 1960s, the city's greatest weakness. Drive around Detroit, and see the twisted skeletons of factory buildings no one can afford to pull down. These derelict factories are often surrounded by neighborhoods similarly emptied of life. Detroit has been left to the poor. The corporations with monstrous piles of capital already invested there are stuck, and try to make the best of it. A walk through the deserted downtown, the sight of large, boarded-up office buildings on block after block, closed hotels, and shuttered stores is a shock. This is where the disease you can see in its early stages in so many other downtowns finally leads.

Today a lot of homeowners will tell you they have bought exactly the life they want, and I have no doubt they believe it. Talk with people about how they once lived, how they grew up, and how they live today. Many people have performed a fascinating sleight of mind. They say life was better "back then," as many remember their own urban past. Because the good urban life is placed in a no-longer-retrievable past, suburban exile is thus made "necessary," and unavoidable. But that former life so precious to them in memory and story is not one they would choose to live today. Making it unobtainable helps sustain the fantasy that the suburban present is an unsought "necessity." The people who made this modern, less satisfying life necessary are always offstage, the blacks, the blockbusters, the developers.

Charles Manelli, more than forty-five years after leaving the neighborhood of his youth around Blessed Sacrament Parish on St. Louis's north side, was still poking around his old neighborhood in the car. He would drive by his house and take the car up the alleys where he played ball as a boy before the war.

CHUCK: It was pretty scary. I just went because I loved it so much, for sentimental reasons. I wanted to look at the old house and the old neighborhood, and reminisce. I don't do it anymore but I did it up until a few years ago. Now I'm afraid to go there.

I have mixed feelings. I'd love to live in St. Louis now, in the same atmosphere we had then. But I know it can't be done. It happened so fast, I mean, my gosh . . . overnight. It was like an exodus . . . zoom, everybody was gone! I'd say it was a five-year period, the whole city of St. Louis changed. And I think it was because of panic. The whole atmosphere of the city changed, and everybody just panicked, and left. Oh, I'd love to live there now, in the same atmosphere as it was, but back then it was just panic.

We don't have that neighborhood life here.

ANNE: It was like living in a small town. We're Catholic, so we lived in a parish. That parish was everything to us. You were like in a small town and everybody knew everybody else, everybody in the whole parish.

CHUCK: You had a parochial school on one corner, and down the street was the public school. It was a neighborhood, and it was like that all over the city. And everybody knew everybody, whether you went to parochial or public school, it was just a big neighborhood; you could walk anyplace in the whole area and you knew everybody. You had places to go . . . drugstores, hamburger places, school grounds. It was unbelievable.

My son's growing up was completely different. He had to take a bus everywhere. It was great. Kids today don't know what they're missing.

In this neighborhood . . . we've been here thirty-five years and we hardly know anybody.

ANNE: The people on the block we know, but the people on the next block we don't know. But, in Mt. Carmel Parish, where I lived, way down, you knew the people who lived in every house on every block . . . you may have lived seven or eight blocks away, but you knew them, I don't know why.

CHUCK: Because you walked those streets. You played with the kids. You knew them. The summer playgrounds were all in the public schools. That's another thing they don't have today . . . everything's organized now. And you've got to drive to it. And you've got to wear uniforms. We just played. We made up our own games. We played ball in the alleys and the vacant lots. We didn't need any supervision.

ANNE: Right now we live right across the street from the parish grounds, and they have this huge park across the street. A ballpark. A soccer field. You'll never see any one person just playing by themselves. When they're there, they're with an organized team, with coaches and the whole thing, everybody's there.

To just go over there . . . a bunch of kids getting together to just hit the ball around, or kick a soccer ball around . . . no. They don't do that.

We lost plenty in those years after World War II. People talk about the closeness, the intimacy of the old urban neighborhood. People talk about their friendships found and lost, the adventures of city life, waiting for the old man to come home from work. We knew each other then. We saw our own faces plainly, in the mirror and in each other's eyes.

Today, with bookstores crowded with new books on the search for lost community, with a whole "communitarian movement" dedicated to reclaiming these lost values, are we ready to be honest with each other about what we've lost? Apparently not yet. We assign to that long list of the differences in daily life in the recent past a particularity that can't survive close inspection. Look at a picture of people today, and compare it with one from "back then." People are people. We were not so different forty years ago. The basic furniture of life was very similar . . . school, jobs, commerce, church and synagogue. We had two arms. Two eyes. Two legs.

So to write this book, I headed out to American cities with a tape recorder and a notebook, and started to gather the stories of families loading and unloading the moving trucks. Often, what people thought, believed, and *felt* simply didn't match what was actually happening on the ground. But an examination of both the interior landscape and the world waiting outside the doorstep is necessary to understand this latest Great Migration.

This is a tour of the places people lived in, loved, and left. These are the places left to face the consequences of postwar America's choice: to run away from home.

The fictional retelling of recent American history as a move toward a color-blind society, the venomous tirades against immigration and affirmative action, the paradoxical urgings of the white middle class to others—be like us, just don't try to be like us and move into our neighborhoods—all call for a dry-eyed accounting of white flight and the hollowing out of the American city.

I have spoken to hundreds of people who mourn the loss of a sense of place tied to block, school, and neighborhood church. When you talk to them further, you may also find that they were busily helping to create the new rootlessness during the years of urban change. Many conclude there was no other way for things to end up. I'll insist until the day they're tossing spadefuls of city soil on my casket that we gave up far too easily, driven by a range of forces in the society we did not recognize.

Chapter 2

Chicago

Heading out to the Southwest side of Chicago on the Stevenson Expressway is an instructive and sobering experience. The landscape immediately gives way to a bewildering network of expressway interchanges. The south Loop, once one of the most densely populated places in North America, is now the confluence point of three great rivers of midwestern traffic: the Kennedy Expressway, leading from downtown to the north and northwestern suburbs; the Dan Ryan Expressway, leading to the South Side and northwest Indiana; and the Stevenson Expressway, leading to the southwest.

The actual "land" that has been able to survive thirty years of relentless highway construction is sliced into oddly shaped, isolated blocks, no longer able to relate to each other. To the west is historic Greektown, now a restaurant-filled rump, home to virtually no one. To the south, the Chicago campus of the University of Illinois system, once officially called the Circle Campus, after the neighboring expressway interchanges, has now been given a more dignified name: the University of Illinois at

Chicago. If you accidentally say the word "Circle," you are quickly corrected by an earnest university public affairs official.

This site, now covered in asphalt, was once the port of entry for tens of thousands of immigrants. It was home to an open-air Jewish peddler's market—the wooden shantytown where the Great Fire began—a teeming Irish neighborhood on the east, and a huge Italian enclave on the west.

In *Chicago: Confidential!*, the authors, Lee Mortimer and Jack Lait, describe premigration Halsted and Maxwell Streets in 1950, "a fantastic riot of smells and colors, a jammed jamboree of Negroes, Mexicans, skull-capped Jews, Filipinos and Levantines. From the reeking cafes come the rancid odors of cheap cooking. You can buy anything on the street from a girl, price $5, to a stiletto, price $2.50." For much of the thirty years thereafter the neighborhood remained a bustling place, the air filled with the aroma of pork chops and fried onions, offered over the din of the street "pullers," men who waited in front of the clothing stores and yanked customers indoors with the promise of a deal.

But as the university marched across the neighborhood, it became clear much of this land was being taken for "future development." The Irish settlement decamped as downtown spread, and the Italian ghetto disappeared, under the auspices of the award-winning, postmodernist nightmare of the university, which also covered the last remnant of the old Jew Town. In the early 1990s, the denizens of Maxwell Street were replaced with vacant lots ringed by cyclone fences.

From the interchange, run your eye south and to the west from Maxwell Street, and you're treated to a landscape of old warehouse and factory buildings, and church steeples. The vista is a reminder of the way lives were once organized in urban America. Workers lived near work. Churches were built where workers lived. The rail yards, warehouses, and canals formed the horizontal boundaries of commerce; the steeples drew the workers' eyes skyward to God.

Today, the few people who call this area home fall into a few distinct categories: the homeless, pushed west by the demolition of skid row; doctors, professors, and other medical and academic workers, drawn to the area by the nearby complex of public and private hospitals and the university; and loft dwellers, attracted to cheap space, downtown access, and the chance to be pioneers. These distinct groups seldom mix. Drugs are rampant. Cook County Hospital, the setting for the sanitized medical drama *ER,* is in reality a setting for countless cases of drug overdose, hypothermic homeless, and incarcerated patients from the massive Cook County jail, a few miles away.

The site of the Haymarket Street battle, which resulted in the deaths of police and workers in 1889, galvanized the international labor movement, and led to trials and executions of left-wing labor leaders, stands unmarked.

Weeds push through the seams in the sidewalk. The drone of the giant highways is an ever-present background noise. There are union halls, some of which remain in business more to administer pensions and medical benefits for workers in long-gone jobs than to organize the workers of today. And there is public housing, lots of it. By 1980, large and dangerous public housing towers had come to symbolize everything white Chicagoans wanted to flee. Remaining city dwellers, down from a postwar high of 3.6 million in 1950 to just 2.8 million, were preparing for a decade-long fight over the spoils.

Public housing provides a place to live for just over 100,000 people in a city that will end the century with some 2.7 million residents. From the symbolic space that public housing takes up in the minds of Chicagoans and suburbanites alike, you would have thought it was two or three times that many. Enormous public housing towers line the Dan Ryan Expressway, one of the main routes into the city. From the swanky shopping and restaurants of the Gold Coast, you were able to scan the horizon to the west and see the high rises of the Cabrini-Green complex. When the housing was built in the 1960s, on the rubble of a white working-class neighborhood cleared in an "urban renewal" project, the real estate north and west of the Loop was simply being written off.

But in the following thirty years, Lincoln Park gentrified just to the north of Cabrini, capital concentrated to create one of America's richest urban neighborhoods between Cabrini and Lake Michigan, and workaday Michigan Avenue became the "Magnificent Mile." Just one thing stood in the way of a seamless garment of gracious, upscale urban living from the Chicago River to De Paul University: the thousands of poor, black residents of the Cabrini Apartments and the Green Homes.

During his 1987 campaign for reelection, Chicago's first black mayor, Harold Washington, visited the notorious Cabrini-Green development, north and east of Cook County Hospital and the University of Illinois. Though Cabrini was far from the biggest development run by the Chicago Housing Authority, it was given inordinate attention because of its location—close to downtown, to gentrifying Lincoln Park, and to the Near North nightspots frequented by suburbanites. It was a few blocks from the famed Gold Coast, and sparkling Lake Michigan. As a reporter covering Washington's campaign, I was glad to be going there for something other than a killing or a major drug bust. The mayor entered the small community center, accompanied by a hot electric guitar and pounding drum kit, his face wreathed in a smile. Here, he could find relief from the relentless criticism of his rivals, the undermining by the press, and the four-year hard march of Council Wars. The four-year standoff pitted a working majority of twenty-nine aldermen from the old machine days against Washington's allies, twenty-one black and reform-minded members of the council. The combo began an improvised political ditty to the bluesy electric guitar—"Nooooo-body, but Ha-rold! Nooooo-body, but Harold!" The mayor, whose waist had ballooned during his four years at City Hall, danced and swayed to the lyric, arms outstretched, as he mounted the podium. "I like that song! I like that song! Noooo-body, but Harold. Well, here he is!"

When the music faded out, Washington told the residents of Cabrini-Green that there were armies of developers who would like nothing better than to come in and bulldoze the place, opening the land for luxury apartments and homes. He said he would never let that happen, that Cabrini-Green was here to stay, and that the answer was not to tear it down but to build it up. There were hoots, hollers, and happy applause. The racism that had created public housing had also created a steady source of votes for black politicians. Washington was victorious in the Democratic primary a few weeks later, reelected a few months after that, and dead of a heart attack before the year was out. In the 1980s, during the administrations of Washington's predecessor Jane Byrne, and his successor, Eugene Sawyer, the white population of Chicago dropped by another 255,000, 20 percent of the previous total.

During the 1980s a lot of the talk among blacks on the political left about a conspiracy to dismantle places like Cabrini-Green was dismissed as scare tactics or a product of racial paranoia no longer appropriate to a city with a rising black middle class and political aristocracy. The idea that Cabrini would tumble just seemed impossible. There it was, an established fact, block after block of high-rise buildings. And the North Side kept on building up, getting more crowded and more expensive year after year with Cabrini right there. Why even bother to tear it down now?

As the U.S. Department of Housing and Urban Development became increasingly involved in the day-to-day operations of the Chicago Housing Authority, CHA's own priorities and plans became indistinguishable from HUD's stated desire to "reinvent" public housing. In Cabrini's case, reinvention looked a lot like demolition. The development's census is down to a few thousand from nearly eighteen thousand when the final phase was completed in 1963.

New housing is planned for the newly vacant land where the high-rises once stood. Fifty percent of the new housing in preliminary plans is to be sold at "market rate" and will stand near some of the most expensive real estate in the Midwest. A fifth of the planned units will be sold as "affordable housing," that is, to families making between 80 and 120 percent of Chicago's median family income (roughly $40,000–$55,000 a year). But only 15 percent of it is reserved for very low-income people (from no income to $22,000 a year) who lived in Cabrini-Green for thirty years. When the "reinvention" period is complete, the people of Cabrini-Green, for the most part, will have been reinvented right out of their homes. Just as the neighborhood activists threatened they would. Just as Harold Washington promised they wouldn't.

During a trip to Chicago I headed down to the South Side to see Dempsey Travis. Dempsey Travis has seen it all and will be happy to tell you all about it. His life as a self-made millionaire, he figures, buys him all the right he needs to annoy people in power with his sometimes less than diplomatic talk.

He has fought against segregation his entire life: as a performer, as a soldier, as a Realtor, and as the president of the largest NAACP chapter in America, the powerful and influential Chicago group. He knows the real, lived history of public housing in Chicago, and after decades of fighting the good fight, Dempsey Travis finally surrendered to what he had been struggling against for many years—the belief that there is an irreducible core of American racism that no amount of struggle will dissolve.

It is important to hear what Dempsey Travis has to say, because imbedded in his stories is a new, "post-integration" attitude now heard among many successful blacks who came of age in the civil rights era and now are tired of a lifelong audition for white acceptance:

"I remember Chicago when in my neighborhood, the doctor lived next door but my father made fifty dollars a week and he never made more than that in his whole life.

"It certainly motivated the kids who saw people like that. Now I can afford to live any damn where I wanted to, if I decided I wanted to live on the moon, and they were selling some moon, I could go. I can afford it!

"You might as well be on another planet in some of these suburbs. Some of our highly profiled stars, nobody ever sees them, except when they're on television! They all live out in Deerfield and Highland Park and waaaayyy back in the woods some damn where. Maybe they don't even see any white people either! I don't know! [laughs]

"Back when I was with the NAACP, we had the largest branch in the United States. Fifty thousand card-carrying members, it was almost like running for mayor of Chicago, it was so political.

"I can remember the night, we had the election at Dunbar High School. There were three thousand, four thousand people inside, and another three–four thousand people outside who couldn't get inside! That was a movement! I then invited, as the president of the NAACP chapter, 160 village officials from all around Cook County, DuPage, surrounding counties, collar counties. I told them, come in, let's talk about how we can integrate these communities, these villages, the townships. Not just me, I got some of the top experts in the country to come in and talk about this. We got professors to come in from Berkeley, out of Philadelphia. How many showed up? Eight! Out of 160 villages and towns! And they were the villages that already had black people! Like Evanston, Harvey, Ford

Heights. The communities that were lily-white didn't respond because they didn't want to hear it.

"Then I went a step further, I didn't want to just walk away from it. I had on these rose-colored glasses. I said we could do better. Then it came time to do a church exchange. I'm invited to go to their church and have dinner in their homes, and they're invited to come have dinner in my home and go to services at my church. And so we went back and forth like that for a year. We became like, what do they call the Quakers again? A Society of Friends. That went on like that for about six months.

"We sent each other Christmas cards. A hello, whatever. Now, fast forward. A few years ago I was on John Callaway's show [a local public television news and public affairs program]. I had occasion to say that I hadn't had a meal in a white person's house in a hundred years, since the 1960s. Before I could get out of the studio and get into my car, that phone at the TV station was jumping off the wire! Come to dinner! Ed Vrdolyak called, he said, 'Dempsey, any time!' Some doctor called. 'Love to have you!'

"Well, I'm really not that anxious to sit down at somebody's table.

"I would say racism is interwoven into the society, it's not a stamp you can wash off. If it's interwoven it's there. Their racism is just plainly interwoven into society and unless you can adjust, and that don't mean Tomming [acting like an Uncle Tom], it gets to the point that you got to make your own bed, you got to fix your own wagon, you got to make your own economic force, your own political force, and we certainly were in the process of doing that. In the sixties, seventies. It was in process.

"I gave up on integration thirty years ago. I didn't feel comfortable being rejected. Why should I be put in that posture? The next thing, you try to do something to make the environment in which you live better.

"If all who make two dollars run away from where the real struggle is then the struggle is lost, because nothing is gained in my opinion from living in a white community. I see absolutely no benefit.

"Within the Chicago area in the last twenty years, we've lost almost two hundred thousand voting blacks to suburbia. Had those blacks stayed in Chicago today we'd still have a black mayor. I think you had the best of all things going right here, and then you followed the Man, and actually . . . you castrated yourself politically!

32

"The Man has built the community for himself, and because of the laws permitting you to move around you're not restricted as you were, thirty, forty years ago. Then the moment you get there he starts to leave. And take what's good out of it . . . then what's wrong with creating your own good? You got to make your own thing. The sooner you recognize that the better off you're going to be.

"Look, let me give you an example. Right now in Chicago there are efforts afoot to take back certain lands, Cabrini-Green would be one of them, Lake Park Towers would be another, and there are probably many others around the city that the people have decided is good stuff, and we want it.

"Let's say this. If I could decide that I would buy a whole square block and develop town houses that are value rated anywhere from three hundred to a half million dollars. By myself. With my own money . . . now these guys certainly make a hell of a lot more money than I do. I don't know how they spend it but they sure make more. . . . They can afford to do a lot of that.

"Let's assume that some of these guys who are making a million, two million, and a lot of them are making a hell of a lot more. They could say, well hell, I'm going to buy a whole block or two and I'm going to develop a lot of houses around my house and we're going to have an oasis of sorts and people could leave. I just think that could be a way to the solution."

For all his resignation and pessimism, Travis still leaves me with these words:

"Is Chicago a cosmopolitan city? One of the best. Of all the cities I've traveled in, and by now I've been to most of the cities in the world, I wouldn't trade Chicago in for anything."

The chief of the Chicago Housing Authority during the late eighties and early nineties was an energetic developer named Vincent Lane. He inherited a corrupt, featherbedded, almost laughably mismanaged shambles of an urban housing authority, and tried several approaches to make public housing work. First, he wanted to stop the use of public housing as the housing of last resort. People want to live in safe apartments, and poor people, he argued, were no different from anyone else. He instituted more thorough screening for prospective tenants, and began eviction proceedings against those tenants who violated the terms of their lease, or whose children violated the rules concerning drugs and firearms.

Several times, in the early 1990s, I stood at the front door of enormous apartment towers as they were sealed off and swept by law enforcement agencies. There were supposed to be some safeguards in place to make sure the police observed the legal niceties involving illegal search and seizure. Officers who were looking for illegal tenants, drugs, and guns always found them—often all three in the same apartment. I talked to tenants who stood awkwardly in the front entrance of their buildings. They were torn between a desire to protect their dignity and their civil liberties, and the desire to take any help they could get.

They were glad to be rid of gang-operated drug markets, high-caliber weapons, and people evading warrants for their arrest out of the buildings, but still felt uncomfortable about waves of cops and dogs running through the hallways. Some complained to me—away from the cameras for fear of retaliation—that rich people, no matter what they were suspected of, would not have to put up with this. And they were right.

Today, Cabrini-Green is being torn down as quickly as the city leaders can mass their political muscle behind the wrecking balls and bulldozers, with the active cooperation of the U.S. Department of Housing and Urban Development. The wrecking crews are bringing down the towers that Housing and Urban Development Secretary Henry Cisneros now insists were a mistake from the start. The secretary aimed for lower-density housing during his tenure in the Clinton cabinet, housing that approximated the low-rise residential neighborhoods of urban America's "good old days." But the math bothers housing activists and advocates for the poor. A smaller number of units invariably rises on these sites, to take the place of tower blocks demolished with so much fanfare on the TV news. Critics attribute the demolition of places like Cabrini-Green, no matter how bestial the life they provided their residents, to a conspiracy to roust the poor from what has become prime real estate, right beneath their feet. Once the damage of conventional public housing and white flight was done, you might think it could not have gotten any worse. But insult was now added to injury.

A few miles south of the Loop, Lane had also tried to take an abandoned housing project to prove that public housing could work. The Chicago Housing Authority had cleared out several enormous buildings, late in the Washington administration, with the promise they would be rehabbed and their tenants welcomed back.

Lane took one of the Lake Park Towers, remade the apartments at considerable cost per unit, filled the building with heavily screened tenants, and tried to show Chicago a different kind of public housing. Lane was right when he said that public housing units were not humane with bathrooms that required one always to take a sit-down bath because mounting a shower curtain rod was impossible in the cinder-block walls. He was right when he said units built with cheap windows that always broke and drove up maintenance costs were stupid. He was right when he said apartments were not good places to live where you couldn't even hang a picture because the walls were concrete. But his solution in Lake Park Towers was so costly it couldn't be replicated anywhere else in the city.

Others had hoped the ill-conceived towers would be demolished, not spruced up. Developer Ferd Kramer drafted a plan to unleash the potential of the neighborhood predicated on the disappearance of the lakefront projects: "I fought to get those buildings torn down. We could have replaced them with scattered, low-rise public housing in small pieces around the area. The mayor had been telling me privately for a dozen years that those buildings were coming down. Recently, he's started to say it in public too, but so far nothing has happened down there."

In well-publicized speeches black politicians, with South Side bases, have told the residents of the towers that they will not come down. But with each passing month the chance that former residents will come back and stake a claim diminishes. The neighbors relax a little more with each month that brings no rehab and return. For years the towers had been the source of much of the crime in the area. The boarded-up buildings were an eyesore on prime land facing Lake Michigan, but their silence was preferable to the noise, violence, and intimidation brought by the street gangs who once lived there. In the streets now facing the empty apartment blocks, owners were doing long-deferred maintenance, sprucing up gardens and entrances. One homeowner told me, "It finally seems worth it."

Kramer, in words free of emotion, political rhetoric, or color-consciousness, puts the case pragmatically: "It costs more to rehab those buildings than to tear them down and build new. They don't know where those people are. They've probably moved three times since then." Parts of that neighborhood, with access to Lake Shore Drive and the expressways, and a terrific view of the lake, have started to spruce up and sprout new buildings even with the abandoned eyesores still standing. Now entering its tenth year, the saga of Lake Park Towers takes its place in an ever-lengthening column of missed opportunities in Chicago, and around the country.

In the 1980s Vince Lane had toured projects with the chipper Jack Kemp talking a mile a minute, and the grave but upbeat Henry Cisneros. The idea of selling these crappy, disgraceful apartments to their tenants, championed by Kemp, was finally abandoned. Cisneros, starved for appropriations, knew public housing was a national orphan and that a new way had to be found to build new housing if there were to be any hope of continued support. The massive apartment towers began to tumble across the country, even in the politically sensitive Cabrini-Green. Public housing peeks into the public consciousness, it seems, only on two days: the day of the latest horrendous crime and the day a local dignitary in a hard hat pushes the plunger that fires the explosive charges that bring the whole thing tumbling down.

Public housing never housed more than a minority of the residents of any major American city. But it is part of the perceptions game, one of the symbols that have helped drive white flight. It may also be one of the things most easily changed. A public housing development in many American cities, with a population that's virtually all poor and all black, expresses in microcosm what many Americans see when they look at the entire city. The housing project and the city itself are seen as places of chaos, crime, and social breakdown. Middle-class people don't see themselves as having the clout or the capital to wall themselves off from poor people in close proximity, the way the rich can. So they use geographical distance instead.

Daniel Lauber sees the threads that bind housing to every other part of the equation. Watching his neighborhood undergo rapid racial change in the early 1960s undoubtedly led to his eventual choice to become an urban planner. He has spent years trying to understand why neighborhood preservation did not work in Chicago's South Shore community in the 1960s, where he grew up, and contrasts it with the sustained integration of Oak Park, an inner-ring suburb on the border with Chicago. Lauber and others who lived through this period in South Shore are highly critical of the Daley administrations of the 1960s and what they perceive as an ongoing effort to maintain a city of ethnic enclaves.

"South Shore was a quintessential example of a community that was receptive to blacks moving in as long as the city made efforts to keep it from turning 'all black.' The pattern that people perceive is that once blacks start moving in, pretty soon 'There goes the neighborhood.' But that pattern is not an accident. It is a result of institutional factors—from the financial industry, to the real estate industry, to the government. The city of Chicago did everything it could to fight the effort to keep South Shore integrated," Lauber said.

"Blacks move for the same reason anybody moves. To be closer to jobs, to be closer to institutions that are important to them. They move for better schools, for safer neighborhoods. The catch is, blacks have fewer choices. That's why communities like Oak Park, and back then, South Shore . . . bear the brunt of all those people who want to move. In Chicago, at any given time, there are six or so neighborhoods they can move into, while whites may have 120 such communities, and if you focus it all on five or six communities, it amounts to a substantial change.

"Juliet Saltman, the urban scholar and sociologist, who's written extensively on this, has found two killer variables that ensure that an integrated neighborhood will resegregate: One is, if there's public housing in the integrated neighborhood, if it's there in any substantial number; two is the schools. If the schools become racially identifiable, you can count on the neighborhood resegregating. That's where Oak Park has just been exemplary. Their elementary schools have been a model for the country where they have worked with the city to assure that no school becomes racially identifiable. They've changed the borders several times. Busing that they have in the community is borne equally by all races.

"South Shore was the suburb in the city. It had an incredible base of supposedly intelligent people. In high school we were hired by the YMCA to do a survey of South Shore's residents. It wasn't just a random sample: we knocked on every door, and we found, in the heart of South Shore, in the single-family home section of South Shore, the average length of education for an average household there was a college degree, and two years beyond a college degree. There was a major effort by the community, through the South Shore Commission, to try to keep it stabilized. It started with the recognition that neighborhood schools tend to overemphasize or exaggerate the number of blacks in the community." Lauber was referring to the tendency for minority children to be represented in the local public schools in disproportion to the number of minority families in a neighborhood. There are several reasons for this: racial change often occurs in areas where aging white homeowners predominate, making them less likely to have children in the local school; black and Latino couples still tend to have more school-age children than white couples of a similar age; and urban white families have a higher, and black families a lower, tendency to use the local Catholic schools. This adds up to the two-to-one rule used by many academics: if an area has a minority population of 25 percent, the local elementary school will have 50 percent minority children. South Shore was a neighborhood of mixed densities, blocks of single-family houses and zones with large apartment buildings. The neighborhood's pattern of school integration, without intervention, would have resembled that of urban areas around the country: elementary schools near the apartment buildings would become almost 100 percent black, and the schools in the less dense areas would inevitably follow as homeowners fled "blackening" schools.

"The first people to sell their homes are those people who no longer have children in the public schools, and they are replaced by families who have a good number of kids in the public schools. So you can get a community that is, for example, like Oak Park, 20 to 23 percent black, been that way for fifteen years. The elementary schools are 36 to 40 percent black.

"The neighborhood started something called the Petal Plan. The Petal Plan was a way of spreading out demand for new places in public schools. It would have clustered elementary schools and sent newly arriving black students to less crowded and whiter schools as well as the ones located in more heavily black parts of the neighborhood. By clustering schools one of the worst parts of busing, shuttling kids to far-off neighborhoods clear across the city, would be avoided. First there was an attempt to do it with O'Keefe and Parkside elementary schools, and that got rejected; The Board of Education wouldn't do it, Mayor Daley the First couldn't stand the possible concept of people of different races possibly living together."

In fact, Lauber recalls, the school administration went ahead with the *exact opposite plan*. "Someone from The Woodlawn Organization," a strong community organization in the nearby Woodlawn neighborhood that was on the way to becoming virtually all black, "claimed that Bryn Mawr, a school in our neighborhood, was a quarter empty—why don't we let some of the black kids in from their overcrowded schools? We couldn't figure that out because Bryn Mawr was a seriously overcrowded school. So that's when I got my first taste. I wrote a letter to the editor at the *Daily News* and it got published. And that's when The Woodlawn Organization stopped trying to get kids shipped into Bryn Mawr."

Even though many in Lauber's neighborhood, through the South Shore Commission, supported the Petal Plan, a neighboring community deeper into South Shore and closer to the steel mills wasn't ready to sign on to gradual, if unwanted change. "But as soon as they started to get immigration [of blacks], all of a sudden they wanted the Petal Plan. It's a white thing. They wanted to continue to be able to live in the community. Because when the neighborhood changes there are massive changes in the institutions. Churches and synagogues move out, stores move out, chains disinvest." In a pattern repeated in aging neighborhoods across America, entrenched white communities thought they could hold off approaching black populations. It was only when the change became inevitable (and its consequences became clear to the white homeowners) that the new assignment moved from resisting change to controlling its pace. In South Shore it was too late for that. The neighborhood may have squandered a one-time-only opportunity to push city hall to back the Petal Plan.

In the worldview of the Daley administration, Jewish liberals were always waiting in his outer office to complain about something in the 1960s, and were easily dismissed. Had South Shore presented a unified front earlier in the game and brought the people from the south end of the neighborhood by US Steel, the support for the Petal Plan could have meant more.

"So, South Shore changed. The synagogues are all churches now. The Greek Orthodox church on Stony Island is now a Muslim temple. Virtually every theater in South Shore is shut down. There's one still standing—The Avalon, and that's live theater. All the landmarks are gone. South Shore didn't turn over, overnight. It took twelve or thirteen years before it became predominantly black.

"There was no big wave of white flight. What did happen, though, is that virtually everyone who moved out was replaced by a black household. The real estate industry saw to it, both overtly and covertly, that only blacks were looking at housing in South Shore. Whites would be told to look elsewhere. Realtors just wouldn't show them. It's been going on a long time.

"There's a tremendous amount of steering. When I got married, twelve years ago, and looked for a house in Evanston, a supposedly enlightened community, a Realtor who was a former president of the Democratic party of Evanston showed us houses only in all-white neighborhoods. We wanted to live in a diverse neighborhood. When we asked to see houses in racially mixed neighborhoods in Evanston, the real estate agent didn't know what to do, because they never show those houses to white people. The real estate industry is one of the most segregated businesses in this country. Their clientele is virtually all white. We finally found a house in a moderately integrated neighborhood, close to Northwestern, and three years later, when we sold the house the value had increased 150 percent, which is more than average for Evanston. The reason was: you finally had 100 percent of the market competing for the house—you didn't shut out blacks, and Hispanics."

Daniel Lauber learned a key lesson about urban change. "You can turn over the neighborhood in fifteen years even if nobody runs. The key is maintaining white demand. So, the focus, a big part of the focus has to be maintaining white demand, and that's what Oak Park has done so well. I'm on the Oak Park River Forest regional housing center board, and it is a constant battle.

"There's a big fear in Oak Park, now with the Multiple Listing Service computerized, and more brokers from outside Oak Park becoming involved, that they're going to steer whites away from Oak Park. If you just have normal turnover a community will completely turn over in thirteen years.

"South Shore first integrated with middle-class blacks, then resegregated with middle-class blacks, who then started to move farther out, and then were replaced by lower-income people. The community was full of people who were trying to stay. My parents were pretty committed. Five years later they were moving.

"I had a thirty-year high school reunion two weeks ago. You did have an interesting mix of people. You did have some people who were just as prejudiced as my parents' generation, and then you had a group of people who were really sad about the changeover in South Shore, and that they didn't feel welcome back in the neighborhood. A lot of people had the desire to see the neighborhood again, and there were people who just didn't want to see it ever again."

What Daniel Lauber watched as a child and young adult—a transition that profoundly marked his life—people of his parents' generation were caught in the middle of, as homeowners, as parents, as people who had to make short-term decisions that boiled down to the binary, "Do we stay or do we go?"

The South Shore that Jeanette Fields remembers so fondly today was a throwback to an idea about urban life that is disappearing everywhere. Just south of Hyde Park on the Chicago lakefront, South Shore was a middle-class neighborhood without fashionable retail, without instant access to an Interstate ramp, and without a cute Main Street.

Fields and some of her neighbors correctly saw the signs of the beginning of the end. To stave off that end she spearheaded the South Shore Commission, an organization that reached out to the city for help in forestalling the flight that had already undermined so many other South Side areas.

Looking back with an odd mixture of pride in a worthwhile crusade, and regret that it didn't work, Fields points out that for a long time South Shore fulfilled its function: it educated postwar generations of city kids in first-rate public schools and sent them on to successful lives . . . somewhere else. She remembers those years, scrapbooks in her lap and photos spread out on a coffee table, in the living room of a meticulously preserved Frank Lloyd Wright house just a few hundred yards from the Chicago city line, in the suburb of River Forest.

"We had the best schools around. Two of the principals, Esther Mulroy and Marion Mulroy, seemed to have a direct line to God and the Board of Education. Anything they wanted, they got. If they wanted the school painted over the summer, they got the school painted over the summer.

"They decided that they wanted to have cooking classes, and manual arts, they got it. So our kids in sixth grade were learning French, cooking, electricity. The housing stock was excellent. There was a variety of housing. In the Highlands area we had mansions, we had apartments along the lake, we had smallish bungalows, which is what we lived in. The services were good. Seventy-first Street had the best shopping outside of the Loop. We had fantastic transportation, the Illinois Central got to downtown in fifteen minutes or so. At that point it had among the highest percentage of college graduates of any community in Chicago. And a dedicated citizenry. We felt we were going to make it work. If any situation is going to succeed anywhere else, it's going to succeed here. We had wonderful churches and a nucleus of people who cared about civil rights and integration. We were gung ho that we could do it, you see?

"Then when the exodus started, and it came like a flood in a way, we still felt we could do it, and we would do it. It meant trying to get people, the whites to stay, to try and concentrate on upgrading the community so people would want to stay. And come up with solutions to the problems as they perceive them. You know, there weren't many examples of successfully integrated communities.

"There were no models, there really weren't. That's one of the reasons we formed the South Shore Commission. Those of us who were involved in it were so thoroughly dedicated to it, to what we were trying to do. I mean, I devoted twenty years full time to this project, I really worked like I'd never worked before. I believed in it so thoroughly. It was so hard to face the fact that it wasn't working after we had worked so hard. My three daughters went through the whole school system in South Shore. From the time that my first daughter entered South Shore High School, it was all white . . . when my third daughter graduated it was all black.

"That was a painful, very, very painful transition. Our block, we were one of the last whites there. We moved in in 1947 and moved out in 1970. We were the last whites on the block. It was painful at the end. It was very, very, very painful. Not only everything crashing down around our heads at the end that was so hard for us, but to look around and realize that there was nobody who appreciated what we were all about. I mean, the blacks, if I had come to the block meetings, looked at me as if to say, 'What are you doing here? We don't care if you stay or not.'

"One of the first blacks who had moved to our block asked us in conversation, 'Are you going to move now?' I said, 'We have no intention of moving.' She said, 'We're so hurt, that all these people are moving. We moved here because we love this area, we wanted our kids to have good schools,' and she went on in this vein. She was testing us to see if we were going to move. When I told her I had no intention of moving I said it because I didn't.

"There were a lot of people who were sure integration could happen in the late fifties and early sixties. By the late sixties they were disenchanted and didn't believe it could happen.

"Why? They saw it would never stabilize! They saw it wasn't happening! The whites were moving out in droves, the blacks were moving in, in bigger droves. Of course, I've spent a lot of time analyzing this, for twenty years. It's very easy, looking back, to understand why it didn't happen. First of all, you've got to remember, physically, where South Shore is. To the north was Woodlawn, an all-black community . . . to the west, a large black ghetto . . . to the south were communities like South Chicago that were violently anti-black and were going to keep them out. And to the east was the lake.

"Here was this pent-up pressure. The blacks needed housing! For Christ's sake, they were coming into Chicago, I forget the exact number, but I think between 1950 and 1960 the black population of Chicago increased by 63 percent. Where were they going to go? They couldn't go to the suburbs. There were too many communities that wouldn't let them in, that they couldn't possibly get into. So those that welcomed them, they overwhelmed. It was just like the gates opened up.

"And then you had added to this, the Realtors who were blockbusting. They did nothing to help us. Nothing! They didn't even pay lip service."

Jeanne Fields's experience was a bitter lesson for the people who look back at South Shore and remember the reward for their optimism. There are some places where the forces at work are so big, the geographic and social pressures so strong, that even if you do everything right, it still won't work.

In many ways, Chicago has survived the triple beatings of suburbanization, deindustrialization, and racial change better than many other cities faced with the same challenges since 1950. Even today, Chicago exerts an irresistible pull to the millions who live in the counties in its orbit, and even over state lines in Wisconsin and Indiana.

Parts of the city are as healthy as any other place in urban America. On the North Side, in neighborhood after neighborhood even the stranger can't help but notice the wall-to-wall construction, renovation, and new businesses. Home values are healthy, and empty lots change hands at higher and higher prices. The North Side rail commuter once got a daily tour of the North Side's rail sidings, small factories, and warehouses. Today, some of the factories are still there, but many of these light-assembly plants and warehouses sport fabulous new kitchens, floor-to-ceiling windows, and the kind of floor plans that find their way into decorating magazines. Starbucks are popping up everywhere. Department stores have become apartment buildings. Ethnic bakeries and delis now cater to a new, younger clientele who refer to the *kolaczki* as "those fruit tarts on the left." It is exciting, and reassuring to see so many people embracing urban life.

These neighborhoods run north-south, following the contours of the lakefront. But just a few miles in it all starts to peter out. Exhausted frame houses quietly sag, begging for a fresh coat of paint and new gutters. A few pioneers incongruously hustle in from the car, laden with bags from the lakefront supermarket they travel two miles to patronize. There may even be a toddler lifted from the infant seat. That is a sign to the old residents that their new neighbors won't be around long.

Some neighborhoods "make it" and others don't. In some cases it has to do with location, transportation, and the economic prospects. In other cases, the built environment—those places left over from another age—dictates whether anyone will give a place a new lease on life. Got a neighborhood with beautiful old houses still sound enough to be snatched back from the brink? It's a start, but never a guarantee.

In many others cases, it has to do with fashion. People will flock to places that seem to have very little going for them, when they get a lot of support for doing so from people just like themselves. Sometimes fashion can combine with other forces, such as land hunger, or development of adjacent areas, to make an area suddenly "hot." But public housing has often become a cancer, gradually stunting and consuming everything around it.

In cities like Chicago, the private market has not built housing for the working poor at the rate it was needed, especially in those areas becoming home to a growing black population. Almost all public housing in the big, industrial cities of the Northeast and Midwest now belongs to minority populations, obscuring the fact that many of "the projects" were built to house young white families in the years just after World War II. In the array of urban goodies available to residents, and in the power and influence structure, public housing "relocated" in many cities, went from being a "white thing" to a "black thing."

When firefighters in the mountains wrestle forest fires, chain saws and fire itself become tools, making what are called "firebreaks"—gaps to hem in the burning forest. In places like Brooklyn, St. Louis, Cleveland, and Chicago, public housing is surrounded by an economic firebreak, block after block denuded of economic activity. Many Chicago projects stand near what were once teeming industrial corridors, now areas falling down the industrial ladder to become "document storage facilities" and "U-Lock-It" personal storage warehouses.

Factories are shuttered. The warehouses where newly finished goods waited to travel by water, rail, and highway to the rest of America are empty. The large number of high- and low-skilled jobs these industrial belts supported, if this region has been able to hold on to them at all, are now far away in the suburbs, beyond the reach of public transportation.

The degree to which economic life can be returned to areas like these is the degree to which sustainable, realistic, long-term improvements can be seen in the lives of people in neighborhoods with heavy concentrations of public housing. The degree to which those changes can be made is—giving extra time for the perceptions to catch up to reality—the degree to which middle-class people of all races will believe that the city can be a better place.

There are now reams of studies on "spatial mismatch" between suburban job growth and urban job hunger. It is true that men and women in concentrated poverty areas would benefit from easier access to vigorous job growth outside the city. But these analyses neatly sidestep the issues directly implicated by the mismatch: Why can't these central-city residents *move* to the suburbs instead of merely *commuting* to them? Will deeply distressed urban areas, struggling to their feet while every effect of deindustrialization piles on, really change that much if economic nomads head off each morning to chase service jobs in the suburbs?

To what degree is the siting of certain kinds of industry far away from sources of cheap, plentiful labor already a judgment passed on the city and its workers? Is the middle class even wooable? Or will mobile Americans, once their make-or-break conditions are met, simply find new reasons to move the target?

From pride of place on a main thoroughfare, to the obvious care in their construction, to the names they carry, it is easy to see how important the church was in the old neighborhood. Churches can be a hint of something long gone—the Evangelische Kirche in a neighborhood where no one has spoken German as the language of daily life in fifty years. Or they can be a sign of newer arrivals—the cavernous Baptist church now living inside the skin of an old synagogue, stained-glass windows with a Hebrew Ten Commandments testifying to another life.

These critical institutions were witnesses to all the changes of a corner of the city, from optimistic beginnings amid growing prosperity when the cornerstone was laid, to decadent old age, or polished marble now echoing with prayers offered up in unfamiliar new tongues. The church often missed the change offered by history, to be the glue for a neighborhood in crisis.

Chapter 3

The Church and the City

Many older church denominations had to cope with the changes in American life, not just the Catholic Church. However, as the preeminent, urban, immigrant church until World War II, the largest American religious institution was pummeled on every front. Along with the massive demographic change in neighborhoods came challenges to the moral and social authority of the church. Suddenly, the Catholic Church had to take its place as a contestant, rather than assume itself to be the central organization setting the boundaries of family life. While the church scrambled to follow its people into the suburbs and struggled to set new parish boundaries, and build schools and churches in communities rising from cornfields, the church also had to figure out what to do in its historic towns.

From the Kennedy Expressway in Chicago, you can see a church dome, rising high above its surrounding neighborhood. The murals in St. Mary of the Angels Church on Chicago's Near Northwest Side show kindly Polish priests smiling at schoolchildren on the streets of Chicago, and Polish devotion to the Virgin Mary. The huge building had been allowed to sink slowly into disrepair by a congregation unable to keep up with the mounting costs of repair. The fastest-growing portion of the weekly communicants spoke Spanish, not Polish. At least thirty other buildings had no future as churches because there was no remnant of the original white ethnic builders, and the neighborhood had not only changed economically but racially as well. When the late Cardinal Joseph Bernardin moved to shutter and demolish St. Mary of the Angels in the late 1980s, the shock waves were felt into the farthest suburbs, where the young people who had been baptized, schooled, confirmed, and married in the church now lived as parents and grandparents. Million of dollars were raised for a first-class rehabilitation of the crumbling but still striking structure.

In the Chicago neighborhood called Back of the Yards, less than a square mile in size, eleven Catholic churches once brought the sacraments to the faithful in Polish, German, Lithuanian, Italian, Slovak, Croatian, Czech, and English (two Irish churches rounded out the eleven). A stunning 70 percent of the people who lived in the Back of the Yards were foreign-born, and nine out of ten were Roman Catholics.

In the early years of the century the archdiocese encouraged the establishment of "national churches" in Chicago. It was more than a spiritual version of "giving the people what they want"; it was a recognition of national aspirations thwarted back home by centuries of empire and conflict. A glance at a map of Europe would have shown no nation-state called "Croatia." But a Croatian church, with mass said in the home tongue, with a vernacular architecture and the adoration of national saints, could create a Croatia of the mind, even thousands of miles away in Chicago. Lithuania and Poland would disappear from the maps of Europe, on and off, but similarly, Poles and Lithuanians could find in the bricks and smokestacks of Chicago a freedom to be Polish, impossible to obtain in Wroclaw and Gdansk; and the Poles built magnificent churches that proclaimed their presence to the rest of the city.

The Catholic churches of Chicago had never had to live by proselytizing. Tradition, fueled by social control, put people in the pews. In the 1960s the Catholic Church was blindsided twice: by religion's new role in the life of the individual and by the rapid change of urban neighborhoods that shut the doors of Catholic churches throughout the Catholic belt, in

Cleveland, Boston, the Bronx, Milwaukee, Chicago, and Hartford. It may be that the "national church" orientation as much as any other aspect of congregational life made the church slow to respond to the challenge of neighborhood change. When an Irish neighborhood stopped being quite so Irish, how quick would the Irish parish church—replete with an Irish priest, Irish cultural institutions, and celebrations—be to welcome the new people in the area? The resulting mind-set, even if it was predictable, was poorly suited to modern America: If there were Polish churches, why shouldn't there be black ones? The church was "ours." Why didn't new people get a church that was "theirs," instead of coming in and changing everything in "mine"? On the other hand, the "parish" system itself—the organization of institutional life along geographic boundaries—meant the Catholic Church has had to stay and struggle with urban change in ways that many Protestant and Jewish congregations have not. It has taken some time for the old, big-city dioceses to frame a response to urban change. Historically a white European organization, the archdiocese in Chicago has had to broaden its own self-image, making room for a new idea about who is a Catholic in the city at the century's end. One sign that they have managed to do it can be found in the population of black Catholics. An almost 500 percent growth in the share of American blacks who call themselves Catholic shows that these two entities, African Americans and the Roman Catholic Church, have found each other. To give the Catholic Church a retroactive, clean bill of health on these matters, however, would be far too indulgent. Most of the Catholic colleges in Chicago excluded blacks, as did the Catholic hospitals.

Father David Baldwin is responsible for overseeing data on congregation size, church attendance, the institutional health and stability of individual parishes, and the Catholic Church in Chicago's gradual restructuring in the face of well-known economic and demographic realities. Along with his work at his diocesan post, keeping the church's database, tracking demographic changes, Father Baldwin is the pastor of St. Benedict the African Church.

"The African-American Catholic population remains rather segregated, though that's really just an extension of neighborhood segregation. The changes that have marked the urban church in the last thirty years in America are, for the most part, still being faced by parish churches in this archdiocese in the nineties. You've got facilities built for large numbers, built with the assumption of large financial support. As the buildings age, and the congregations change, you've got a greater need for resources, which have been declining over the years. This is not to say anything about the faithfulness and loyalty of the new congregations. But, while they may be Catholic, they are not in the same position to support the church, as it had been supported in the past.

"At first there was money, and there was staff, along with a sense of mission. The church could maintain itself in the face of changing circumstances because it would use the same structures it had already built up. Then costs started to rise, like energy in the 1970s, and realities started to set in. Look at Engelwood. It's six square miles. You had twelve parishes in six square miles. When the neighborhood was Irish and German, all the churches were full, and all the congregations were large. As white flight began, new immigrants from the American South continued to pour in. And the churches on the South Side emptied out. African Americans were not welcomed in the neighborhoods, and not welcomed in the church communities either, though there were some exceptions. People would have preferred that they would go back to where they came from. The churches already there weren't particularly good to worship in. Back in Engelwood, for instance, what we heard from parish leaders was growing dissatisfaction. The community was saddled with large, expensive old buildings. The old structure had built-in mechanisms for keeping the black Catholic population very small. But when the African Americans finally felt accepted, there was a surprising sense of ownership, and investment in a church that wasn't built by them, and didn't serve that community very well.

"Schools were an important witness. They were probably the biggest contribution the church made to the wave of new immigrants to Chicago's South Side from Europe. That system flourished and grew in the twenties, thirties, and forties; every church eventually built a school. These were groups that arrived in this country with no English skills. At Sacred Heart, some classes were taught in German, all the way up to the 1960s. You didn't hear too much controversy about bilingual education back then.

"The schools also made a major contribution, as vehicles for evangelization. Let's stay with Engelwood. There were ten parishes left in 1983, and there were still nine schools, expensive, older buildings that needed heavy maintenance and capital improvements. Not only were the buildings more expensive to maintain, but increasingly, tuition couldn't cover the cost of education. Back then, the Archdiocese was faced with a choice between closing all these schools, or keeping them open. The Archdiocese chose to subsidize.

"So in 1983, we merged five parishes in the east side of Engelwood and renovated St. Benedict the African and established the Academy of St. Benedict the African. We developed a model of a church that better served the community that's there now. It was built by their own people, it reflects their ideas, and is, I think, strikingly beautiful. The school was remodeled, the faculty and administration strengthened, the quality of education was boosted as high as we could get it.

"That process grew and grew through the sixties, seventies, and eighties, and we still do it today. When, in the mid-eighties, the Archdiocese made its announcements of church and school closings, one of the factors was the level of subsidy, which had risen to eighteen million dollars a year.

"Of course, we knew we had to deal with people's attachments to the old worship spaces. We said to people, look, you're struggling all week, you shouldn't have to struggle at church, too. We have to think in a new way about how we construct churches, and structure them, too. I would ask them, Is this what church should be? How could it be better? Instead of spending thousands to heat a building that isn't even warm when we enter it on Sunday, what could we be doing to make better use of that money? We inherited these buildings, those old buildings were the product of different times. When I was responsible for merging those five parishes, education was the key component in helping people tell us what the church could really be.

"But changing symbols is a difficult thing. Not too long ago, you wouldn't have found anyone who wanted to offer a new approach to black Catholics. Among black Christians, there is a different style of liturgy, a different approach to the liturgy, a different style of speaking to the congregation. What we were offering then was not as connected to people's lives in the direct way it is today.

"Today the door is open to leading thinkers in social justice policy, to priests in the front line of the social justice movement. And at the same time, the church is getting better at articulating its own policy. For priests, there are some new assignments. You have to understand the population you serve. We need leaders who can pastor in a culture other than their own. Today, the Archdiocese employs ethnic ministry consultants—African American, Asian, Hispanic, and East European. One of the biggest challenges the Archdiocese faces, even in relatively small communities, is for leaders who can handle bilingual and trilingual congregations. There are 377 parishes in the Archdiocese. One hundred have weekly Spanish masses. Forty-three parishes are predominantly African American. Thirty-five are predominantly Hispanic. Twelve are predominantly Asian. Seventy-three have very clearly identifiable mixes of those populations. The shifting populations are at the top of our list: Does it make more sense to meet Hispanic needs with a few large, well-staffed churches with Spanish-speaking staffs, or, should we try to meet the spreading need?

"With the National Church route [opening churches to meet the needs of specific ethnic groups], the pastoral service was better, but what if you're in Crystal Lake [a suburb far from the large centers of Spanish-speaking population]?

"The church also had to find a way to focus its resources, in order to better serve the needs of the poor. We could not create a Catholic Church welfare system that does not recognize and appreciate the resources available in poor areas. In Wilmette, the parish can subsidize the school. It can't in Engelwood. In that case, how do you finance elementary education?"

That question may be answered by the Supreme Court, as test cases slowly make their way toward the court, that could define the boundaries for the use of public money in parochial schools. The collision of need versus mission versus the law has already come to a head in New York City, where, in response to a dare from Mayor Rudolph Giuliani, Cardinal John O'Connor has offered to enroll some of the hardest-to-teach kids in the New York City public school system in archdiocesan schools—promising a better result. Many of those children have been transferred, and the money for their tuitions is being raised through private donations and sponsorships.

While ministering to a small Catholic majority in black enclaves is one kind of challenge, coping with a sudden tidal wave of new Catholics is another. Bishop John Manz presides over the vicariate in the Archdiocese of Chicago that is home to the lion's share of Chicago's Spanish-speaking Catholics. A son of working-class German parents, the bishop is bilingual, has worked in Spanish-speaking congregations throughout his priesthood, and has watched as parishes moved from needing one, small, Spanish Mass on Sunday, to deciding how to schedule the remaining English one. He still has plenty of couples seeking prenuptial counseling, widows needing funerals for their husbands, and newborns requiring baptism, but his fast-growing congregations are poor and sometimes unable to meet the financial demands of maintaining aging church buildings.

The bishop concedes that the church's response to urban change has not been comprehensive or well thought out. Too much was left to the pastor at ground zero, coping with keeping the doors open and the heat on, and watching his old familiar flock disappear.

"Look at the West Side, you have St. Mel's, St. Thomas Aquinas, and Resurrection parishes. In their heyday, each had eight thousand to ten thousand members. Our Lady of Sorrows on Jackson and Kedzie, another huge congregation, has become a tiny one. Through our schools, we are ministering to largely non-Catholic populations. So we have a situation where the young people of the neighborhood are educated by the church: then they leave the neighborhood too!

"In the central city, there are just too many churches. St. Joseph's was Slovak. Providence of God was Lithuanian. Sacred Heart was Irish. St. Procopius, St. Pius, and St. Vitus were Czech. Trinity was Croatian. St. Adalbert's was German. There were twenty-five parishes in Pilsen alone.

"How many medium-sized churches would you need today? Let's say ten. So even if you close ten, you're still left with too many.

"People are now willing to travel. They don't necessarily identify 'territorially' with a place, but it's significant to them as the 'place where I got confirmed' or 'the place where I baptized my kids.' I don't think that's necessarily bad, going by what I hear from the white middle class, and even the upper class, economically. That seems to be more of a reality in the Catholic Church today—breaking up the old allegiances to the old ethnic neighborhood church.

"For example, I started out at Providence of God, and when I got there in 1971, . . . they still had one mass with the readings in Lithuanian, and then by the time I left, seven years later, that was long gone. It had been a small percentage when I got there, but it had totally disappeared by the time I left. At Providence of God the first Spanish mass was probably in 1961–62. It was similar when I went west: at St. Roman's, it was in Polish. It wasn't radical. When I was at St. Agnes of Bohemia, in 1983—my last parish—the percentage was 85 percent to 90 percent Hispanic, and 95 percent when I left. Their first Spanish mass was in '75. I stayed there for thirteen years. The big change in Pilsen was more in the sixties; in Little Village it was the late seventies, early eighties.

"There was that slow movement west. Little Village was a little harder to crack.

"I remember telling one Polish lady in the hospital, when I was visiting her—she was complaining to me about all the Mexicans moving into the neighborhood—'First of all, for anyone else to come into the neighborhood, whether they be Mexican or anything else, somebody's got to move out, don't they? If you want to start blaming somebody for what's going on in the neighborhood, blame the ones that moved out!' She got my message.

"We talked about it from the pulpit, on occasion. I can remember, back in [the] seventies some of the changes going on were in my own attitude, even. We used to try to encourage people to stick around—I'm talking about the middle class, the solid folks. People would complain about gang problems, and this and that. In East Pilsen, in those days, the housing was worse too; as time went on, I began to see that I didn't know if I could really plead with people with children to stay in an area that's got more violence, if they could find something better.

"You know, it was hard. Because a lot of the good people that are active, that are helpful, in the church—you hate to see them go. There was a time when I lamented that, and asked, Why here? Then I said, Well, it appears to be fairly common. Even people in the suburbs, who've invested in a great big home, eight to ten years later, they're gone too, on to an even bigger home. So, that's part of a larger social change.

"Generally, the most tense time in a neighborhood is when it's fifty-fifty or sixty-forty. When I came to my earlier parishes it was well beyond that. What I encountered was people who were already in the minority—whether it's Polish descent, Lithuanian descent, Czech descent—who felt somewhat embittered. So I found myself trying to console them, and just listen to their anger. They weren't happy being in the minority.

"Even when an area goes through several years where it ends up sixty-forty Hispanic, the people who are most active, or have positions of leadership in the parish, are probably disproportionately from the former group, and they don't want to give up the reins."

We discussed the situation faced in his vicariate, where one group of Catholics is having what could only be described as an un-Christian response to the other Catholics—the newcomers. A priest may understand what the older residents are going through, and yet, as their pastor, must talk them out of it.

"It's not really an ethnic or racial hatred. You could fill in the blank, whoever they are, I know that my neighborhood, my home, my block, is not what it used to be. And I miss that. So that's the challenge to a priest, when you are ministering to that person, to walk with them and yet not leave them there. You have to help them realize this kind of bitterness is not good for them."

In neighborhoods turning black, in which the newcomers were mostly non-Catholic, the church could become a kind of bunker, a place where people understood each other's trials. In Bishop Manz's Southwest Chicago domain, the church is not emptying out. The new people in the neighborhood are also the people you see coming out the door from the mass just before yours. They're not strangers. They are the same people you perceive as the source of your problems.

"There were some pretty sad episodes in the parishes where new black neighbors were moving in during the sixties. I know Hispanic people definitely felt rejected in some places. Around here it was Mexican people wanting to come to church and either getting cold stares from some people, or wondering if they could have the mass in Spanish, and hearing from church members, 'No, why don't you just learn English?' Europeans have also come and heard that over and over again but that doesn't make it right. That history is no consolation to anyone who's arriving today. What? We got treated shabbily so now we're going to treat you shabbily too?

"One of the unique things about the Hispanic immigration here—as distinct from the Polish, or the Italian, or from other heavily Catholic countries—was that no clergy came with them. That made a big difference. The biggest immigration was in the sixties and especially in the seventies: There was a vocation crisis, here, and in Mexico, too.

"At my residence, the Archdiocese has 'Casa de Jesus,' which is for young Hispanic men from nineteen and twenty, up to thirty-five years old, who are interested in going out for priest. It's been going for seven to eight years. This year we may have our biggest year—twelve men are coming there to live. They'll spend a year studying English at UIC [University of Illinois at Chicago], deciding whether they want to go to the major seminary at Mundelein. Next year, when I go to Mexico, I'll be talking to bishops down there, who have said, 'Why are you coming to take our young guys?' You know why? A lot of the people from here are up in Chicago and they need priests.

"The ironic thing is, I talked to a young man today who's attending seminary up here—and just like in the early days, and in that spirit of 'Go West, young man,' there are a lot of young men down there in Latin America who are interested in coming up here. They see the church up here as a little bit more liberal, for another thing. We are interested in trying to get young men before they're priests, so we can acculturate them. To try to act like it's the church in Mexico—you can't do that here. For better and worse, there are differences, and it's a whole different ball game.

"Because no clergy accompanied them, all we had been able to get before was a number of Spaniards, but that wasn't the answer. The language is the same but there are a lot of differences."

Even with expanding rolls of teenagers now making an early commitment to priesthood, Bishop Manz is not giddily optimistic. He's guessing that 5 to 10 percent at the most will make the entire journey, which ends with lying prostrate before the cardinal on the cool marble floor of Holy Name Cathedral, at ordination.

Even for clergy with the best intentions, institutional reality can clash with prophetic mission. Urban churches, especially Catholic parishes in the old neighborhood, are formidable physical plants in need of constant attention. As the neighborhood changes, the building gets older and more expensive to maintain. The school begins to run at a deficit as enrollments decline, or as enrollments balloon, with students from families less likely to pay full tuition.

Eventually, even the stalwarts begin to weaken. Church members who might have formed the nucleus for the resistance to continued erosion fall prey to the realities of fighting a battle in which everyone around you has long since thrown in the towel.

Tom O'Connell remembers the changes on Garfield Boulevard and Back of the Yards in Chicago, and the impact they had on his home church, where he was an active layman. He watched as suspicion replaced the closeness parishioners felt before. "You need to have community in one sense, to know that people are together, it's almost like a circling the wagon train mentality, in any community whether it's this community where we're standing right now or anywhere. You need to know that if I call you and you're my neighbor you're going to be there for me, or, at the very least, that you're not going to be perpetrating anything on my family or my house. We didn't have that anymore."

Unlike many Catholics who told me that their neighborhood crises were never confronted by their clergy, O'Connell points out that in Back of the Yards, many of the neighborhood organizing and integration projects were spearheaded by religious leaders of many denominations, including his own priest. "Marty Howard was here then and he was just a great guy. I think his death came in part as a result of the trauma and the stress he had in this community as he was trying to pull people together. He was just really a good man. He would have been a bishop. He transferred out of here as it was really falling apart, and went . . . to a parish up north and died of a heart attack within six months. He was just fifty-five or fifty-six."

Chapter 4

Philadelphia: The Most American City

I headed to Philadelphia for a look at a city said to be back from the brink. Healthier, more stable, better governed, Philadelphia is still watching the moving trucks head over the city line to healthy and growing suburbs. I sought out tour guides who were experts on the Philly far from Independence Hall, Society Hill, and the Liberty Bell.

The journalist Lincoln Steffens called Philadelphia "the most American" of our cities. The muckraker wasn't referring to the sacred sites of American liberty: Steffens had cast his eyes to the other great cities of his day—Boston, New York, and Chicago—and seen the way a surge tide of European immigration had shaped their characters, while Philadelphia had quietly passed through these decades fundamentally unchanged. From 1870 to 1920, when Ellis Island groaned under the weight of new arrivals, Philadelphia was home to a smaller percentage of foreign-born adults than any other Northern city. At the height of European immigration, its share of foreign-born residents peaked at 27 percent, compared with Boston at 34 percent, New York at 50 percent, and Chicago reached 36 percent.

As with so many of the original urban giants, Philadelphia's population reached its maximum in 1950, at 2,071,605. Its subsequent population decline trailed that of other cities, but Philly remained virtually unchanged throughout the 1950s and began a slow descent after 1960, leaving about a million and a half souls within the city limits today. There was no spectacular Detroit-like meltdown, no Chicago-style widespread warfare over racial turf. As the nation as a whole feasted on rapid economic growth during the 1950s, the cradle of nineteenth-century industrialism, Pennsylvania, had the second-highest unemployment rate in the United States between 1950 and 1962. Philadelphia's trades—leather, shipbuilding, consumer electronics—were all going to be reinvented in those years, and the City of Brotherly Love was not going to get a piece of the action when the restructuring was over.

The seventies were not only rough on the central city but on the surrounding suburbs as well. The metro area, which dips into Delaware, spans the Delaware River, and steps into New Jersey, did not grow fat on Philadelphia's decline: While the city population was dropping by a quarter million, to 1,688,210, the suburbs were also losing steam, dropping a hundred thousand by 1980 and coming to rest at 4,781,494. After the 1990 census it was revealed that Philadelphia, which had been America's third-largest city for much of the twentieth century, was now in fifth place, behind Houston and Los Angeles. In many ways, Philadelphia represents American urbanism's past, with its dense downtown, grid pattern streets, the city hemmed in by old suburbs. Houston represents the future, not centered on an historic downtown, growing by annexation, laced together with freeways.

The absence of entrenched ethnic ghettos home to an economically insecure white middle class might have pointed to a different outcome from that of other cities. However, decline did not spread from Philadelphia's urban core to the inner-ring suburbs the way it has in many other metropolitan areas. Like many older American cities, Philadelphia is small: It has within its borders some older communities, absorbed over the centuries. In its history and self-concept, it is a city of neighborhoods. A high degree of social tolerance was part of Philadelphia's past: in colonial times, it was one of the few places to freely admit Jews and Roman

Catholics as settlers. From the beginning of the twentieth century, Philadelphia was also home to the largest black community in the North, larger even than that of giant New York, just ninety miles away.

Unlike New York, Boston, and Chicago, the white ethnic progress to political power in Philadelphia was slow. The city did not elect its first Irish mayor until 1963. Its first Italian mayor came eight years later. It was the earliest major American city to create a human relations commission, an influential body that has helped determine urban policy for decades. Philadelphia made an early foray into public housing and built its first large projects in the 1930s.

But the promising start, gradual integration, and a tradition of social tolerance were all swept away. Residential segregation, begun before World War II, had created crowded black ghettos similar to those elsewhere in the North. As in other cities, the percentage of the public school population that was black strongly overstated the share in the overall population; white withdrawal from the public schools presaged white withdrawal from the city itself. Meanwhile, the suburbs remained virtually all white.

By the 1960s, the Philadelphia Story was much like that of other big Northern cities. The riots of the late 1960s led to the election of former policeman and self-proclaimed law-and-order candidate Frank Rizzo. At the end of his second term, Rizzo was defeated when he tried to amend the city charter and remove term limits. The Rizzo years were followed by a single term for Bill Greene; and then, like Cleveland, Chicago, Los Angeles, Atlanta, Gary, and Detroit, Philadelphia elected its first black mayor, Wilson Goode.

Philadelphia remains politically potent because its population is such a large share of the metropolitan total. But its clout is undermined by its neediness: more than a third of its households are headed by single women with children, and a third of its young children are in poverty.

It would be hard to come up with a better guide to the streets of Philadelphia and the fringe neighborhoods that form its borders than Elijah Anderson, a sociologist at the University of Pennsylvania, the author of *Streetwise*, and an observer of gentrification from ground zero, as a homeowner in an area between the University of Pennsylvania and Mantua, a poor neighborhood in steep decline.

During the 1980s, the professor developed friendships with his neighbors on the middle-class frontier and spent hundreds of hours with young men living on the other side of the economic divide. He chronicled the tense, watchful years during which both sides observed, and failed to understand, the other.

We met at the university on a beautiful fall afternoon and drove through west and southwest Philly, the regions of the city where he has conducted his fieldwork for years. He watches the streets with the trained eye of the scholar and historian, and with the sympathetic eye of a black man at century's end, raising young children and wondering, like the rest of us, where it all goes from here. Anderson has a soft voice, but occasionally his world-weariness, coming from his deep understanding of the terrain, can give way to flashes of anger. We wait while a crowd of white Penn students cross a street near the main bookstore, and head into a gentrified area of beautiful late-nineteenth-century homes.

"Students come from all-white high schools and go to college around *here*. It changes their outlook. Here's Powell School—an integrated school, a deseg school. The ratio is kept at about fifty-fifty. But in order to do that, they've had to import white kids from other areas around the city to come to this school. They have good facilities and good teachers. It's one of the best schools in the city. But by the time the white parents get their kids through to the fifth grade, they start to dribble out, and we lose some who decide they've got to move their kids to private school or leave the city."

As we head across the neighborhood, to our left stands the old residential area, complete with new infill housing (new housing built in spaces left empty by previously demolished structures) and heavy restoration, while off to our right is a mix of old factory and warehouse buildings. Infill housing is often a sign of market viability for a neighborhood. In other places, when an older house is lost to fire, decay, or demolition, the resulting vacant lot stays vacant. When a new house rises among seventy-five-year-old structures, somebody thought it was worth spending money to build it.

"This is Lancaster Avenue . . . take a right, then take a left at this corner. You'll see all the old Victorian houses, the gingerbread. This is one of the most integrated areas of the city. It has been for a long time, and has had the reputation. Integration is not without its tensions. One of the most important has to do with negotiating one's way around the street. As you can see, these are well-kept houses—mostly middle-class people, some working class. Make a right here."

We turn a corner on Lancaster Avenue and roll past an eye-popping set of fully restored nineteenth-century beauties, with highly detailed, lovingly painted gingerbread facades, gas lamps, and period curtains framing gorgeous first-floor parlor windows.

"These are beautiful structures. The people who live here are middle class, and liberals, who find themselves becoming more and more uptight as they run into problems on the street. People get broken into, mugged, robbed on the street. Their liberalism creates a lot of ambivalence in dealing with young black people on the street. On the one hand, they want to be accepting, but on the other hand, they don't know how to distinguish between a young guy on his way home, and the guy who's going to hit you over the head. And that speaks to the distance which really exists between the blacks and whites. Even though people are liberal, you go to some of the parties, and the parties are all white; and I'll be the only black there. That's how it is. People mean well, and I've got a number of friends in this area.

"You see, black people from the old manufacturing era live in this area; when they pass on, the house will go to a relative, who probably won't be able to keep it up, because the person who had it kept it up with money saved from the manufacturing era. It takes money to keep the place up. The person who passed on is seventy-five to eighty years old. When they die, the relatives who get it will sell it to someone not likely to be a minority. The black middle class is not interested in being here, at this point . . . you'll find a few, but the black middle class is far more interested in the suburbs.

"Look at these new houses here. Certain developers have gotten land, and quasi-government sponsorship, and they're building low-income houses—Section 8 qualified [where tenants can take advantage of a federal rent subsidy]. It's a real problem if it's too concentrated, because middle-class people won't buy here. The first MOVE house was over there, right over there, back in '78. [MOVE is the black political group whose stand-off with police brought an aerial bombardment, and an accidental fire that resulted in an entire city block burning down. The block has been completely rebuilt.] Students live in some of these low-income units. In many ways, they bring positive things to the neighborhood, because they occupy the streets. They walk on the streets, and keep the streets safe, but they also make a lot of noise."

As we continue down through the neighborhood, the influence of the re-habbers, and the University of Pennsylvania, is beginning to fade. As we move on, it looks less and less like a neighborhood where Ivy League students, even the cash-strapped or adventurous ones, would rent an apartment.

"I'm looking at this neighborhood now. Powellton looks blacker than when we lived here. Maybe it's become blacker in the last few years."

During the years that Anderson lived in this area and did his research, one place for whites and blacks to work together toward common goals was in block clubs. "When you get middle-class whites and middle-class blacks together there's comity, there's exchange. The problem with the integration here had to do with the fact that the blacks were working class, and the whites, for the most part, were middle class. It didn't always go well. Take a right over here, on Spring Garden. This is the boundary between Powellton and Mantua. Mantua is a really tough area."

By now, we have clearly moved into a different zone. "Here you get a sense of the boundary . . . there are two empty lots. There are more dilapidated houses once you get over here, though developers are starting to take a look at this area, they hope to build housing for students here. Drexel University has a policy of encouraging the students to live in this community, which helped the whole process along. This is poorer here, this is the edge over here. You can see these rehabbed units over there. Possibly, the developer who did that was waiting for a middle-class person to come in and buy this, but they never came. He settled for someone who is poor. Many of the blacks who own these houses came out of the manufacturing era. They were making good money. They can afford a nicer house. We're into Mantua now. Here you can buy drugs, you can do everything you can do in the worst areas of any city—all right here. The houses back here are occupied by very, very poor people."

As we head deeper into this West Philadelphia neighborhood, we pass a large antidrug mural painted on the exposed-brick side wall of what was once a row house but now is surrounded by abandoned lots. I told Anderson how in New York, Chicago, St. Louis, and Cleveland the press pays a lot of attention to popular movements to retake the street, to exercise some social control over the illicit activities in a neighborhood like this one. Yet these efforts rarely amount to much. "Mantua Against Drugs" says the sign. All very nice. All very noble. But effective?

"Project Pull was started over here by George Bush. He came out and met with the old heads—the older residents—who wanted to eliminate crack houses and all. And they really did push the crack houses out. They made it a lot more difficult for the drug dealers here. They were battling with these guys. They were knocking down doors and marching with grandmothers, with the old heads really putting their foot down. In the short term, it worked. But it wasn't a solution. Certainly, it made it difficult for these dealers to carry on their business as usual. When they stopped, of course, the dealers went back. The people tried. Project Pull got it started—a lot of that was cosmetic."

We have turned onto a wide commercial street. Above us are suspended the electric wires that power the streetcars; below us are the rails, shiny from constant wear of traffic. Stretching to the horizon is an undistinguished mix of one- and two-story buildings—storefronts mostly—occasionally with residential rental property above. There was once a solid neighborhood economy here: coin-operated laundries; grocery stores; clothing stores for men, women, and children; hardware and home-improvement stores. Now the frantic cross-pollination of the old neighborhood street is struggling against giving way to the too common monoculture of small, badly capitalized fast-food stores, hairdressing shops, and empty storefronts left behind by failed businesses.

"This is the main drag here. You can see how things have come down. It's late afternoon, and already a lot of businesses have their gates pulled down. But during the day there's a lot of life through here. There's community here."

I ask Anderson if the businesses hanging on in Southwest Philadelphia offer much to a young high-schooler from the neighborhood looking for a summer job, or some work after school to contribute to family finances. He tries to be optimistic.

"Look at how many carry-outs there are. They can be a problem. And the more they proliferate, the more problems they create for a street. They become centers for drugs, and all kinds of things. But you can find something to do on a strip like this."

Anderson suggests that may be less of a problem than in earlier years. The sense young blacks, especially boys, had in so many poor neighborhoods in the urban core of being unwelcome and open to abuse downtown may be declining. "Some of the boys—seven, eight years of age—you can find downtown, just walking around. Which is interesting. Because a middle-class kid of the same age you would never find downtown, by himself. This neighborhood along here is very, very poor. Certain people who run these places do hire kids from the neighborhood. There's an old Italian man who owns this faucet company here. He hires only young black men from the neighborhood. It gives him a certain legitimacy in the neighborhood, because he becomes a presence here. People would not look askance at him for being here.

"There's a lot of drug activity in this area. This is a bar I used to go to. This is the center of the action, right here. When you get to Thirty-ninth make a left. A lot of the Koreans have moved in here, which is interesting. There used to be a lot of tension, but it seems a lot of it has subsided. Take a left here. You can see some houses being refurbished along here, and a couple being demolished. This place has been buffeted by deindustrialization. It might be interesting to talk to these guys on the corner here, but not during a crap game! Those guys—they're seventeen, eighteen years old. Standing around, shooting craps, you can imagine that there's still spirit in them. There's a lot of shooting in this area, a lot of killing over the drug trade, and that's mostly young people."

We come to an intersection of two main avenues, and because the main drag meanders on a diagonal through this end of West Philadelphia, a six-way intersection has been created. It is a good place to get something to eat, have a check cashed, or switch from the streetcar to the bus. According to Anderson, it's a good place for illicit business as well.

"This is the staging area, where you can come and get into something.

The side streets feed into here. There's persistent poverty, drug dealing, and hardworking people, decent people, who are trying to make it.

"These new businesses do hire people from the neighborhood. But I've come here year after year for supplies, and you always see the same thing: the boss taking the money is white, and the men cutting the lumber are black. A lot of the businesses remain because they get cheap labor in this area, and can continue to draw their trade from throughout the city. But there's still fear, and insecurity. They barricade their stores—make them locked down and inaccessible—like this one here, with the fencing and the wire."

We pass a derelict train station, once part of a commuter line from downtown. "Another thing about this place: People will just go at you. They're quite aggressive here. It's so easy to get into a fight around here. If you continue out that way, you get to City Line Avenue; if you continue out that way, you'll hit Ardmore. There's a large number of black middle-class families out there."

After large-scale white flight kicks the institutional and economic struts out from under a neighborhood, black flight often follows. The families of strivers, with stable family lives and long-term job tenure, see the neighborhood becoming the very thing their former white neighbors feared. The emerging black middle class finds itself facing the consequences of the self-fulfilling prophecies of white flight. Along with a departing black middle class, heading for the city line, more and more immigrant families are cutting out the middle step, in the time-tested story of assimilation and upward mobility.

"Take a place like Merion, as an example. It is an increasingly integrated area. It's predominately Jewish, but you're starting to see Indians, other Asians, black middle-class people, some Hispanics. It's becoming a really mixed scene. It used to be predominantly Jewish, and it had been for a long time. It's a near suburb, and the kind of place that takes in people who are leaving the city. You've got lower tax rates, and better schools. You don't have to deal with the city taxes, and you get a break on the wage tax, though it's not that much, if you live across City Line Avenue. That's the phenomenon we were talking about. You pay a commuter tax, but it's not significant.

"Here's Thirty-second Street. In the old days of gang wars, this place was hot—shootings, that kind of thing—even today, the drug dealing and turf battles go on. It's a lot of stress on the decent folks, I can tell you that. They just don't come out at night. Don't hang out. They arm themselves."

Anderson returns to the centrality of the "old heads" in the maintenance of family stability. "He is this older, decent family man, worked in the factory, kept his family together, sometimes worked two jobs, and he's not there today. When you do see him, he's sixty, seventy years of age, and he's not being replaced. The problem in large measure is: that person doesn't have a job—that solid middle-class job. He doesn't have the money to take care of a family the way he would like. He's so proud." Anderson maintains that the loss of steady, unspectacular jobs, like school janitor, letter carrier, housepainter, since the 1950s, in many black neighborhoods, has deprived the community of its "decent daddies."

"When there was a single woman in the community with children, these daddies would help raise those boys. But now, you don't have that critical mass of the decent daddies the way you used to. It has implications for the social organization of the community, for whether kids will get the right outlook that will help them negotiate the system. Of course, now you find more and more women who have babies and don't have husbands."

We stop at a red light at the corner where a small park begins. It is a "common," a square patch of green with a stand of mature trees, fenced in by wrought iron. The park is a mess. The grass has not been mowed in a long time and is infested with weeds. Bottles, cans, and food wrappers are strewn throughout the park.

"This square is the same as Rittenhouse Square," says Anderson, "but look at the difference between how this is taken care of and how Rittenhouse Square is taken care of." Rittenhouse Square is a landmark in central Philadelphia, near some of the city's most exclusive shopping streets.

In reply, I suggest that the people who run the parks might place some of the responsibility for the square's appearance on the people of the neighborhood. "There are those, certainly, who individualize poverty, and would say, 'Well, what's the point of the park district spending scarce resources to keep up *this* park when people piss in it? *They* throw beer bottles, and *their* litter?'"

Anderson replies that the park authorities making an effort to keep up this park would send a potent message to the neighborhood. "It's a chicken-egg thing. These are people who have become so angry, and have been disenfranchised for so many years, that they've adapted to a situation of lack—adjusted to persistent neglect—by doing the kinds of things that, I suppose, conservatives would say brought about the problems in the first place. In fact these people are responding to structural conditions that were already there. Basically, we've got many, many people who require some sort of resocialization, in order to deal with some of these issues, that go way back. People no longer know how to take care of a park like that, and when I say that, what I mean is, that the people around here are so used to not having nice things. Real social learning would have to go on here before this problem was settled."

"So, it's a bourgeois value, taking care of a park?"

"It is! In the old days, when all the adults could get jobs, you had Mr. Johnson out on the street, Mr. Thomas over there—making the young boys heel, pick up papers, not throw trash. That's an important part of keeping the park nice. But those men are not there the way they used to be. And if a passerby asks the young boys not to throw bottles, they might break them instead. They'd say something like, 'You ain't my father.'—You hear this kind of thing—'You ain't my daddy.' I've seen that happen. You still have some of these Mr. Johnsons around. It's interesting to see how some of them carry on in this situation of social deterioration."

As we continue to make our way toward the edges of the city, moving farther south and west, we pass pockets of streets ravaged by economic collapse and abandonment. They are microenvironments, a cluster of four or five blocks where deterioration is advanced: Then, like people huddled against each other for comfort and security, you find blocks where the houses are very old, but residents have taken the time to paint their front gates, or plant a few geraniums in a planter made from abandoned tires.

"Southwest is one of the toughest, poorest neighborhoods in the city—a lot of the violent crime, a lot of the shootings you hear about take place around here. The real defining characteristic of Southwest is, I think, the social isolation."

We talk for a while about the impact of isolation. The isolation is not physical or geographic. In fact, in some cities, it grips neighborhoods a few blocks away from city hall. In less isolated poor populations, people often realize they are being cut out of the action: grassroots groups form, or outside organizers channel the outrage, and the neighborhood actively resists neglect. People tell their council member they want the city to come and fix this street or respond to a dangerous condition near a school. Sometimes poor people do not organize as effectively as their middle-class neighbors, but they try to push the buttons that keep the city moving. However, in the most isolated neighborhoods, there's a frightening entropy. Nobody bothers to call a council member because nobody expects anything to be fixed. "That's the key right there," Anderson says. "Expectations. If someone started caring for that park, people would say, 'What?' They wouldn't know how to react."

We are now in the heart of Southwest Philly. "This used to be a predominantly Jewish area, about thirty years ago. The other whites were Irish, German—all working class. When the riots came in the sixties, the Jews picked up and split. There were some middle-class blacks living in here by the sixties. Longtime residents say that after the riots, when the rapid departure of Jews left a lot of vacancies behind, poorer blacks started moving in. The middle-class blacks then started to split. They moved up to Yeadon, which is a black middle-class community today. So the area quickly became blacker, and poorer. And that's what we have today. The houses—they don't look occupied, many of them—but there are families in there. See that sign—'We Love You Barry, Rest in Peace'? That's a graffiti memorial.

"Then you pass a block like this. . . . It looks pretty good.

"It looks nice, but what's going on inside is something else. There was a shooting in this building here, three or four years ago. Shotgun killing. Right here. This church used to be a synagogue. You can see the star of David up top. . . . Now it's a Baptist church. You see that again and again in the city—signs of transition. A large, elaborate Presbyterian church, that's now a Baptist church, with an all-black congregation—and these are the decent folks living in the neighborhood. See the Chinese takeout there? That used to be a store, owned by a Jewish man, who was shot and killed by people from North Philly about five years ago. Now they have that bulletproof Plexiglas between the server and the customer. This pharmacy used to be owned by a Jewish family, and there was a doctor's office right above it—a Jewish doctor. Now both are Indians. Where are we—Fiftieth? Take a right here.

"Interesting, there were Indians in this drugstore here when I visited just six months ago, now it seems they're gone. You're beginning to see more and more black solidarity, vis-à-vis the Asian and Indian business people, which sometimes spills over into real violence. How does a 'Kim's Market' open, how does it survive in a place like this?

"This community abuts a white working-class area. You can see the transition from black to white—you can see the line, right here—and how the border is moving. These houses are about 1930 vintage. Pretty good houses, really. Hardwood floors, solidly built, about 1925. A lot better than houses that are built today. It would take a lot of money to bring these houses back. Talk about alienation, and anger, and bitterness. Talk to young boys, they feel it, you know. You can see it in their faces. And yet the same boys have to go out into the wider society and basically participate, in order to make a living. They have to negotiate their way, and yet they still have all this bitterness, and anxiety, and anger. . . . There can be fights at work. Or they can be fired very easily. They'll punch out a manager. There's so little at stake in very-low-wage work, they can say, Take this job and stick it. There's a real suspicion and mistrust on the part of so many of the young people toward the wider system—toward any authority."

We end our tour in a neighborhood called Cobb's Creek. It's a largely Irish neighborhood, but the Irish are leaving, heading over the nearby city line, and the area is now, increasingly, black. Turn a corner and you find eight, ten, twelve FOR SALE signs; turn another corner, five, on the next street, nine. But on a corner, a cluster of black and white preteens laugh uproariously and horse around. Black and white girls are jumping rope. As we wait for a light, two boys come by on an adult-sized bike. A white boy is standing on the pedals, straddling the bar from handlebars to seat. Hanging on is his black passenger. Same size. Same school shirt. Same sneakers. It is a rare enough scene in urban America to be striking, and both of us remark on it, as the boys pass.

As the children negotiate the street-level realities of the world their parents give them, the parents themselves carry a different universe around in their heads. With each subsequent FOR SALE sign that changes to SOLD, with a deed in black hands, the chances that white families will see these quiet, clean, neat streets as a good place to raise their children declines. For the moment, there is integration, and peace.

"You never hear about real problems around here. It's all happening very calmly and slowly. There are occasionally fights in the school and that sort of thing, but this is not panic peddling or blockbusting," Anderson told me as we walked at the neighborhood's edge, near the park and creek that gives the area its name. There would be no moving vans in the night in Cobb's Creek, burning crosses, or anonymous threats on the phone. It is as if an agreement was made long before about how all this was to turn out, and even after two different groups of people realized living together was not so bad, all were obliged to play out their part in the drama.

Representative Chaka Fattah has been called one of the rising stars of the Democratic Party. He grew up in an all-black neighborhood in Philadelphia and represented a largely black district in the state legislature in Harrisburg. He now represents a mixed population in the U.S. Congress, including historic center-city Philadelphia, the University of Pennsylvania, and gentrifying Powellton, struggling Mantua, and comfortable Wynnefield, nestled against the city line.

We spoke in the district office above busy Walnut Street in West Philadelphia. The cream of American collegians—the students of the University of Pennsylvania—pass underneath the window on bikes or glide by on in-line skates. Just beyond the bounds of this neighborhood stretch distressed black neighborhoods to the south, west, and north.

As a visitor, you could be lulled into thinking Fattah's district is going to be just fine, if you went on the strength of what you could see from the office and the surrounding blocks. Fattah isn't ready to conclude that the worst is over for his district, or Philadelphia as a whole.

"If you look at the population that's left the city, it's for a multitude of reasons—there's the job loss, the fear of crime, there's the perception of city life. But I think race, correctly, has been identified as the number one contributing factor to how national policy has been shaped around cities, and how people view their own neighborhoods. Right here in Philadelphia there are both examples of the real capacity for people to live together and the reality that there's still a great deal of racism that exists at a basic level.

"Primarily, you have the majority that assumes that to the degree that their neighborhoods are—how did Jimmy Carter say it? 'ethnically pure'—things are moving in a positive direction: and to the degree that it changes, so does their view of the neighborhood.

"Part of the struggle in building communities is how you get people to see beyond their differences and focus on what brings them together—their need for strong schools, a good economic base. Twenty years ago Wynnefield, for instance, this was an integrated community. Today it's still racially integrated, except it's really not. There's a part of Wynnefield that's mainly white, and Jewish, and there's a part that's mainly black. Yes, it's mixed, but there are definite lines of demarcation between the races.

"Some very high-income Asians—Koreans basically—have moved into the suburbs, where they aggregate themselves, as all ethnic groups have done. As the Irish settled, they settled in enclaves in the cities; the Italians did the same thing. If you go to our Chinatown, there is a fabric to the community that works well, because people do feel they have the support systems.

"We have immigrants from Russia, who are Jewish, who have settled in the northeast section of Philadelphia, and not in other parts of the city. We have Cambodians and Laotians who have settled here in West Philadelphia, and when people come over from Puerto Rico they go over into North Philadelphia, because that's where their family relationships are, that's where they're comfortable.

"It's only when the aggregation of people together with people like themselves turns negative that I think it really deserves our condemnation. You cannot deny the fact that there hasn't been a year that's gone by when we haven't had front page stories about African Americans or other minorities moving into neighborhoods and being run out of those neighborhoods with racial epithets, threats, and the like. The bigger point is about people's attitudes. If I raise my son to believe that automatically he's better than any Latino, any Asian, or any Native American, then there's a certain thing that happens when anybody else moves next door. Those kinds of attitudes have been communicated in white communities for a very long time. They're better. Even irrespective of income or educational attainment or anything else.

"The chamber of commerce did a report about how they saw as the greatest drain on productivity people's inability to get along with each other, to get along with people who are different from them in the workplace. So, that was causing a real problem. It's not just housing patterns, because people really don't have to live together, but they probably do have to go to school together, and they have to go to work together, and there are things people have to do in unison with other people who might be different from them, religion, or ethnic background.

"What happens when these kids get to college campuses? At the University of Pennsylvania, you've got a student calling young African-American women names, yelling out his window, you've got bomb threats against a dorm where black students stay.

"The issue, and its significance to the white community, is that they are the overwhelming majority of the country. They control the power and the wealth. So their racial attitudes lead to more than a school-yard fight, you know? It's not just kids calling each other names. Their attitudes impact people's ability to get jobs, or to get business loans, mortgage loans. It has a greater impact on the life chance of minorities who are looked down upon. My district is big. CIGNA's world headquarters is in my district, so is Smith-Kline Beecham. It's downtown Philadelphia, and it's wonderful. But center-city Philadelphia is not the place where there's the greatest need. But I also have one of the six empowerment zones in my district.

"Part of the difficulty between cities, suburbs, and neighboring states is that we're all competing for jobs. So we all offer these packages—'Come here, we'll give you the land, we'll give you a tax abatement for five years, ten years.' What businesses have learned to do is come here, set up a plant, use up all the tax benefits, and then move somewhere else. What would be preferable would be if we were playing on a neutral playing field, if there wasn't any financial disincentive to locate in a city or an urban community or even a rural poor community.

"We can't have a situation like we presently do, where in order to set up your business in Philadelphia, you've got a 5 percent wage tax, and if you set up on the other side of City Line Avenue, your payroll just went down 5 percent. Irrespective of race, that's going to be a strong incentive for people who have a business operation with a lot of personnel.

"I got this one guy, David Broverman, years ago, when I was the state rep, to move his business from the suburbs into Philadelphia. Young white guy. He makes gift boxes for all the department stores. He called me up after two years and he says, 'I'm still out here, doing business, things are wonderful. But I just got my insurance notice, and all of a sudden, I've got a problem with my bank.' So I asked him, what's the problem? He says, 'Look, we haven't had one claim, but my insurance carrier is going to cancel my policy because they don't want any policies in this neighborhood. I've been in business twenty years, never missed a mortgage payment, never been late, we've got a million dollars wrapped up in this building here, and my mortgage banker says he's calling the note, because he wants to get out of West Philadelphia.'

"Look, these decisions, these decisions that bankers make, that insurance officials and mortgage lenders make about the worth of a community, are racially based. You got a businessman—he's done exactly what you want him to do, he moved a business into the community; and he's having problems, not from forces inside the community, but forces that are external to the community, yet control needed commodities. So that in maintaining and retaining jobs and creating businesses, how we combat people's wrongheaded impressions based on race is still very, very important. It colors everything.

"I heard the drug czar speaking to the U.S. Senate last week, and he was explaining that, if you profile the average drug user in this country, you're talking about a white male. But that is not the impression in people's minds. Not only is it not the impression in people's minds: When you look at the justice system part of it, even though the majority of people arrested for drugs are white, the majority of people convicted on drug charges are not white, and the sentences are race-influenced, all through the process; and the evening news helps convince you by constantly showing black males under arrest every night. So people may have a stereotype that does not come from their parents telling them that black people may not be all that they should be—they're not patriotic, not courageous, not interested in education, not hardworking, or whatever their father may have told them. Their *own* viewpoint of the world is colored by the perceptions and images that they get every day. They don't see on the news, or in the newspapers, the stories of success in the minority community.

"The minority community is not getting the information on which minority kids can build their own hopes and aspirations, and the majority community doesn't get this information either. Therefore, the people they hear about, for the most part, who don't look like them, are people who are not successful. But the facts are: Black college enrollment is shooting up. Black home ownership is up 48 percent. African-American unemployment is at a twenty-year low. The five hundred largest black-owned businesses in the country had a larger profit margin last year than the Fortune 500. But not everybody reads *Black Enterprise,* and people are not focused on this. My son, who's thirteen, met a friend of mine who owns a number of McDonald's. He was just amazed to meet someone who owns McDonald's, not who works at McDonald's. Yet, if you saw the Howard University debating team walking down the street, black and white, you might move to the other side of the street, just based on a stereotypical viewpoint about what a group of young blacks, who are casually dressed, might be up to."

It is paradoxical to hear all this from a member of the U.S. House of Representatives who came to Washington after successful terms as a state legislator in Harrisburg. He is the very example he maintains no one gets to see. I asked how his new neighbors would regard him, if he moved into a previously all-white neighborhood.

"They'd say, 'He's an exception.'" Fattah would not be the black man next door, he said; he'd be the congressman next door. "You're not one of *them.* You're not one of what they perceive to be the group. They carve out an exception for you, for Michael Jordan, or for whomever else, and then they still hold this view of the group.

"We really have to, in some ways—and now I sound like Bob Dole—return to the past. There was a time when parents told their kids: You have to be better than everyone else in order to be equal—you have to do 110 percent. You have to go to school, unless you are dead or dying, and that's the only way you're going to make it. Like Dr. King says, if someone started out a race before you, you've either got to run faster than them, or just agree, concede that you're going to be behind forever. If you view this as a generation after generation relay race, a group of people, who happen to be white, got a two hundred year head start. Then two hundred years later, African Americans got a chance to start running in the race. Up until that point, when we started earning money for our work, we weren't in the wealth-chasing business.

"Anybody who studies wealth in America knows there are very few examples of wealth being generated in one generation. It is the Bill Cosby who does well, whose kids then benefit by him doing well, who then invest in businesses. To inherit a position on the Big Board just doesn't happen very often for African Americans.

"If you're not in the culture, and you got a system that's designed to promote the majority culture, then you're going to disproportionately fail, unless you understand the nature of the game, and get at it with a greater degree of zest than might normally be brought to it.

"My high school counselor told me, Listen, you're not college material. This is on day one. First day in high school, rousting me into wood shop. You're not college material. This is sight unseen. Never met my parents. Didn't know anything about me. The surprise of it, which shouldn't be a surprise, is that it's not an isolated incident. You go around to schools where the majority of kids are minority, and you will find counselors today, and plenty of examples of people my age and older who faced the same thing. Mayor Wilson Goode's counselor told him the same thing.

"We have to accentuate the positive. That is: not to deny that there are negatives, but put more emphasis on the positives in order to give people some sense of what's possible in their own lives.

"I've done a program for the last five years, each year we honor one hundred African-American men on Malcolm X's birthday. We do it at seven o'clock in the morning, and there's always standing room only in the church. It's widely supported. We've got plumbers, carpenters, college professors, bank loan officers, radio DJs. The idea is to show the great diversity among the men who are making a contribution, raising their families, being responsible. Even if you take into account the statistic that a quarter of all black men are in the criminal justice system—either incarcerated or on parole, or on probation, which is an abnormally high number—that's still three-fourths who are not.

"The first thing is you have hundreds of thousands of black students at college campuses all around the country. If you try to get into Spelman, or Morehouse, or Hampton, any of the historically black colleges, there are twenty applications for every one that's admitted. Period. Spelman is a school for black girls, you have SATs of 1400 getting put on the wait list. It's amazing what's going on out there, and at the University of Pennsylvania and at the Penn States a lot of these kids, that are part of the same generation these other people want to write off, are matriculating through.

"These dire circumstances call for some kind of change. I don't believe that we should write any group off. You have people at a number of extremes. Militia guys, Freemen—they're off in their own little world too. These guys lost their farms to foreclosure, the farm their dads left them when they were young. They are loners, these Timothy McVeighs . . . and you find very, very sympathetic comments about them. When it comes to youngsters in my community, who may show antisocial tendencies, or criminality at some level, you don't hear any of that sympathy. What you hear on the floor of the Congress is, 'We're going to pass the Juvenile Predators Control Act.' Very, very interesting dichotomy. That's because racism influences even how we begin to cope with people who are at extremes in this society."

We turned to the University of Pennsylvania, a major presence in Fattah's district. I pointed out that I had noticed a workable kind of peace on the streets, especially in the commercial areas, where a sizable population of poor blacks rubbed shoulders with America's elite students. But these students, once out of college, will likely not make their lives in neighborhoods like this one. "What you have here is very interesting. You have a black community here, a Cambodian, and Laotian. Penn has basically decided to invest in the community at some levels. It's got 525 buildings, the legacy of being here, and it's gonna be here way into the future. The university has decided to be an impact player at the neighborhood level to some degree. Last year, Yale didn't have one student from New Haven, and it's right smack in the center of the city. Penn is somewhat better: they have a focus on recruiting Philadelphia students. They made a deal with the city years ago to swap some land with them; in exchange, they give out a hundred full scholarships a year to Philadelphia students. They have a mortgage plan that allows people who work for the university to buy a home here."

That desire to be an impact player is not driven only by altruism. Fattah says the number one crime corner in Philadelphia is Fortieth and Walnut, right near where we're sitting. "This is where the neighborhood and the university meet. There have been some horrible incidents. One young man, a Ph.D. candidate in math, was accosted, assaulted for a few dollars, and killed on the street. The same thing happened ten and fifteen years ago, with the same headlines—same big splash.

"So, Penn has to do more. They've started to reach out, working with high schools in the community—creating scholarships. They've just launched a major program to get their students involved in community service. This is the kind of normal back and forth going on around the country. It's not just racially connected. Take Howard University in Washington, a city that's predominately black, a university that's historically black. There's the same kind of tensions between the community and the school. When you mix a bunch of young people who have everything going for them with young people who are not so certain they have anything going for them, it's going to happen. When you add race to it, it just becomes more probable.

"This neighborhood's got a lot of different sides to it. On one side, it's the well-to-do, university faculty and administrators, but within a couple of blocks of the university, on all sides, there are distressed communities. There are young people running around these streets who don't perceive themselves as having a significant future. Add that to a group of kids who assume that they're going to rule the world. It can be interesting. We have a high school near here, University City High. We've had some significant problems between African-American and Asian kids. The racial tensions in the inner city are not just black and white anymore."

After reviewing the long litany of distressing trends and signs of decay, Fattah can still be upbeat about his city's future. "Mainly because I see people reconnecting at the block level. Having said that, we're still losing more jobs than we bring in. And the new jobs that are being created here are ones that require a college-level education. If you're unemployed in my district you're likely to have no educational credentials at all.

"The other day, I spent time with juvenile offenders. These particular kids are on the fringe of things. I am amazed at the intellectual prowess of the young men I met in jail. It's not formal education. But they are bright young men. They are convinced that people like me have no understanding of what they have to face in their everyday lives. Many are in prison for serious crimes. But virtually all are going to see the light of day again someday, outside those walls. What's out there for them?

"Listen to the words they use. They talk about 'living large,' and 'blowing up.' They don't have a very optimistic view of life. They don't have a trust fund waiting for them when they get out of prison. So when they hit the streets, they will again start to act based on their own information. They take risks based on expectations that they will die violent deaths, or die very young."

Our conversation turned to the changing political fortunes of black politicians in big-city America. In the 1980s, with higher office the exclusive province of white politicians, the country's biggest cities elected black mayors. The elections of Tom Bradley in Los Angeles, Harold Washington in Chicago, Wilson Goode in Philadelphia, and David Dinkins in New York were taken as signs of a shift in the power equation of urban America. If whites had decamped to the suburbs, went the thinking, then black voters would have a chance to send a black politician to the mayor's office.

All four of these mayors were succeeded by white men, which led to the despairing cry of black activists, "We lost city hall!" In all the above-mentioned cities, and in Kansas City, St. Louis, Minneapolis, Cleveland, and other major cities electing black mayors in recent years, there was speculation about black mayors "taking care of their own," and predictions of further losses in white middle-class population.

"I think people are very, very uncomfortable with shifts in power, that empower people that are different from them. I don't think it's much of a surprise that we have a dearth of women in elective office, and minorities, and when you have elections take place like the Wilson Goode election, you had people threatening to move out of the city, you had people talking like the world was going to come to an end because an African American was going to be sitting in the mayor's chair.

"I wrote a response to an editorial in the *Inquirer,* it's dated now, there was a comment in the paper, blacks had taken over the city, taken over the party, and I wrote a piece that showed that even though Wilson was mayor, on the city council, seventeen people, I think there were six African Americans, I think there are still six today. On the school board there were two African Americans out of seven or so, and I just went on down detail by detail to make the point that even though Wilson was mayor, power was still pretty well dispersed in the city, and that was a fairly abnormal thing for me to do, because I usually don't respond to those senseless comments. But I thought it was important because there was this feeling that Wilson was in power, and so trash was only going to get picked up in the black community, that the only people who were going to get jobs or contracts were blacks.

"People know that in politics it's not enough to be in the room, you've got to be at the table, and when people get a chance to make choices, they are arbitrary choices. African Americans and Hispanics were never in the investment banking business until they started winning minority seats, and city halls started deciding which investment houses, which law firms, were going to manage the bond deals. Every city's got to borrow money, every school district's got to borrow money, every turnpike, every government entity borrows money, for its operations. They go into the bond market in New York and borrow hundreds of millions of dollars at a time, and the people who orchestrate these deals make tens of millions of dollars in fees.

"Every year Goldman Sachs is number one in the country in municipal financing, and Merrill Lynch is up there and a few other firms are up there, and as African Americans and Hispanics started winning seats a few other firms started getting up there, you know, Brigsby, Brandfordson, and Malcolm Priors; Cisneros had a firm, Cisneros Asset Management, there was another one out of Texas. The SEC gets together and says, no more political contributions, none of these investment banking houses can give any more political contributions, then you see all these minority firms have dropped off the map because they don't have the access and the wherewithal.

"But before Dinkins became mayor of New York no black firm had ever done an investment banking deal. When Wilson Goode became mayor that brought the first time an African American had ever been the manager of a financing deal. This is a simple, everyday deal in local government, you have to borrow money to get things done, take a loan until you get the property taxes, or wage taxes at the end of the quarter, but this is the kind of white-collar patronage that is never, never, sprinkled over. There are all kinds of fields just like that. Once people take political power there's a sense that some people are going to be moved out of the political gravy line to make room for new people, just as it was when the Irish lost control to the Italians and so forth. New people were added to the mix, but there seemed to be a great deal of concern about that when it was African Americans.

"Even though Dinkins and Goode did a great deal, they never could have done business the way their predecessors had done. When Bill Greene was the mayor of Philadelphia, literally one firm did 90 percent. Wolf, Block, Shore and Cohen did all of the city's work, essentially. When Wilson came in he said, we're going to rotate law firms, we're going to rotate investment banking firms, so yes, African Americans were included, Hispanic firms were included, women-owned firms were included, but they were rotated. The concern was to deal with the criticisms, or expected attacks that were obvious.

"As a consequence the minority electorate is not as enthused. You saw it with Dinkins, you saw it with others. When the second time comes around, or the third time . . . they have not seen the same degree of benefit, and even though you know their expectations are off the ceilings anyway. They expect more.

"I think there have been 123 mayors since Philadelphia existed, and there's been one African American, and you can't correct everything that's happened across those 123 mayors with one mayoralty. So African Americans and other minority politicians have additional burdens on them to figure out how to get those things done."

The changes on the street—the interplay of longtime residents and newcomers, black and white, Latino and Asian—are all mirrored in changes in the calculus at city hall, at the chamber of commerce, and at the school board. Change can be managed, by individuals and institutions. Not all ethnic succession carries with it the inexorable weight of entropy. Not all whites hang on to every last shred of clout past their time. Not all blacks yearn for a return to the mayor's office to begin settling scores. New ethnic dispensations—on the street and in the halls of power— have come with time, along with the admission that things are better now, and will never go back to the old ways again.

Chapter 5

Side Trip–St. Louis

When Veronica Evans is asked, "Would you leave this neighborhood, if you had the cash? If you *could* go?" she gives a surprising answer. "No, I wouldn't leave. I couldn't leave now." She had been working on her block, working on her neighborhood with a brave little band of home-owners in a blasted landscape.

Reporters ask a lot of questions already prepared for a specific answer: They want to get it "on the record." I had assumed Veronica Evans wanted the first thing smoking out of town. I hadn't reckoned with people caring so deeply about their crumbling streets, shuttered shopping strips, and dim prospects for the future that they would stay even when going was a possibility. A lot of people I had met while traveling around the country were engaged in a daily struggle to bail out the leaky life rafts their neighborhoods had become. In the Wells-Goodfellow section of St. Louis, the damage was already done. But Veronica Evans, like many of her neighbors, wanted to stay.

The contrast between the conditions in the city of St. Louis and its vast suburbs is stark, and stunning. Large sections of the city are now virtually empty. Children thread their way through vacant lots in the morning, converging on the neighborhood school in Evans's area, Pierre Laclede, named for the French founder of St. Louis. Standing adjacent to the vacant lots are the board-ups, stout brick houses once home to one, two, and four families. Now the generous front porches are permanently empty, the windows covered in plywood, the houses empty except when colonized by squatters and drug dealers or stripped by salvagers.

The board-ups are so frightening to the neighborhood that many decide a vacant lot is better. A common and effective focus of grassroots activity centers is on demolition petitions. You can tell a lot about a neighborhood when there is general rejoicing after another intact building tumbles to the wrecker's ball.

For Veronica Evans, watching her own back is one thing; worrying about her son Chris is another. "He's eleven now, and he's a big boy, very big for his age. When we first moved to this area, gang members were always stopping him, punching him, pushing him around, asking, 'Who are you claiming?' He would always tell them, 'I'm not claiming nobody,' or, 'I'm just claiming myself.' Now he says, 'I claim Jesus,' and most of the time they leave him alone.

"But last year some boys were bothering him for his Chicago Bulls jacket, and he didn't want to give it up. He came running home, and he came in all upset, and I asked him, 'What's wrong? Tell me what's wrong!' And just then, I heard gunshots and we had to get down, somebody was shooting up the side of the house with an AK-47. I said, 'It's time to call the police.'

"The police came and started questioning my son about his gang affiliations. You know, they assumed, because he's big and black, and he has a sports jacket, that he's got to be in a gang.

"I understood why they were asking him those questions, and I know why they were asking me, too. In a community like this one, where we've got kids who are dying, and their parents denying, telling people they're not in gangs, but they are. Chris has lost five friends to gang violence. Their parents aren't necessarily bad parents, but they just don't know what their kids are up to. I can't tell you what my child is doing right now. You never know."

As we walked around the neighborhood, Evans's compassion shone through her disappointment at the cruelties some of her neighbors inflict on each other. "Some of them really want to be good parents, but they can't. They have dependency problems, and they just can't do better. When their children get locked up, they are at a loss too. And when their children shoot somebody, it's like a death in their family, too. At the same time as you're angry at them, I feel sorry for that mother. Once she sat up all night rocking that child, like any other mother did.

"Everybody talks about the drug problems in this neighborhood. But where is that problem coming from? We don't grow no dope here. We don't own the planes that fly in with drugs in them. You see on the TV those problems with North Side people with crime and drugs. Who are these young people selling to? When you see vanilla people sitting in a car in the neighborhood, they aren't tourists. You know it's a drop. They're either dropping or making a buy."

I know what she says is true. In some of the places in America where you are least likely to see a white face, white kids in cars make the trip. Sometimes they drive a sports car, reeking of parental wealth and privilege; sometimes they drive a responsible, suburban hand-me-down family car. From either windshield they gaze out, navigating a world that is not theirs, scanning the street for a contact, driving a little slower than someone who wants to be inconspicuous should.

You can sit on the porch of graystones on particular blocks in Lawndale, one of Chicago's most devastated neighborhoods, and watch the suburban white boys drive by. They cruise the blocks a few times, then stop at a corner. A short time later, a local quickly walks to the car from a building you might otherwise think was abandoned. After a short conversation, a brief touch, or handshake, the car takes off, to return for a quick visit a few moments later, before speeding off again in search of the city line. You don't need to be a detective to find the same activity in Manhattan's Washington Heights, where drug buyers from New Jersey can score right after coming off the George Washington Bridge. You can find such commerce in southeast D.C., where easy access from the suburbs and close-by yuppie enclaves of Capitol Hill provide a ready market.

Just after her son's run-in with the local gangs, Evans, a short, stout woman of thirty with a gentle manner and an easy smile, started trying to enlist her neighbors in the fight for control of the streets. She meets regularly with a dozen neighbors who keep tabs on everything happening on their street and surrounding blocks. The police, once regarded with suspicion (and often enough, with good reason), are now allies in the wars against fly dumping (the clandestine dumping of building supplies, industrial waste, or bulk household waste on vacant land), crack sales, gang violence, and the general disorder that can break out in the widening gaps between the inhabited buildings of Wells-Goodfellow.

Evans points with pride not only to the community garden, where the children of Laclede School spend their spring and fall learning about botany and nutrition, but to the boarded-up two-family home directly across the street from the main entrance of the school. "They were selling drugs in here. We called the police, and kept calling, and kept calling until we got them out of here. But it was sad. The other tenants weren't involved in selling drugs. They was probably just as scared as us. They left too. It was also difficult because, in that same apartment with the people who was selling the drugs, was an older person and a little baby."

She has no idea what happened to any of the people who once lived in this large brick building. After the tenants were cleared out and the building was boarded up, squatters moved in. They ran an electric line from the alley and began cooking over wood fires. Knowing that such buildings become a petri dish for street crime and a danger to adjacent neighbors, Evans and her partners leaned on the police again, and today the building is once more shut up tight.

"I think it doesn't make any sense to have a nice building like this just sitting here when people need places to live. It couldn't cost that much to fix this place up to make it good enough to live in." But the longer the buildings stay empty, the more they deteriorate; floors buckle from summer expansion and winter contraction, broken windows let in the water that wrecks walls and floors, intruders set fires, water pipes burst with the cold. The real problem with a brick building like the one across the street from the school is that it is a leftover, a relic from a past economy. "It's a shame when they got to knock them down, instead of fixing them up. But if nobody wants to fix them up, there's really nothing else we can do."

There was once value in every square foot of the building. Somebody bought the land. Somebody paid for the construction of the building, which not only has room for one large family but for an extended family or renters. As a neighborhood slips down the rungs of the economic ladder, the human resources to keep a building whole constantly decrease: the number of people with the wherewithal to buy at a price that would be satisfactory compensation to the landlord, the number of people with sufficient income to pay a rent that covers costs in full and on time, and the number of owners able or willing to keep an aging property in working order, with the occasional large capital investment required.

Sometimes the failure of a boiler, the need for new electrical wiring, a flood in the basement is all that it takes to tip a building from a rough equilibrium between costs and revenues to an economically irrational asset. Absentee landlords can read a balance sheet as well as any other owner. The farther they live from the apartment, the more they are shielded from the economic brute force of their decisions. The cost of taxes, maintenance, and the occasional repair gets leveraged against declining and sporadic rents at the "going rate" in a neighborhood and, at some point, the value imbedded in a property eventually reaches zero. There is no cannonade . . . no bugle sounds . . . no banner unfurled from the second-floor porch. A multiton bundle of bricks and plaster, paint and pipes and wire, has just quietly moved from the asset column to become a liability, not just for the former owner but for the city of St. Louis and the entire neighborhood. Preventing the building's slide into criminal activity, putting out the fire that will someday be set there, cleaning up the asbestos- and lead-laced rubble left behind by the demolition crew all cost money a struggling city like St. Louis can ill afford. The abandoned buildings house both real crime and the worst fantasies of suburban whites that drive their perceptions of inner-city life. For all the buildings that do become home to shooting galleries, crack kitchens, or gang flophouses, others sit, mute and decaying. The pictures of these homes are a staple of the evening news in big metropolitan areas, acting as potent symbols in the minds of many Americans. To a marked extent, people who left in the Great Migration or the sons and daughters of those who did harbor beliefs based on a grain of truth. But these beliefs are more stubborn than anything based just on statistics.

Greater St. Louis, huddled around the confluence of the St. Charles and Mississippi Rivers, is the fourteenth-largest metropolitan area in the United States, with some 2.5 million residents living in two states—Missouri and Illinois—spread over eleven counties and the city of St. Louis. During the nineties, the city of St. Louis has earned some dubious distinctions: the urban core makes up one of the smallest percentages of the population among the thirty-five largest metropolitan areas, trailed only by the relatively healthy Minneapolis, the anemic Atlanta, the intensive care–bound Washington, D.C., and the Boston metro, which now splays out into New Hampshire, Rhode Island, Massachusetts, and Maine. That small urban core, the city of St. Louis, has lost more of its population in the 1990s than any of the other cities. While Atlanta's population has remained stagnant, its metropolitan area has boomed, posting the largest net in-migration of all American metros. By comparison, the city of St. Louis has continued to shrink, and its metropolitan population, the most sprawled in America, posted one of the smallest overall population changes in the country, a loss of twenty-nine thousand. The St. Louis region has one of the highest median ages, one of the smallest working-age populations, and one of the largest shares of elderly people in all the largest metropolitan areas.

There is bittersweet irony in St. Louis's historical confinement between North and South. In the North, the suburbs closed in early around the big cities, hardening their permanent boundaries before the twentieth century began, while in the South and West, cities like Houston, Dallas, Atlanta, and Los Angeles have continued to grow through annexation. During the nineteenth century, St. Louis was a Northern-flavored city on the edge of Southern-flavored Missouri. St. Louisans' fear of political domination after Reconstruction, by the strongly Jim Crow "Little Dixie" region surrounding it, brought a vote for complete independence and separation of county and city functions in 1876.

They could never have imagined they were signing their own death warrant, these local worthies who froze their borders and took on home rule with St. Louis at sixty-one square miles, and nowhere to grow. By the 1920s, business leaders saw the writing on the wall and sponsored a referendum to incorporate St. Louis County into what would have become the world's largest city. It was approved by city voters and overwhelmingly defeated in the county. There have been periodic attempts in the decades since to move the city-county divide, but as the city decayed and power shifted to the county, change became less and less likely. Despite the full blast of regional boosterism contained in brochures, videos, and annual publications from the East-West Gateway Coordinating Council, a regional business development organization, the outlook is not promising. Once the country's fourth-largest city, St. Louis now hovers around thirtieth place.

On a bitter cold December night, I headed over to a community meeting with Veronica Evans. It is held in a space donated by a landlord unable to rent the unit, as a block club headquarters. The owner can only hope that grassroots work can make his properties desirable again. Around the table sat retired city workers, young parents, representatives of local church-based not-for-profits, and the local police precinct commander. Over coffee and cookies, the block association reviews its work with police on a host of problems. The commander had theorized that the people who dump bulk trash for free in the neighborhood's vacant lots, rather than pay for the privilege at the landfill, were suburbanites who faced rising tipping fees in their own and surrounding communities. He was wrong. "I am sorry to report," says Commander Thomas Hegger, "that when the antidumping task force assembled all the zip codes for the arrests and summonses for dumping violations over the last six months, the majority are from the city of St. Louis." But the commander also brings good news: Crime against persons, like muggings and assaults, is down 10 percent from a year ago. This announcement is greeted with applause around the table.

The neighbors are worried about a local grocer near the school who intends to apply for a liquor license. Several block club members have already registered complaints with the alderman, and Commander Hegger has gone one better, writing a letter to the licensing board announcing his intention to oppose the granting of the license, if and when it comes up for a hearing. Veronica Evans reports that drug sales from a persistently troubling house on the next block have started up again—from the apartment of a woman whose son was recently arrested by Commander Hegger's officers for the gang rape of a young teenager.

The neighbors talk about derelict properties and demolition orders. They talk about the tactics used by another block club nearby to speed up the demolition process. They talk with the representatives of the not-for-profits about restoring units instead of tearing them down. Throughout the meeting setbacks are met with concern and a plan for tackling them. Good news is met with real satisfaction and optimism. In spite of everything they're up against, it seems, these people who inhabit what would look like America's urban nightmare on a newspaper cover, or during the late news, really believe they can control their blocks, and thus take more control of their lives.

Some twenty miles away, in St. Charles County, the attitude seems less upbeat. The residents of a recently built suburban subdivision have gotten together to organize a neighborhood watch and hear from the local police about how residents and the police force can work together against crime. There is a strange juxtaposition between this block meeting and the one back in St. Louis. In Wells-Goodfellow, the people live with the daily possibility of sudden, convulsive, dangerous crime and worry about their children making their way in the streets. Here in St. Charles, where it would seem you have a better chance of getting hit by lightning than over the head by a mugger, the fear of crime is intense.

One neighbor new to St. Charles from the Illinois side of the metro area says, "I never feel safe. Sure, I feel safer here than I do in other areas, but I don't think you can ever feel safe, that crime is something you don't have to worry about. Look at the news, look in the newspaper, it doesn't matter where you live."

This is a community started from scratch. Many of the people gathered in Pat and Lisa Petroff's living room moved to St. Charles from the northern part of St. Louis County, from the suburbs closest to Wells-Goodfellow. They've pulled up stakes from previous hometowns and home states to come to an area with a low crime rate and a total absence of the urban madness that crowds their late news each night. And they're still afraid. Their benign landscape seems to offer little reassurance.

What makes these people feel such palpable danger, such threat while living in comfortable homes strung along semicircular drives laid over what was once rolling farmland? A woman says, "To me, there's no real place you're going to be able to go to get away from crime. It's gonna be wherever you go." They all feel that "having good neighbors is the key to having a safe neighborhood."

One man, who recently moved from the north St. Louis County town of Florissant, explains what he wants from his new home. "You work hard, and you want to be comfortable and safe. As a matter of fact, I've run into six people I graduated from high school with who are now living in this area."

At the community meeting, the police representatives do not reassure these homeowners or dispel their fear of crime. The chief, a uniformed patrol officer, and his community relations representative were all on hand to say, in effect, "You're right. It's out there."

The word *drugs* isn't even mentioned in St. Charles. There are complaints about the drivers who speed through the lightly trafficked streets, questions about front-door locks, and a lively discussion about the fines levied when a home security system is accidentally triggered, summoning police needlessly to the house.

This is the world they bought by moving, putting up with the traffic jams to and from work. They do have property to protect. They do *not* have to face gang rapes, fly dumping, crack houses, and drive-by shootings.

Pat and Lisa Petroff hosted that meeting. Pat is a firefighter in another suburb. Lisa's a registered nurse in a nearby hospital. Pat told me: "One of the biggest factors why we were moving in the first place was to leave a higher crime area. I was involved in local politics in that little town in St. Louis County, across the bridge and maybe ten miles north from where we are now—so I heard a lot more about crime through the police chief and the police department than the general public. I didn't want to raise my daughters in that environment. I work twenty-four-hour shifts as a firefighter, and I definitely didn't want to leave my wife and children home alone in that environment. That played a big factor in why we wanted to leave that area.

"The school districts are much better here. The insurance rates are a drastic drop out here from where we were, not only for homes but for cars as well. My insurance agent said it was the low level of crime in the area."

I suggested that even though the crime rate in this area is low, and the national crime rate had dropped, national polls showed that regardless of the statistics, people worried about crime at a consistently high level. Lisa Petroff remains cautious. "I think crime is going to happen no matter where you live. I don't think you should ever put your guard down, even though the crime rates may be lower there's still crime going on."

Her husband agreed: "I don't think any of us with any common sense can afford to say, well, on a piece of paper, my odds are less than 10 percent to be attacked—in my environment—where I live. That doesn't do me any good.

"I have worked in the City of St. Louis. I still have a lot of friends who work down there, and that combination of my past experience and their present experiences and the media's experiences are enough for me to put two and two together. That's enough. I know what's right and what's wrong and I make my judgment based on those.

"As far as the lifestyle out here, and the lifestyle in the inner city or wherever goes . . . I think we all live in our own little worlds. We're all interconnected, and help each other in different ways. Police and fire services, other services work together. I think we coexist, but there is an element of separation."

Lisa Petroff indicates that her family is cautious about visiting the city: "There's a few areas in the city with the theaters and what not. We love to go to them, we love to visit, but we won't bring the family down there because we have that sense of the possibility that it's not a family environment, or we don't want to expose our children to that area."

The Petroffs are optimists. Whatever the problems of the city or any other neighborhood, they are not dystopian. Lisa talked about their married lives, and the crazy work schedules of a firefighter and a nurse. Their new home gave them a sense they had turned a corner. "We've come a long way to get where we are, and with us working as hard as we do, I think we'll be in good shape five years from now." One thing you won't hear is hesitation, or a tone of apology about moving farther from the city.

Both Petroffs were disappointed by the 1996 referendum defeating a proposal to extend the St. Louis Metrolink system out to St. Charles. Pat said, "I was in favor of it myself. One of the biggest issues was crime, that it would have brought crime to this area. I guess people thought it was cheaper for the crooks to pay a dollar and come out here on the Metrolink, as opposed to taking a taxicab for fifteen! It was definitely one of the big issues, and in our opinion, a poor excuse. In this case, I think fear overrode rationality."

Perceptions about crime are long-lasting. St. Louis has been a part of the dropping urban violent crime rates of the 1990s. Yet here, as in cities across the country, there's been a lag time between the drop in the crime statistics and a rise in the comfort levels. A national survey conducted in 1996 by the Pew Center for the People and the Press reported that almost two-thirds of Americans believed the country was on the wrong track when it came to dealing with crime. Yet cities as different as Boston, Dallas, and San Diego experienced major drops in violent crime. New York's murder rate dropped to a near thirty-year low.

Rick Rosenfeld, a St. Louis criminologist, thinks about the conundrum in personal and professional terms. He grew up in St. Louis and now lives in an inner-ring suburb.

"I think there's two reasons why concern about crime remains strong. One is, crime rates remain very high. We're coming down off a terribly high plateau, and compared to other Western industrial countries, crime rates in the United States—serious crime, violent crime—are still very high. I don't think Americans are typically comparing the United States with other societies when they answer questions about their fear of crime. But the sense that we have too much of it is realistic.

"Why don't people get a little less anxious when the crime rates come down a little bit? In many places in the country, St. Louis included, crime rates have come down more than just a little bit over the last few years. I think there the second reason comes in, and that is, that people have a sense that crime in recent years, in the last decade or so, changed in fundamental ways.

"Offenders have gotten younger. That perception does, in fact, fit the reality. Offenders in violent crime are considerably younger than they were a decade ago. There is, however, a perception that people are more likely to be victimized by a stranger in a violent offense as well as in a property offense. That perception tends not to be as true. It is true that fewer criminals are processed in some way by the criminal justice system. Fewer serious crimes are solved through arrest. And that goes for homicide, too. That doesn't mean that the person was victimized by a stranger, it just means the police have a harder time closing cases now.

"I think that if people did have a sense that violent crime was still an activity that flowed through the 'normal' interactional channels—that you are more likely to be victimized by someone you know—that you're more likely to be victimized closer to home rather than farther away from home—if people had that sense, I think some of the free-floating anxiety about crime would dissipate.

"The real homicide reductions have occurred in the U.S. over the last twenty to twenty-five years in the age group twenty-five and above. A good example is the dramatic decline in intimate-partner homicides over the past twenty-five years in the United States. What's contributed to that reduction is the reduced rate of marriage, the increased age at which people marry, and a shortening of the time in which people engage in non-marital cohabiting relationships. In a variety of ways, adults have arranged to make it much less likely that they are going to do serious harm to one another.

"But when you think about what those changes in living arrangements mean for a family, and what traditional families have meant for children, in terms of the care, and supervision, and support, and nurturing provided by adults, we're in the process of creating a reconstituted family that in some ways offers more protection to adults at the expense of children.

"St. Louis is a city in many ways in trouble, like most large central cities in the United States. And I think people tend to use the crime rates, and even pump them up a little bit, as an indicator of a much broader set of concerns about the place they're living in—about a more general deterioration in the quality of life. I haven't seen people standing on the corners applauding the lowering of the crime rate in St. Louis or where my brother lives in D.C. I think a lot of people realize the crime rate has come down, but there are other things happening to their city that continue to make them anxious. So if you ask them questions about quality of life, anxiety gets registered, even for people who do know, objectively speaking, that things are a little bit better now."

I told Rosenfeld about my visits to the community meetings in St. Louis and the suburbs and the arm's-length relationship the Petroffs now had with the city. Were the maps accurate that suburbanites carried in their heads when they visit the city? "People have a grainy sense, a rough sense of where to drive, and where not to drive—and they're not far off.

"The problem is the sin of overgeneralization. What they miss coming through areas their neighbors would refer to as dicey, are all pockets of safety, and block groups—the collection of streets that are quite unlike what they think of as high-risk areas."

We talked about the widely shared idea that one of the best things you can do for your family is move out of the city. Even though there are now more blacks with that kind of mobility, moving out is generally a white option. I wondered if Rosenfeld thought crime was used not to mask a host of other concerns about city life but as an excuse that will always be supported.

"It is clear that crime is an impetus for much of that mobility, on the part of families with prospects—both black and white. Blacks still face discriminatory barriers that white families don't, in moving from the cities to the suburbs. This is, after all, the United States. This is a society that, since the beginning, has always equated moving up with moving out. We happen to be in a city, St. Louis, where if you move west, you're making progress. That's a smaller version of the story of the United States. So crime rates can be used to explain mobility, and I think they do to a certain degree. But it transcends crime. The problem for the society and its crime rate is: What happens to the people in the communities who get left behind?

"It would be the height of bad faith to counsel people to stay where they are, to continue to put up with whatever problems they define as problems in their own communities, and not move. What I don't like about mobility in the United States out of cities into suburbs, and now increasingly from inner suburbs into outer suburbs, is the throwaway attitude that goes along with it. That once you move from a community, the larger metropolitan area or the larger community has no responsibility or not much for what got left behind there. What they leave behind is much worse without them. The tragedy of mobility here is not that people leave the city of St. Louis: it's that so few resources go into the communities left behind to make them attractive to the families that are one or two cars down the line, who themselves might want to move into that neighborhood. I don't think mobility is the issue. It's our unwillingness to do anything about the tragic conditions that occur once people leave.

"Chasing people out of the city and reminding them of their moral and community obligations, as desirable as that might be on some level, is something of a lost cause. I would prefer that we work on strategies with a better chance. There are thousands of people in the suburbs who, right now, are waiting to be brought into some kind of coalition, who would like to see more pennies in tax dollars spent to make sure that the community, and its center, hold. I think that can happen without chasing all the exurbanites down, and forcing them to pay their fair share."

People on the run aren't the best neighbors. Does the way we live at century's end contribute to what Rosenfeld called "free-floating anxiety"?

"It is true that people in communities, all else equal, who know their neighbors, are people who are less fearful, holding constant the crime rate in the community. So clearly there are lots of good reasons why it's important to know your neighbors. I have to tell you that I don't know many of my neighbors and I've lived in my neighborhood for several years now. That's because I'm rushing in and out of my house to get to and from work and to get to and from all the other places that I do business and live my life." To see people getting the balance right, Rosenfeld says, he looks at his teenage children.

"My kids have a sense of the city that's not unlike the one that we've been using as an implicit model, as a place that has a vital center. At that point, their view of the city as a livable place, and as a safe place, differs from the traditional one that I continue to hold. They're more mobile. Their sense of the city is much less rooted to single geographic poles."

I left Rosenfeld with a final story about my tour of Wells-Goodfellow with Veronica Evans. While we talked about her block club's struggle to wrest control of the boarded-up building from the junkies and whores, she told me that if there was a similar house in St. Charles, where people were selling drugs, it would be taken care of much more quickly than it is on her street.

He didn't hesitate: "She's absolutely right, there's no question about it. And there are two reasons: St. Charles has the political will and resources to do it, to a greater degree than many neighborhoods in St. Louis, and it doesn't have the volume of that kind of problem. If you are the St. Louis police department and you're in contact with a dozen community groups that have just identified a dozen crack houses to take down, it might not get taken down as rapidly as you'd like. That's not the case in St. Charles."

So Veronica Evans must work hard in concert with her neighbors, sometimes for months at a time, to accomplish what might be taken care of with a phone call just a few miles away. This will not strike many millions of Americans as unjust, since their understanding of the rewards system in society intimately ties possession to worthiness, and poverty to unworthiness. In the current culture wars any attempt to question today's rewards system is called "class envy" or "class warfare," while the defenders of widening inequality have no problem at all with discussing the sloth of the poor.

Eventually, public perceptions will catch up with what's been happening with central-city crime. It may be too much to hope that cities will eventually be thought of—and portrayed in the culture—as "nice, safe places to live." At least the national crime trends of the 1990s have given the cities a chance.

Perceptions on their own won't save the cities. But getting the Petroffs and Veronica Evans and her son into the same mental universe could help remind everyone of the ties of mutual dependence that bind the fate of the cities and suburbs, even now.

Chapter 6

The America Factory, Brooklyn, N.Y.

I t covers just seventy-one square miles on the western tip of an offshore island of the United States. It hasn't been a city in its own right in one hundred years. It hasn't had its own daily newspaper since the *Daily Eagle* folded in the 1950s. It hasn't had its own major league baseball team since the last day of the 1957 season. These few square miles loom large in the American mind. Though a little less than 1 percent of all Americans live here when John Travolta crossed the disco floor in *Saturday Night Fever* and Thomas Wolfe wrote, "You can never go home again," and Jackie Gleason growled, "To the moon, Alice!" and Neil Sedaka sang, "Breaking up is hard to do . . . ," and Walt Whitman wrote, "I hear America singing," and Spike Lee brought us inside Joe's Bed-Stuy Barber Shop, into pizzerias and brownstones, and Woody Allen drove Annie Hall across the bridge to show her Coney Island—that was Brooklyn talking to you, America.

Excuse me if I break the bounds of journalistic restraint and rhapsodize a little. Brooklyn is my hometown. Within its watery boundaries live some two and a half million souls, making it larger on its own than most of the ten largest American cities. It was once a mighty factory town. It made everything, employed prosperous, overall-wearing masses, and turned people from everywhere into Americans.

The factories are for the most part gone. Like members of a vanishing species, some hang on in tiny ecological niches, near the canals and expressways and docks. You'll see places that once provided work and money and new shoes and Catholic school tuitions for generations of families still standing in clusters, gently tumbling down the economic evolutionary scale. . . . Heavy industrial plants now house "assembly" operations of components from other places, factories now serve as warehouses . . . warehouses become empty and gutted.

New York is the biggest mouth in the world. It appears to be the prime example of the survival of the herd instinct, leading the universal urban conspiracy to deprive man of his birthright (the good ground), to hang him by his eyebrows from skyhooks above hard pavements, to crucify him, sell him, or be sold by him.

Frank Lloyd Wright, 1958

Perhaps the crusty Mr. Wright would have been softened by some time in Brooklyn. Let's start the story on my street—Pacific Street—in the late fifties. The apartment was on the top floor, cost fifty dollars a month, and had 750 square feet of living space. The building was completed in 1908. Along both sides of the street were similar big, boxy apartment buildings with small front staircases that ran right out to the sidewalk, without the buffer of a lawn. The apartments had big rooms and many of the amenities that now turn up in the real estate section of a big-city paper as "details": French doors, ornamental door frames, moldings, parquet floors. Not much of a place for gardens, this part of Pacific Street, on the edge of the Crown Heights section of Brooklyn. From the stoop you can hear the rumble of the New York subway, climbing out of a tunnel onto elevated tracks that ran west through Brooklyn and into Queens. Today the block itself is quiet, even desolate. Many of the windows of the apartment buildings are bricked up after fires. Some of the buildings without fire-scorched brick aren't fully rented.

Here my mother used to roller-skate and walk home from school. My father delivered the *Eagle* and met my mother on his route. He had arrived from Puerto Rico just a few years before. She was a Yankee, a Brooklyn native. They married in the mid-fifties. He headed off to sea, and she took the train to Wall Street. I started life on the same block where my mother grew up.

When the 1960s began, my mother was pregnant again, and the family concluded that the long-term prospects for the area were not good. The people you saw shopping, in school, and at the church on the corner all your life were disappearing. The elderly were urged by their children to come to other parts of Brooklyn, to Long Island, to New Jersey, and to the fancier sections of the Bronx. The impact of all those people making their decisions, in effect, forced you to make your own.

We moved from Crown Heights to Bensonhurst, also in Brooklyn. Both sets of grandparents also left white-flight areas of northern Brooklyn and settled in new neighborhoods, Bensonhurst and Flatbush. The new neighborhood was much like the old one physically—apartment buildings and row houses and nearby blocks of single-family homes. But everything in Bensonhurst was newer. Once home to a Dutch settlement and, later, truck farms, this part of Brooklyn only revved up and developed after the streetcars and subways had extended out to the rest of the borough from its historic heart near the Brooklyn Bridge.

Unlike other national foundry towns—Youngstown, Pittsburgh, Detroit, Cleveland—Brooklyn did not shrink. Somehow this vast world of apartment houses, parkways, docks, and elevated trains has remained full, dense, bustling. Today the borough's population is not far below its historic high.

One of the best places to see Brooklyn is from the elevated trains. From where I grew up in Bensonhurst, the distant vista of the Manhattan skyline floats just above the tops of apartment buildings in the foreground. The shrieking rails are your Yellow Brick Road, the skyline your beckoning Emerald City. Today, I'm heading toward Coney Island. There, I'll change trains to ride through the heart of Brooklyn for a look at what recent decades have wrought. I've ridden this line nearly all my life and rode it daily from the time I started high school to my mid-twenties, when

I got married and moved away. What I left in 1980 was old Brooklyn. What was waiting for me on the train was new Brooklyn. Chinese have moved by the thousands into the south and west of the borough, Hasidim have spread out of the small enclaves in Borough Park and Crown Heights and made the sight of men in long black coats and side locks (*peyes*) more common throughout the city. Two men huddle in one corner, having an argument in Russian, and right across from them a young Puerto Rican woman locks her stroller wheels and smiles at her baby as the train jerks into motion. At one time all these people would have called vastly different parts of Brooklyn home. Now, the lines of demarcation are fainter. Fewer areas are ethnic ghettos where different kinds of people are unlikely to set eyes on each other or hear another language.

We rumble along above Eighty-sixth Street, the main street of Benson-hurst. The din inside the train is exceeded only by the roar on the side-walks. This was once a family shopping district, a place where a car was unnecessary. The boom families of the 1960s strolled Eighty-sixth Street on the prowl for kids' shoes, baked goods, jewelry, and ladies' clothes—"popular" and "better" in the jargon of the garment district, where many of the men in the neighborhood made their living.

The train passes over busy stores, over the "two-up, one-down" three-family brick houses (buildings with two apartments stacked at the top of a flight of stairs, with a garden apartment at ground level next to the garage) that rose all over this part of Brooklyn during the 1970s and 1980s. The homes are in orderly rows along the side streets which end in huge apartment buildings on the main streets. The "nicer" part of Eighty-sixth Street had always been known as "The Avenue," and the discount stores, odd lots, and fruit-and-vegetable stands that start on Bay Parkway were called "the Market."

I'm above the Market now. The Italian-born greengrocers have now given way to Korean families with Mexican employees. In the distance I can see K Mart, inside what was once EJ Korvette, a middlebrow retailer for a middlebrow neighborhood. It was predicted, in the sixties, when Korvette's opened its doors, that it would destroy Eighty-sixth Street. Family-owned businesses catering to shoppers on foot had been hurt by the opening of department stores in many other parts of New York City.

But it didn't happen quite that way. What brought down Eighty-sixth Street was the same change that eventually brought down Korvette's itself: the transformation of consumer taste—the "un-middling" of retail, as merchants were forced to head way up- or way down-market or close their doors.

Macy's thus transformed itself in the late 1970s and early 1980s from a middle-class department store to a high-end emporium, devoted to meeting the needs of that newly emerging person created by the baby boom and a few decades of steady economic growth: the yuppie. Korvette's, Alexander's, Abraham & Straus, and many other department stores that neither followed Macy's up nor remade themselves as discount marketers eventually closed their doors. Sears and JC Penney, faced with many of the same pressures created by the evacuation of the middle range, held on only because of their huge size, market penetration, and, eventually, their aggressive, creative management.

Though a shopper strolling Eighty-sixth Street's market would be less likely to hear the Italian and Yiddish of the 1960s than today's Russian, Chinese, Korean, and Spanish, there are still plenty of cues to indicate that the Italian presence remains strong. Italian social clubs proclaim their allegiance to a particular town or province in Italy. You can buy a first-rate espresso on Eighty-sixth Street, and it's unlikely Starbucks will ever open anywhere near here.

If you're wondering why you know that name—Bensonhurst—there may be many reasons. Most benignly, I suppose, is its fictional role as the home of *The Honeymooners*. (Though the neighborhood was and is home to many Ralphs, Eds, Trixies, and Alices, the real Chauncey Street, television home to the Nortons and Kramdens, is clear on the other side of Brooklyn, in Jackie Gleason's own neighborhood of Brownsville.) Bensonhurst also served as the set for *Saturday Night Fever* on the big screen and *Welcome Back, Kotter* on the small one. When the Italian-American woman who falls for a black colleague in Spike Lee's *Jungle Fever* heads home, she takes the very same train I'm riding through Bensonhurst. When *The French Connection*'s Popeye Doyle made his terrifying high-speed run under the elevated tracks in Brooklyn, he was screaming up Eighty-sixth Street, and when a drug dealer met his end, shot in the back while running up the stairs to the elevated track, he did that at the front entrance of my own alma mater, John Dewey High School.

Less benign is Bensonhurst's membership in a litany of names that includes Montgomery, Selma, Birmingham, and Howard Beach, where particularly shocking race-based crimes, or racial confrontations, have made it possible to invoke outrage by using one loaded word. Bensonhurst. In 1989 a black teenager, Yusuf Hawkins, was shot to death by Bensonhurst teens when he and some friends came to the neighborhood to look at a used car. The crime set off months of racial confrontation, with that professional protester, the Reverend Al Sharpton, leading marches through the streets of the neighborhood, jeered at and baited by local boys and men.

Much of the reportage at the time, in local papers and from national networks, portrayed an all-white enclave where strangers and minorities were rarely seen. Those reporters may have been working from memory; *that* Bensonhurst was already gone. Today quiet young Muslim women in *hijabs* (head scarves), Indians in electric-colored saris, and Caribbeans of various complexions are searching the bargain bins in "the Market" for a good buy, jostling newly arrived Russians who've traded in their old lives, never-ending scarcity, and food lines for a streetscape promising endless "Sales!" Yet the killing of Yusuf Hawkins did tell the world of an angry and unreconstructed racial bias that still exists on many streets. But the lily-white Bensonhurst of newspaper reports and TV documentaries, where a lone black teenager could count on an invigorating sprint to the train station with white boys hot on his heels, is gone and has been for a long time. At a late-night pizza parlor in Westchester County, I recently observed a young Italian man from Bensonhurst asking for directions for home. The pizza maker asked how things are going in Bensonhurst, and the young man answered, "It's totally gone. All we got left is Eighteenth Avenue."

Brooklyn's white underbelly, which ran all the way from Sunset Park, overlooking Upper New York Bay, along the waterfront past Coney Island, Brighton, and Manhattan Beach, to Bergen Beach, Mill Basin, and the border with Queens, is no longer very white. Over the decades the Finns, Norwegians, Irish, Italians, Jews, and Italians who inhabited the broad crescent of southern Brooklyn have moved in the hundreds of thousands, and in doing so made room for the Puerto Ricans and Dominicans, American and West Indian blacks, Russians, Pakistanis, and Indians, who quietly infiltrated once-closed parts of Brooklyn. A piece of folk wisdom has grown up in many of these neighborhoods in the decades since World War II, often repeated as a boast or an indictment. "Jews run," Italians can still be heard to say, "but *we* defend our neighborhoods." But the zeal for battle appears to be sagging. Nowadays, as our man in the pizza shop would indicate, many Italians see themselves locked in a war of attrition. Many of the streets where "we" once held sway are, alas, "gone."

But from my perch on the B train, I can still see the backyards where Italians grow grapes on trellises, and the front yards where delicate fig trees will soon be bundled up to weather another winter in a climate where they don't really belong.

Continuing toward Coney Island, with the ocean now visible in the distance, we pass the town-sized public housing development—acres and acres—that make up the New York City Housing Authority's Marlboro Homes, while on the other side Bensonhurst's Lafayette High School, once virtually all white, now uneasily integrated, looms as large as the projects.

People who grew up in school districts where a whole town, or sometimes half a county, would feed the local high school wouldn't be ready for Lafayette High. It is a huge, blunt building. Metal screens—the kind you often see in factories—cover the windows. The daytime home of three thousand students, its population is itself larger than hundreds of school districts in America. Lafayette is really three schools; one institution prepares the college-bound for higher education, another slaps the patina of education onto people heading out to work, and a third provides custodial care to young people who are in school only because it is required by law.

Across the tracks, Marlboro did not use as its model for public housing the large, apartment-block towers so prevalent in other cities, and even in other parts of New York City. Perhaps because they had space to work with, perhaps because the surrounding community would not have supported them. Marlboro is built to human scale. The entryways to clusters of apartment buildings face each other. Built in 1958, the project is so old the trees are actually mature, and give one an idea of what the architects probably had in mind: small parks, shady trees, and lots of paths for strolling. But that sun-dappled vision, quickly built for a city in the midst of a housing shortage, has not exactly come to fruition. Once an integrated development, Marlboro is now primarily black and Latino. Once the home of middle-class and working-poor renters, it is now more uniformly poor; thus it is a frightening place to people who have never seen anything but the outside of the development, who drive by on the two main drags that border it and mutter about "the projects."

Next to the projects sits John Dewey High, a public high school that draws its student body from all of Brooklyn. On a recent graduation day, you could see the changes in the borough, in flesh and bone, as a smiling queue of seniors snaked its way to the risers set up on the school's front lawn to receive their diplomas. On this particular June morning, more than twenty years after my own long march to the platform, with many of the same teachers seated in folding chairs and looking on, came a fascinating parade of Indians and Pakistanis, Chinese and Vietnamese, Russian-born graduates, and young Muslim women who wore mortarboards over their head scarves, as tiny Asian grandmothers craned their necks for a glimpse of their own American Dream. The Latinos in line were no longer exclusively Puerto Ricans; they now had company from the Dominican Republic and the rest of the hemisphere. If you looked at my own yearbook you would have seen page after page of Jews of Eastern European extraction, Italians from two or three earlier waves of immigration, and scattered among the grandchildren of European immigrants, blacks (American-born and Caribbean), Puerto Ricans (island- and mainland-born), and Chinese (rarely children of American-born parents). Now the black faces were not scattered here and there but were a major presence in the class. In the hundreds of names in the columns of graduating seniors, only a few were Italian, Irish, and Jewish—the names that had once formed the majority of the class.

From my train car now, you can see Coney Island in the distance, a view bracketed by enormous apartment complexes wound in highway interchanges and elevated tracks. My train crosses reeking, stagnant Coney Island Creek and pulls into the station that millions before me have rolled into—a bathing suit and a towel tucked under the arm—ready for a day of swimming, the amusement park, fried clams, and Nathan's hot dogs and fries.

You can still see, in the faded advertisements painted on brick walls, and in shuttered storefronts, what fun this place was thirty, forty, and fifty years ago. The bathhouses and the restaurants, the attractions and the Atlantic. After the war, with low unemployment and a winning ball club, and the diversions of Coney waiting at the end of a short train ride, Brooklyn must have seemed like the best of all possible worlds for many of its residents. "It was a great place to grow up, and a good time for Brooklyn," says my mother, Prospect Heights High School, class of 1955. "Who knew about drugs? Who was afraid of being murdered on the street? We went everywhere, and we weren't afraid. Coney Island. Ebbets Field. The Fox. The Paramount. I saw Alan Freed at the Brooklyn Paramount, and I waited for hours in the freezing cold for a ticket."

Today, the bathhouses are gone. George Tilyou's Steeplechase Park, granddaddy to today's theme parks, is gone. Ebbets Field is gone. The streetcars that my parents rode on dates are gone. So are the Fox and the Paramount.

By 1998, much of the middle class had little interest in the attractions of Coney Island. In Coney's heyday, only a wealthy few could fly to places like Florida, California, or the Caribbean. The ancient, creaky rides can't hold a candle to modern theme park rides for gravity-defying terror, or to Disney and Universal for high-tech polish. Those who have grown up with the ability to fly to interesting places, who are not prisoners of this island for recreation and are not drawn by the gypsies offering to guess your weight, the Wax Musée, the cotton candy, or the fried clams, can find it hard to remember that Coney invented a form of beachside recreation, surf, and fun for the masses.

The beach was a leveler, a democratic piece of public real estate where a young clerk or salesman could play handball with a garbageman or ogle a domestic or a shop girl. The swimsuit made them all equal. Barriers of neighborhood, social distance, the inhibitions of Old Country ways could be dropped in that strip of blocks between the subway and the surf. While the amusements sought might vary a bit according to education or income—music halls for some, dance floors for others, hootchie-kootchie girls for still others—it was all a nickel away by subway for everyone who needed a break from the sweltering streets of crowded, pre–air-conditioned Brooklyn.

One of the last vestiges of the old "beach resort" shoreline has finally thrown in the towel. The Brighton Beach Cabana Club, the in-town vacation for generations of Brooklyn Jews, watched as its clientele slowly aged and departed this world. There were no longer leathery brown ladies in cat's-eye glasses kibitzing over mah-jongg tiles, watching children swim and play ball from the corners of their eyes. Their children are scattered to the four corners of the country. The people who once rented cabanas year after year have a much wider choice of entertainment open to them elsewhere. Flying is no longer only for the wealthy.

The land where the Cabana Club's showers, courts, pools, and card tables once stood is now more valuable as housing: A high-rise, ocean-view condo complex is proposed for the lot, responding to the sudden demand for new housing. As my D train rolls into Brighton Beach, I can see the billboard and business signs in English and Cyrillic: There are more than a hundred thousand Russians in Brooklyn now, and Brighton is a locus for their community life.

There are immigration lawyers and computer schools, nightclubs and smoked fish stores. If you stroll under the train tracks, above the din of Coney- and city-bound trains, you can hear women coo to their babies while pushing strollers, men talking business, and kids running along, all chatting in the new language of commerce for Brighton Beach Avenue: Russian. At the Brighton stop, whole families board the train. The children still look foreign—sandals and socks, very short shorts, and small-brimmed sun hats. The older children have quickly taken to American hip-hop wear: Nikes and baggy jeans, headphones around their necks, portable cassette players on their hips. The young women are more likely to be heavily made up, wear "done" hair, and have elaborately painted nails, than the other Brooklyn women on the train.

One of the business niches now filled by Russian women in many neighborhood storefronts is the nail salon. With few capital costs and almost no overhead, a nail salon is the perfect immigrant business. The business gets its revenue from hundreds of hours of labor put in by young

Russian women hunched over tables, squinting through tabletop magnifiers. The money to open the nail shops and other businesses comes from the pooled capital of family and friends, which blossoms into an array of businesses based on lots of sweat equity. There are many signs for PECTOPAH, that is, "restaurant" in Russian script, and plenty of signs reading MAGAZIN, the "grocery store" filled with Russian-style breads and canned goods from back home.

This is the kind of neighborhood renewal that can never be created by urban planners or dreamed up by urban economic development commissions. Until the late 1970s, Brighton was on the wane, a largely Jewish neighborhood watching its children move on to greener pastures and its aging move on to retirement communities. But the thaw in Soviet-American relations, American pressure in the form of the Jackson-Vanick amendment, and the mobilization of American activists to "save Soviet Jewry" brought waves of Russian-Jewish immigrants to Brooklyn. Once in New York, they found a long list of voluntary agencies ready to smooth their entry into American society: language classes, social workers to fill out food stamp applications, Hebrew schools to teach thousands an only half-remembered faith.

Brooklyn's future has been built every bit as much by the State Department and the U.S. Congress as the U.S. Department of Housing and Urban Development or the city's own government. When America threw its doors open wide in the early years of this century, Brooklyn filled up with people from Cork and Calabria, from Oslo and Oswiecim. When the Depression and a shrinking tolerance for open immigration slowed the flood to a trickle, these immigrants and their children assimilated, and the Old Country became a place in fading photographs. But in the 1960s suburbanization, changing immigration laws, and American involvement in places like Haiti and the Dominican Republic brought recurring waves of their people to Brooklyn. Think of Brooklyn as the America Factory. It finished with the children of Naples, Bialystok, and Bergen, and watched them move on. Today Brooklyn is fulfilling the same function for migrants from Gaza and Bangalore, Santo Domingo and St. Petersburg.

The panic-peddling and blockbusting of the 1950s and 1960s, and the wholesale white flight and economic turmoil of industrial decline, have given way to something far more subtle than those brutal methods of bringing urban change. One day a new shop opens on Coney Island Avenue. It might have been a clothing store, or a kosher butcher. It might have sold car stereos or kids' shoes. Now it bears a business name in Urdu, while larger letters above it proclaim Halal Meats. Not too long ago it didn't seem as if there were very many Pakistanis in the neighborhood. You might have occasionally seen mothers in head scarves, loose trousers, and long, flowing tops talking to their children or getting into a car. Now there are enough to support a butcher for ritually prepared meat, and the clients don't come by car from far-off parts of Brooklyn but stroll through the door from the surrounding neighborhood.

Little by little, the D train moved from having a few Chinese passengers, loaded down with groceries from Manhattan's Chinatown, to carrying entire cars full of Chinese traveling between lower Manhattan and what everyone has taken to calling "Brooklyn Chinatown."

After making a long, lazy loop through Brighton toward Midwood, we begin our descent. For the next several stations, we'll roar through backyards and underneath street traffic. Kitchens and bathrooms look over the tracks. Sometimes you can catch a glimpse of a woman in a housedress watching a pot on the stove, or kids in pajamas hunched over a bowl of cereal.

This part of Brooklyn is an odd mix, of gentrified housing, now included in a historic district, built early in this century as "suburban" housing, on beautiful tree-lined streets. These houses would look at home in Brookline, Massachusetts, or Scarsdale, New York. A few blocks away you then confront massive ranks of apartment buildings—row on row, block after block—an immense parade. I have never seen anything like them, in this number, outside Brooklyn. This density of construction, thousands of families housed in the space of just a few blocks, was why Brooklyn, not even the largest borough, is the home of almost one out of three New Yorkers. Many of these apartment houses suffered in the 1960s and 1970s as both tenants and landlords moved away. Farther east, toward the border with Queens, some Brooklyn neighborhoods have hit bottom. But these buildings have storm windows and working intercoms, clean lawns and working laundry rooms. They don't offer much in the way of luxury, but they are decent housing a working family can afford.

From our ride through backyards we roar into a tunnel. If you stay on the IRT, you will not see daylight again until the train crosses over the East River on the Manhattan Bridge. I get out at the corner of Prospect Park, Frederick Law Olmsted and Calvert Vaux's masterpiece in the heart of northern Brooklyn. Here the great architects and landscapers built their Champs Élysées, their American Arc de Triomphe.

The east side of the park is talked of as the "bad side" in the white parts of Brooklyn. "Bad" is a designation saved for neighborhoods that are now mostly black. The lexicon is simple. When "we" lived there, the neighborhood was good. Then it started to "get bad." That's when "we" left.

I climb the steps from underground and reach a sun-drenched street. There's a coin-operated laundry (very few tenants can have washing machines in their apartments), a locksmith (an important business in a neighborhood where property crime had been rampant), a pizzeria (no matter what neighborhood it is), and a McDonald's. When I pass through the golden arches into what is arguably the most American-associated of fastfood chains, a quiet calypso is playing on a radio. The bunting over the counter sports Haitian, Guyanese, Jamaican, and Dominican flags. These are the big four of central Brooklyn's immigrant groups. From a small strip of neighborhoods along Flatbush Avenue, the West Indian presence has radiated out through the center of the borough to become a powerhouse on the local scene. In Community District 9, Prospect/Lefferts Gardens, Crown Heights, and Wingate, a third of the 110,000 residents in the 1990 census were West Indian. In Community District 14, Flatbush, Midwood, and Ocean Parkway, it's one out of five. In Community District 17, East Flatbush and Remsen Village, it's pushing one out of two.

As Italians, Irish, Germans, and Jews left the neighborhoods around Prospect Park for other parts of Brooklyn, or left the city altogether, the median family incomes were not drastically reduced, putting the lie to the perception that things were now newly "bad." In fact, in Flatbush and Midwood, real per capita income rose almost two thousand dollars per head, nearly 20 percent. In East Flatbush, household income rose by a third in constant dollars, as did per capita income. This occurred while whites were pouring out of Flatbush and East Flatbush, and against stereotype and deeply ingrained belief, blacks replaced whites, with more green, too.

Mary and Phil Gallagher moved to East Flatbush just in time to watch their white neighbors leave. Phil was a professor at nearby Brooklyn College. The row houses lining the streets of East Flatbush were well kept and affordable, a magnet for a young couple with a child looking for a home, and the local elementary schools had terrific reputations. Mary's older neighbors didn't see it that way. "A lot of people who lived in this neighborhood grew up here; their parents had moved into this neighborhood long before, and anyone who was from the outside, anyone who looked different was a threat. We moved in here shortly after our daughter was born in 1974; we lived in an apartment just a few blocks away, and at that point we were completely unaware of the dynamics of this area. Neither of us is from New York.

"A lot of things had happened here during the sixties. Previous legislation on FHA and VA mortgages [mortgages provided or underwritten by the Federal Housing Administration or the Veterans Administration] had specifically proscribed that you couldn't use a mortgage to destabilize a neighborhood." Federal mortgage programs were openly racist for decades, and later denied blacks housing assistance by prohibiting loans for the purchase of existing housing. This meant that blacks, who lived in areas underserved by savings and loan associations and heavily in the market for limited urban housing, were virtually shut out of home ownership. But during the Johnson administration those limitations were removed and went too far in the other direction. FHA loans were written willy-nilly, without enough regard for family income or the condition of the home. Federal housing assistance had earned the resentment of blacks by shutting them out of the market, but it turned out that running headlong in the opposite direction didn't work either. The combination of housing-hungry blacks, whites desperate to sell, and sloppy administration from the FHA was like a wrecking ball in many older cities.

Mary remembers the process as more benign in East Flatbush. "When those provisions were removed, all of a sudden people could get government-insured mortgages to move in here. There was also a significant wave of immigration from the West Indies. Many of the white people who had lived here from before had gotten very used to the idea that this was their neighborhood, and they began to feel they had completely lost control of it."

In the heart of the neighborhood also sits an enormous housing complex, the Vanderveer Estates. Fifty-nine buildings, 2,500 units. Well into the 1960s, the use of heavy screening and plain old racism kept many blacks out. The John Lindsay administration forced the management of this project, financed by the U.S. Department of Housing and Urban Development, to take welfare tenants. Within a few years, the vast complex turned over completely, earning a well-deserved reputation as a dangerous, sometimes fatal place to be. On a summer night, drivers waiting for a red light at the project's edge could hear gunshots in the distance. Capital fled the nearby commercial streets. Aging homeowners took what was happening in Vanderveer as a sign.

Phil Gallagher found it was tough to work against "urban lore," once homeowners were convinced they could not stay. "One of the rumors that went on in regard to this was that there was a murder a week over here that never made it into the newspaper. It was just what people three, four, five blocks away would say, and they believed it. They would repeat it with some certainty. I suspect there was some violence in here . . . occasionally, I'm sure, people were shot. The people on our block didn't talk so much about this. They were worried about their children, like anybody else would be."

By the time the Gallaghers moved in, the main shopping strip, Avenue D, had declined. There were many empty storefronts. Burglar bars, the kind of roll-down barriers that covered the entire window, became the rule, giving a sinister air to the street. The local elementary school, despite its good reputation, was finding it hard to hang on to white, middle-class students. The Catholic churches were watching parishioners who had been baptized, schooled, and married here head for Queens and the suburbs.

Phil and Mary became part of a small group of people who decided the neighborhood did not have to become a slum. The issue was not race but income. If the banks persisted in redlining East Flatbush as whites left, capital's loss of faith would become a self-fulfilling prophecy. They embarked on what would be a fifteen-year labor of love, stabilizing their neighborhood with the Bank on Brooklyn campaign. The racial rules of commercial investment in those days were ironclad. As the black portion of the population rose, longtime merchants left, and national chains would not move in. Mary remembers, "one of the major fears was, if the neighborhood goes black, then the neighborhood would go to hell. What we were trying to do with Bank on Brooklyn was say, 'We want access to credit for qualified buyers, whatever their color; and we want them to have mortgages. We don't want some sort of absentee landlords picking up these properties and renting to people who are totally unable to manage a home in the sense that they're on drugs.' This is one of the tactics that was used in the multiple dwellings around here. Seed it with a couple of drug dealers, and drive out the tenants."

Phil is adamant that the appeal was always grounded in the bottom line—not an appeal to the better nature of bankers. "Our argument was: We're not asking the banks to be *eleemosynary* institutions. We were asking them to behave as responsible business people, and back up the investment they had made in this area, and not lose it, by continuing to invest in it. Not to walk away from it. We told them we didn't like the idea of throwaway neighborhoods, any more than we liked the idea of throwaway beer cans. This was totally irresponsible. We were asking them to act as good businessmen, we weren't asking them for any giveaways."

It worked. The housing is solid. The sidewalks are swept clean. Sharp new cars line the streets. You'll still see a white face here and there, but this neighborhood is now home to a stable population of middle- and upper-middle-class West Indians: civil service managers and dentists, beauty shop owners and police sergeants. The area bursts into music and block parties during the autumn Carnival season. The subway stop and major intersection are known as "the Junction," where two major streets—Flatbush and Nostrand avenues—meet; the smells of jerk chicken, curried goat, and meat pies waft from open shop windows. Jitney cabs pull up and their minivan doors swing open. These private services are unregulated, unlicensed, and a source of concern for city fathers. They mutter, sometimes loud enough to hear on Flatbush Avenue, about regulating the jitneys or shutting them down. I stand at the Junction, for some time, watching the smooth operation of a business you would find on the streets of Kingston, Jamaica, or Bridgetown, Barbados. There are no signs saying This Is the Place. There are no route numbers, ticket takers, or cops. An older lady pushes up those last few steps at the top of a long staircase from the IRT platforms below the street, her arms pulled down by shopping bags. She peers along Flatbush and, seconds later, steps from the curb. A green van pulls over, the driver helps her in, the door bangs shut, and she's gone.

In other cities public transportation consultants are commissioned to do six-figure studies on how to get people to use "intermodal" urban transport. A regional authority pushes ahead with public transit plans and somehow services the loans while waiting for the customers to come. Here in Brooklyn, on a busy Saturday, West Indian shoppers easily move around in a world they understand. When the businesses around the Junction were all owned by Jewish and Irish immigrants, and Brooklyn College students poured from the trains to walk to class, this place did not look very different. The heavy traffic on the broad streets, the massive apartment blocks, and the rows of small shops marching up Flatbush toward the Brooklyn Bridge *have* shaped the American Dream of thousands of Barbadians, Jamaicans, Guyanese, Haitians, and St. Lucians. Now the Junction is being shaped by them.

The Gallaghers look at their neighborhood today with tremendous satisfaction. At the height of their activism, Mary specialized in the commercial strip, Phil in housing. New regulations, and a new spirit among some bankers, led to a de-escalation of the 1970s conflicts over housing. "We shifted gears all together, and got the same banks that we'd been picketing, with whom we'd developed personal relationships over the years, to come in and fund neighborhood housing services. Between 1980 and 1990 we rehabbed about a hundred-and-some houses here. It all worked out well, as far as we're concerned. We're delighted with the feel of the neighborhood."

After they had done their bit, Phil figured, it was time to hand on the cudgels, for other reasons. "When I was forty-eight, I realized, hey, one quarter of my life, I've been doing this. It's time to resign. The second reason—we felt strongly about this—you really shouldn't have corporations in neighborhoods like this that are 95 percent black with all the leadership coming from a couple of white people."

More than twenty years after coming to the neighborhood, Mary still "can't help but wonder if the racial issue in America will ever be solved. I have complete faith that, if I ever needed anything, all I'd have to do is ring the doorbell next door, and I'd have it—like that. We live with wonderful people."

One longtime friend was a young engineer named Felix Bartholomew. Like many of Phil and Mary's new neighbors, Felix was a West Indian immigrant, who came to Brooklyn in 1962. After finishing college and starting a career and family, Bartholomew took what you might call an engineer's approach to picking a place to live.

"I went about buying in a sort of methodical way. I got the demographics. I *wanted* to move to Brooklyn. I didn't want to move to Jersey, I didn't want to move to Long Island, I wanted to stay in New York City, and Brooklyn was for me a nice area, I didn't particularly care for Queens or the Bronx. I got the demographics from the *New York Times* on the seventy-eight precincts, that gave the information like, what was the population makeup of each precinct, what was the percentage white, the percentage black, the percentage Hispanic. It gave you information like, what was the income level. It told you what the percentage of families on welfare was. It gave you homicides per thousand. All that information.

"From that, I selected a precinct that I thought had a nice racial mix. A precinct that I thought I would be able to fit in and live comfortably. At that time what we did, my wife and I, and by that time I had my son, we began to drive through these precincts, and look at these different areas.

"We would drive through at different times of the day . . . on different days of the week, but especially on a Friday evening, Saturdays, and Sundays, to see what the community was like. To see if there were people standing outside, whether they were making noise on the sidewalk, whether there were drums and whatnot. Based on these analyses, and visual observation of the area, we picked out East Flatbush.

"Then I went to the real estate agent, and said, 'I'm looking for a house. I wanted so many bedrooms, and I'd like to have a garage, I would prefer something with a fence, and I was prepared to spend between forty and forty-five thousand dollars. And this is the area that I would prefer.' I gave her the precinct. I mapped out the blocks that I thought I would like to buy in. And something strange happened.

"The real estate agent took us riding on Kings Highway, though we told her we wanted to look in East Flatbush, and she would take us all the way to the East New York section of Brooklyn. She would show us one house after another, and then she would ride us back *through* the East Flatbush section. We would say, how much is one of those houses over there? She would quote us some number that she knew was way out of our price range. . . . I didn't feel like I could afford sixty-five thousand dollars worth of mortgage, or she would say that the people were not yet prepared to sell. Those were the two answers I got.

"And then one day my wife made contact with someone who knew somebody who was selling a house, and that's how we finally found a house within that same locality. On East Forty-eighth Street and Clarendon Road, and we liked that house. I didn't just say, suddenly, one day, here we go, we're moving to Brooklyn. I studied the matter. There was a method to my madness."

Bartholomew says he realized his agent was purposely steering him away from blocks of white homeowners. Not the confrontational type, he politely asked about houses he found out about on his own. "I wanted someplace where I could afford to live, and someplace I could fit in and be comfortable. When the real estate agent took me someplace else, I would say, 'No, that's not what I want,' and bring her back and point out, how about this, how about that, hoping that she would realize what we were looking for. I wasn't angry, but I looked for ways to get around her. It might have been that I still had a certain amount of naïveté, I didn't know. So the real estate agent taking me to those other places was no surprise. I wasn't as militant as I would become later in East Flatbush. I didn't really know what was happening until after I moved.

"There were tree-lined streets. Very clean. The trash was picked up three days a week. It was a nice neighborhood. It was a neighborhood I enjoyed living in. The block where I lived was approximately sixty-forty . . . 60 percent white, 40 percent black. The block just north of where I lived was almost all white . . . but I don't know why my block was different. I'm not sure.

"Then one morning as I was driving north I saw these signs farther up East Forty-eighth Street, on the doorways or in the windows of the houses. The signs said, 'I Am Staying!' 'I Am Staying!' I wanted to know what was going on. People who saw me on the block every day would talk to me, so I inquired about the 'I Am Staying!' signs. I had an idea of what it was, but I needed to verify my idea. What had happened, there was the first black family that bought a house on that block. When they moved in a number of families on that block received a real estate agent's letter soliciting their homes, indicating that the block now had a black family and things were going to change . . . things were going to be different from now on. And that block, I guess, the people got together, and people began to put signs in the window, 'I am Staying!' The real estate agents were trying to infiltrate that block. But over time, the people who had declared 'I Am Staying!' saw their neighbors move, saw their friends move, and then, what happened? They moved. The real estate agents were able to do exactly what they set out to do.

"That's what I saw in a changing neighborhood. A neighborhood that was primarily white, after about five years becoming a neighborhood that was predominately black. You saw the changes in the schools, you saw the changes in the grocery stores, you saw other changes in the shops around.

"At first what I saw was their loss being my gain. Because what I discovered in those black families that moved to the neighborhood . . . they were like myself. They were young families . . . they were professional . . . they were people who had the same aspirations, the same dreams that I had. They were people who were willing not only to invest in their homes but were willing to maintain their homes to the same standards that were in force when they met it. Living was still comfortable. Living was still easy. The guy next door was white. He was a teacher, a principal, his wife was a teacher, but he still lived there. . . . he's still living there today! We would stand around and chat in the morning. Whenever I go back to Brooklyn I always stop in to visit. There were many [white] people on my block who continued to live there. There was a dentist and his wife. . . . They were comfortable living with me, and living with other people like me. They were older, they were professional people. You learn something from living with them. But it's those people who were ignorant who just see something coming, see you coming, and just run across the street without really knowing who you are."

Bartholomew wrestled with one of the central paradoxes of white flight for the black middle class. Yes, wholesale flight often causes economic dislocation and wrenching adjustment for those leaving, those arriving, and neighborhood businesses. While recognizing that the departure of frightened white homeowners was bad for the neighborhood, Bartholomew recognized that their staying put would have been a mixed blessing as well.

"Did I really want to live with someone who was as prejudiced as that? Who didn't want to know who I am? Who didn't really care to know who I am? Do I want to live with that person? Not necessarily." Yet Bartholomew is quick to add that his experience did not sour him on the possibility of peaceful, sustainable integration.

"During that period I was able to meet some people who I was able to work with. I got introduced to community groups. . . . It was the first community group I joined after I had lived in the area for about three years. It was called the Farragut Association. The group worked to maintain the sense of decorum that exists in the neighborhood. In the summer we had house tours, where people who were interested in living in East Flatbush, similar to what they do in Brooklyn Heights and Boerum Hill, would come in and see what it is East Flatbush had to offer. This Farragut area, we called it 'a small town in town.' Because it was a community in which people began to live together, to do things to not only uplift their own homes, but the area surrounding their homes as well.

"There was an ice cream parlor on Avenue D that burned down, and the people began working with a block association to create the first community garden in that space. That was the first time I ever knew about community gardens. That was my first experience with people coming together to work on beautifying the neighborhood.

"We had a group called Bank on Brooklyn. Then Peg Horneckle decided to create the Flatbush East Community Development Corporation, where we were now concentrating on an even bigger area. Very early, through the efforts of the Flatbush East Development Corporation and the efforts of people working with us, and some of the businesses, we were able to petition the city and we were given six million dollars for capital improvements and for commercial revitalization. Once that money was approved Flatbush East went out and got a contractor. We had to develop some kind of program. We worked with the merchants to improve storefronts. The city undertook the capital development on the strip—the new sidewalks, the new gutters, the new crosswalks, the new lighting, the new signs. The Flatbush East Community Development Corp. created a program where a merchant would receive up to 25 percent of the cost of refurbishing the front of a store. Anything on the front. Many of the merchants at that time were not really willing to spend money on improvements. So here was an opportunity for them to get something.

"The merchants formed the Avenue D Merchants Association, and they had Alan Spiro. Alan was a very energetic carpet store owner. He eventually moved out but he got the merchants to come to meetings and he would get them together with the development corporation, and tell them all these beautiful things we were going to do and what was going to happen, and many of the merchants did agree to participate in the program. Without that deterioration and that blight setting in that shopping strip started to turn around and people began to see results.

"Instead of people getting in their cars and driving to the mall at the south end of Flatbush Avenue, or getting in their cars and driving even farther away, people were beginning to walk with their shopping carts on Avenue D, and walking to the different stores."

Racial integration in East Flatbush was to be a lost cause. Longtime white families remain, and the neighborhood's overall viability helps keep nearby residential areas from catching the infection of panic. Most intriguingly, the economic models regarding resegregation and neighborhood decline were not valid in this part of Brooklyn. Usually, the momentum of decline is easy to see: once black homeowners arrive on a block, every subsequent white-owned house going on the market becomes increasingly unlikely to find a buyer at the asking price, since the house is increasingly less likely to attract all qualified buyers in that price range. Instead, once a block is believed to be "going black," only the market subset of buyers, black buyers, will likely browse, bid, or buy. In this way two of the main props under home prices, desire and competition, are kicked out. Bartholomew reports that with price this was not the case when he reluctantly sold his house.

"My house in East Flatbush cost forty-five thousand dollars. I sold my house just recently. I held on to it even though I have been living in the Washington area for some time now, because I love Brooklyn, and I love that house! I got one hundred seventy thousand dollars for it. I think a white person who would buy in that area would get something you might want to call a steal."

Bartholomew concedes, with some regret, that his area will attract few white buyers of similar education, income, and aspirations. "But we share the same concerns! About five years ago rap music had just come into vogue. There was a young man who lived right across the street from us. He and his friends were on my side, where our house fronted onto Clarendon Road. They were blasting the music, screaming obscenities, and making rude jokes. My wife came out of the house and said, 'Darwin, I don't stand in front of your house and scream and make this kind of noise. And further I do not talk this kind of talk. If you and your friends want to talk that kind of talk you can take it to your house, or just take it out of here. But not in front of my house.' Those kids got up. They were young kids. If we all just take that approach . . . they don't want it, we don't want it either. It's not that whites are more concerned than us. We are just as concerned about the same things, and we have to exercise our rights. I was a little concerned about my wife confronting these kids, but I guess those are just chances you have to take."

When our conversation turned to the future of Brooklyn, and where and when neighborhood decline was reversible, Bartholomew got a twinkle in his eye and smiled broadly. He counseled patience and said history was on his side. "Take a look at what has happened in the Crown Heights neighborhood. In 1962 my brother moved from the Bedford-Stuyvesant neighborhood to Crown Street. I think it was 421 Crown Street. Right on the corner of Crown Street and Brooklyn Avenue. When we moved over there I saw a change in that neighborhood from a Jewish neighborhood to a black one. Blacks began to buy the houses and the Jews began to move out.

"Years later a friend in the area told me about his house, that at that time he was able to buy for sixteen or eighteen thousand dollars. The Jews sold, the blacks bought. Then, years later the blacks began to move out, too, because they considered that part of Brooklyn no longer desirable; they started to move to Long Island, too. And who began to move in? A new group of Jews who were now buying on that street! The neighborhood is not necessarily a better place. . . . I guess because of the religious beliefs of the new Jewish neighbors it may be a little quieter. . . . You don't have so many kids running up and down the street. I remember Jim telling me, 'Someone just offered me eighty-four thousand dollars for my house,' after he paid sixteen thousand dollars for it! Could that happen to the East Flatbush section if people realize what's there? It began at one time. I remember families who moved from the area where we were and went to Long Island. Five years later some of them were looking for houses again in the East Flatbush section. They didn't necessarily come to the same streets, the same community where they had lived before, but now they were a little lower down, near the bay.

"If you go out there to Long Island and you're disillusioned, you may want to come back, and if you can't afford to live in an expensive seaside community, well, hey man, we have affordable houses in East Flatbush. And you know those houses . . . you know they're strong houses, well built, clean. So? Who knows!?"

While Crown Heights has been remade by an influx of new white buyers long after the area was written off as a desirable home, the relations between black and Hasidic Jewish residents have struggled toward civility. If the name Crown Heights strikes you as familiar, it may be the recollection of murder and racial strife after the accidental killing of a young black boy by a driver in a Hasidic motorcade. For a place like Crown Heights—which has seen its fortunes rise as segregation declines—to become a model, there have to be changes in much more than home prices.

There must also be new neighbors like Felix Bartholomew, who believes new arrivals will share his goodwill. "I don't know about a change of heart, maybe a change in expectations. Maybe things didn't live up to their expectations out in Long Island. Remember, when they moved to Long Island, I could have moved to Long Island also! Who knows? I never really investigated . . . but I know it is not beyond my means to purchase a house next door to them, wherever, in Hempstead. Where are they going to go? What are they going to do?"

Chapter 7

The Persistent
Significance of Race

From King Day speeches, to debates over affirmative action, to Supreme Court arguments about the Voting Rights Act, we are assured that race doesn't matter as it once did on the American social scene. We are further told the country would be a better place if race didn't matter. But race remains central to all kinds of transactions we wouldn't even expect to find it. It's there. It matters. And despite the appeals to our better nature, it isn't going to disappear quietly.

I was in an all-white Chicago neighborhood covering a community meeting at a park field house. The meeting was called to discuss recent break-ins, believed to be the work of "outsiders." As my camera crew packed its gear and I prepared to leave, one of the neighborhood residents hit me with a question: "Do you know what integration is?" As I waited to hear his answer I played along, telling him I didn't. With raised voice and dramatic flourishes he recited his answer.

"Integration [insert a pause for effect here] is the period of time between the arrival of the first blacks, and the departure of the last whites."

I couldn't quibble with his (borrowed) definition because a lot of places I had seen in America were confirmation that this cynical snapshot of the inside of the national heart was accurate. In community after community, the idea of people of different races living together in a sustainable and stable way was as impossible as sprouting wings and taking off from the roof.

It wasn't always ugly bias or active racial animus that made people think this way. Instead it was the life they saw with their own eyes, far from city hall or Washington, D.C.

In the late eighties, long after I stopped wanting to believe this sort of thing still happened, the Waheed family's new home was scorched by arson. The house was still livable; the damage was minor and the building needed only cosmetic repair. The outrageous act committed by Shirley Waheed was buying a home west of the widely understood dividing line between whites and blacks on Chicago's South Side. After her damaged roof shingles were repaired, after the burned window frame was replaced and painted, the only damage left was to Shirley Waheed herself.

Shirley Waheed asked me, again and again, "Why hurt me? I didn't bother anybody!"

We squandered what might have been an opportunity, in 1958, 1965, or 1971, to find a new way for Americans to live with one another. We blew it one family at a time. The chance that American race relations might have been altered by personal discovery was lost in a way that is hard ever to create again. We are reaping the results of those blown opportunities every day in the 1990s, in celebrated show trials, like that of Rodney King's assailants in Simi Valley, and in the corrosive drip, drip, drip of the bile that runs through our national conversations on race.

In the late fifties, the sixties, and the seventies, countless thousands of white families felt chased and threatened, and thousands of black families felt despised and marginalized. The story continues to this day in scores of urban neighborhoods and inner-ring suburbs. The increased presence of black homeowners erodes white desire to even consider shopping for a home there. Flagging white desire for a place means capital abandonment. Capital abandonment means urban decay. Urban decay in one neighborhood leads to decay in adjoining neighborhoods. It's the only "domino theory" from the sixties that really worked.

White flight remade many American cities. While the Sun Belt cities were in many cases "built segregated," the older cities of the North, the destination of black migrants for fifty years, were transformed by it. White flight was the midwife to the modern American suburb. It also had a tremendous impact on public schooling and attitudes about taxes, racial understanding, transportation, and the "mainstream" attitude about urban life. Yet newspapers, television, movie theaters, and bookstores are largely silent about this wrenching, traumatic era in American society. I have long wondered why. That silence about the past is mirrored in a lack of comment today. A small army of true believers still keeps an eye on lenders and real estate agents, and forces institutions to comply with housing laws already on the books.

David Shucker is a fair-housing specialist at the Leadership Council for Metropolitan Open Communities in Chicago. Shucker told me white owners watching the action in other neighborhoods, or themselves scarred veterans of flight from other areas, can have hair-trigger responses even to minor change in the complexion of their community.

"The latest problem we've seen has been in Hiawatha Park, where there's been a lot of local press coverage of an attempt by the Chicago Housing Authority to buy a three-flat in the neighborhood.

"There have been four community meetings on the subject, each drawing six hundred to seven hundred people. Add that to the wide coverage, and you can tell this is on a lot of people's minds. So that's the set-up. It never had to get to race. You don't have to talk about race. It's already there, it's been laid there as the predicate.

"This is my area, this is what I've worked with on a regular basis. So I worked with them on this for months in advance, though I've got no official connection to the project. From my point of view, when you talk about panic, you have to look at different neighborhoods . . . there's no panic in Lincoln Park. Yet there is panic, or could be, in Hiawatha Park. The whole thing is more subtle than it was in the fifties or sixties, when real estate people hired African Americans to walk up and down targeted streets. I learned a lot of the tricks when I was training real estate people in fair-housing law. Maybe panic peddling wasn't invented here, but it was certainly honed into a high art.

"The testing is not complicated. We represent ourselves as buyers and renters to real estate agents and see what happens. When we are doing a seller test, we get a neighborhood homeowner to invite seller's presentations to hear what real estate agents have to say. One agent told a tester, 'It's really too bad. You waited too long to sell. If you were a couple of blocks west of here I could still probably get you a good price.'

"Fear, not reality, plays the biggest role in driving neighborhood change. Fear is what drives whites, not actual market conditions. Once your wife says, 'We've got to move to protect the kids,' they're gone.

"Take a look at Hiawatha Park. We had several meetings with the Northwest Association of Realtors. They were open meetings on several Saturday mornings, not only with Realtors but with anybody who wanted to come in. Those meetings calmed fears about property values. Here's an interesting part of it . . . three out of five people who were at the last meeting used to live in Austin." The Austin neighborhood on the west side of Chicago is legendary for its rapid racial turnover. "They all had horror stories of things that had happened to them or to someone they knew. When they left Austin they moved two miles north. Now they were dead sure the same thing was going to happen. They wanted to believe it.

"I always ask people in that position: Where are you going to move? The only answer they could come up with is farther out. It would be better farther out. It's part of a cycle. People talk, and a folklore is created. That drives perceptions, creates beliefs, which further drives perceptions.

"Some neighborhoods are growing around immigrants to the United States who are settling in Chicago in large numbers. The newly arrived minority buyers still place a large emphasis on language and culture. A couple of months ago there was an editorial piece in a local paper. It was an infuriating column creating projections of city and near suburban demographics completely based on race and ethnicity. The writer was invited to come out and speak to the Niles [a northwest suburb bordering Chicago] council.

"They ate it up. What they weren't dealing with was when people first get here they will choose to live with people like themselves. But what happens next? Yuppies don't all move together to their next neighborhood. As families, as groups are in the country for generation after generation, other things become important. Third-generation Asians and Hispanics don't live in ethnic ghettos in large metropolitan areas.

"Most whites don't want to live in majority black areas. Real estate people know that and try to find an accommodation without talking about it. We catch 1 percent, the other 99 percent continue to sell the way they always have. Steering isn't specifically mentioned in the law. For many buyers and sellers, it isn't really necessary. The culture of the community teaches real estate agents what it's important to know."

The dreary "definition" of integration supplied by the amateur sociologist in Chicago has been lived by millions, in hundreds of neighborhoods in dozens of cities. People on all sides of America's racial divides feel they were made victims by the process. Some reach that conclusion out of a clear understanding of what happened to them, some as a way of escaping culpability for the demolition of much of urban America.

For a generation, those who made this disaster possible have explained it away as something that just "happened." The cause often seems to lie elsewhere. But this is, and has always been, a story with victims and victimizers, heroes and villains, winners and losers. It happened. We did it. We let it happen.

At its heart, this is a story of people making individual and mass decisions about the ability of different Americans to live together. A lot of new attention is being given to the predictive value of class and socioeconomic status in urban America, as an alternative explanation to that of race. But history, not self-consoling revisionism, tells a different story.

The rapid churning of neighborhoods came not when whites of one class found themselves living with whites of another class, or when blacks of one class were watching new neighbors of a different status move in (indeed, pre-civil rights–era black neighborhoods were economically integrated in a way hard to find in any other American communities), but when whites of any income and educational level had to confront black neighbors of any income or educational level.

Racial steering has been a powerful tool in widespread neighborhood resegregation. As a new legal approach to housing tightened the grip around the real estate industry in the late 1960s and early 1970s, white flight had more polite, more academic names like "ethnic succession" or "neighborhood change." Pick any name you feel comfortable with. The phenomenon has blasted the urban landscape into its current form. It has remade older American cities large and small, and shaped today's policies toward urban America. When Congress sits in session, aid for the cities is now help for "them," not "us." Urban programs are portrayed as hand-outs to the unworthy, instead of investments in a shared future. The in-tense infusions of public cash, which made and sustained the American suburb, are rarely seen as handouts or subsidies. The recipients are not portrayed in our media and popular culture as parasites, destroying their hometowns and taking out of America more than they put in. In the clos-ing years of the twentieth century, to be "urban" is to be unworthy. The very word *urban* is becoming a coded synonym for "black and brown," and rarely for "urbane."

At the same time, the city lives in an ambivalent place in our national consciousness. The writers and casts of *Seinfeld, Mad About You, Friends, Ellen, Caroline in the City,* and other popular television programs extol the excite-ment, sophistication, variety, and sheer with-it-ness of urban life. But these shows seem to exist in urban environments unrecognizable to millions of their nonfictional neighbors. Most Latinos in the United States live in large urban areas. Most blacks in the United States live in large urban areas. The networks beam their vision of white urbanity and cozy consumption into the homes of millions of white suburbanites without having to recognize or apologize for the real black-and-brown world that exists just beyond the camera frame occupied by Jerry, George, and Kramer.

The dramatic urban landscape is another matter entirely. Unlike the melanin-free zone of Caucasian sit-comedy, the urban jungles of *Homicide, The Commish, NYPD Blue,* and other programs feature brown and black characters galore. They are cops, secretaries, victims, and, most notably, suspects. The membrane between late prime-time and your local news grows thinner with each ratings period, as the clench-jawed realism of black-and-brown urban pathology segues easily into the mayhem of local news. It must be a comfort to an increasingly suburbanized reportorial staff, management, and audience that the "alleged" wild men in their cen-ter city are far, far, away.

There may be a simple explanation for the unreality of comedic television's all-white New York: So many millions of Americans live segregated lives that this white planet of Manhattan never provokes a "what's wrong with this picture?" moment. The all-white world of *Friends* isn't that different from the all-white world of *Friends* fans.

To ask in 1999 that this way of showing ourselves to ourselves somehow take account of the actual New York where a million Puerto Ricans or two million blacks live is to risk being accused of that dangerous of modern sins, being pc.

I'm not pc. I just want us all to face up to what we did in the last forty years. We turned millions of people's lives upside down and only occasionally stopped to ask ourselves why. We marooned our children in isolated communities and told ourselves we were really doing it for them. We told ourselves we weren't racist, just protecting the only valuable thing we had—the house—from the inevitable decline in values that "integration," however fleeting, would bring.

Was it worth it? Did we end up with the country we wanted? Did we end up living a life we cherished? If we did, what did it cost us? If we didn't, what happened? It's important to ask those questions now, because we seem to be in the midst of a transitional period in American life. The ideas about government responsibility, community, and the role of the individual in society are all being requantified, argued over, wrestled with. Ideas that once looked pretty durable—public education, government housing assistance, food aid to the poor—are now openly questioned and under legislative assault. Now more than ever, the poorest populations in America are singled out not to understand why this country's abundance has not reached them but as examples of the absence of personal qualities or values, in the mythology of the American Right, that are all that are needed to pull the individual out of poverty.

One idea that has been taking more than its share of knocks is integration. You no longer have to look very hard to find people trashing integration as that most pathetic of notions, "another failed sixties program." Integration is now casually dismissed by both whites and blacks as an idea that "didn't work." It is no doubt a relief to many whites that America is preparing to discard the notion of residential integration, before anybody really had to seriously try it.

Since the Supreme Court handed down its decision in *Brown v. Board of Education of Topeka, Kansas,* in 1954, and since the civil rights legislation of the Johnson administration, black isolation in urban areas has been growing, not receding. The laws that freed striving black families from the confines of the ghetto also freed them to be the first arrivals in a wave of black residential resegregation. That process left many Americans feeling they had already tried integration, as they watched moving trucks fill the streets and the number of white faces in their children's elementary school yearbooks start to dwindle.

That was not integration. By using superior mobility and access to capital to put the maximum distance between themselves and black urbanites, white home buyers made blacks more isolated in the modern city than they had been in the Jim Crow South, and more isolated than any group of European immigrants had been in the history of the United States.

In their eye-opening study, *American Apartheid,* the sociologists Douglas Massey and Nancy Denton point out that white attitudes made integration impossible from the outset. In 1942, whites were asked by an opinion researcher, "Do you think there should be separate sections in towns and cities for Negroes to live in?" More than eight out of ten answered yes. In 1962, poll respondents were asked to agree or disagree with the following: "White people have a right to keep blacks out of their neighborhood if they want to, and blacks should respect that right." Six out of ten agreed. When the choice was given again in 1970, the slimmest majority disagreed for the first time.

The idea that the willingness to drop everything and run belongs to an unfortunate past doesn't stand up to much scrutiny. Massey and Denton crunched numbers from twenty thousand census tracts in the sixty largest metropolitan areas and found that white antennae are so sensitively tuned that a jump in the black population of a neighborhood up to twenty-five miles away raises the likelihood that any given white family will decide to move.

What these two scholars have concluded from the reams of census data and observations of decade-to-decade change is this: In the old Northern cities, black Americans are now more isolated than ever, and are thus less likely to be able to participate in the wider society in ways that enable them to move out of poverty. Many times while I was working on this project, people asked me, "White flight? What about black flight? They're leaving the cities too," as if the idea of urban degradation becomes more acceptable once the culpability is spread around. But blacks have played a reactive role in urban change, moving into places white capital will allow, responding to market forces created by white capital. Denton and Massey insist: "The emergence of severe racial segregation in the North was not primarily a reflection of black housing preferences or a natural outcome of the migration processes."

You could call what is happening at the core of large black urban enclaves "hypersegregation." What is happening at the edges is that neverending process of better-off blacks buying their way out of the ghetto, only to find that their new white neighbors are thus encouraged to leave. With each white family that leaves a neighborhood that is perceived to be "changing," the chance that the next buyer will be white declines. This withdrawal from the market sets into motion a cycle that can only end with a new black neighborhood in the place of a white one. This newly black community only increases the physical distance between predominately white commercial and residential centers and the most isolated, poorest blacks.

Among the neighborhoods most vulnerable to rapid flight and resegregation are those where retirees and people in the last stages of their working lives are concentrated. These areas were once bursting with children and home to the kind of neighborly spirit remembered with sentimental longing by people in their fifties and sixties. These areas are open to stampede because the houses, cheaply purchased forty years ago, don't feature all the bells and whistles of today's new suburban construction.

Yet the aging homeowners are depending on the bricks and mortar, mortgage now paid, to retain value and help finance a secure retirement. The stakes are high, and a wait-and-see attitude becomes a commodity in short supply. Each time one of them sells to move to a retirement community, a warmer climate, or the suburban homes of their children, the neighbors hold their breath. Who will buy in?

Though the housing stock is sound and the proximity to downtown makes a potential commute a lot easier, white buyers with ready cash are few. Having grown up in the neighborhood, young married couples aspire to "something better." The extended family is already in the suburbs and loath to take a chance on the city. The plants around which these neighborhoods were first built are long gone or offer little steady work, and downtown jobs are no longer the only game in town for second- and third-generation kids who have lightened the color of their collars.

Besides . . . the kids are all going to want their own bedrooms, even if you don't have any kids yet. There's only one place to go. Out.

Do the old gray heads endure the everlasting wrath of their neighbors and "sell black"? Do they rent to a relative and try to survive the long search for a white buyer?

In places like Brooklyn, Chicago, Philadelphia, and elsewhere, the old binary, black-white view of race and residential space is also getting more subtle. Latinos and Asians are held up to the neighborhood as, yes, different but "a lot like us" in ways that matter most: taking care of the property, valuing religion and family.

Aging Eastern European families in Chicago have told me of the "very nice" Mexican families moving into the once all-white enclaves of Gage Park and Chicago Lawn. One of the delicious ironies of the suddenly admirable qualities of Mexican buyers is that just a generation earlier, Mexicans rushed to fill the vacuum created by fleeing whites in the largely Czech neighborhoods of Pilsen and Little Village.

In several Brooklyn neighborhoods Asians, mostly Chinese, are forming new residential buffers between expanding black and Latino neighborhoods and shrinking white ones. As in Chicago, these buffers serve to slow the pace of racial change in a radical departure from the frantic "tipping" of the 1960s and 1970s.

For any American who has ever loved city life and worried over the present and future of any urban setting, it is crucial to factor in the depth of American racism. The abandonment of urban America is portrayed over and over as cause, rarely as effect. Did whites of varying classes run from Washington, D.C., which then created a growing inability to cope with crisis? Or did the city's increasing inability to cope force the decision of so many to leave? As early as 1980, in the large and fast-growing D.C.

metropolitan area, an astonishing 91.7 percent of the whites lived outside the city, which still functions as the region's economic and cultural engine, compared with just 46 percent of blacks. The numbers are even higher now, with the total growing among blacks as well as they cluster in the rapidly resegregating Prince George's County, Maryland. Prince George's, home to one of the largest concentrations of middle-class blacks anywhere, has tremendous problems attracting high-end retail or fine dining to the county's commercial areas, despite the fact that any census tract analysis would show a market waiting for it. A coincidence?

While it would be naive to maintain that racial animus played no part in early suburbanization, it must also be conceded that something else made men sleep in line to sign up for a house in the new Levittowns in Long Island and Pennsylvania. A society that chased its working women back indoors after World War II and lined the pockets of its working men in the largest peacetime economic expansion ever had revved up to meet their yearning for "the new": new kitchens filled with new appliances, and new televisions displayed in that new place called the family room.

These same pent-up desires drove black families, too. The women had worked hard in the war industries. The men had drawn the worst duty and fought hard in the still-segregated armed forces. But their revolution of rising expectations would have to be satisfied in other ways: the cities that had become home to millions of blacks in the previous forty years were not ready to extend the privileges of citizenship to all their citizens.

In the cities of the North, mobs of white men drove back moving vans and stoned family cars bringing recently discharged black GIs and their families to new housing developments in or near white neighborhoods. If that demonstration of force didn't make blacks turn back, their cars were vandalized in the dark, their living room windows smashed with bricks.

During the first wave of white flight the dimensions of the ghetto began to change in Philadelphia, New York, Chicago, and elsewhere. For the most part, however, black families, also enjoying relatively good economic times, were still hemmed in by the invisible walls of the ghetto.

Race was a force in the first big wave of white migration to the suburbs. But it is the central motif of the subsequent era, with the core years of the 1960s. It is the second wave that created the metropolitan area of century's end: a declining city of black and brown floating in a sea of white suburbs.

The process has completed what was already under way in 1944, when Gunnar Myrdal, in *An American Dilemma,* identified the hardening ghetto as "an artificial city . . . that permits any prejudice on the part of public officials to be freely vented on Negroes without hurting whites." Myrdal saw what political officials must have known in the cities of the North: that the level of consultation, municipal services, schools, and attention was far inferior in black neighborhoods.

What white society did, said the Kerner Commission, twenty-four years after Myrdal's dire observations, was to create, maintain, and condone the ghetto. But having done that—confining those it identified as problem people—it also locked the strivers behind the ghetto walls that Massey and Denton say grew ever "thicker and higher." Well-to-do blacks "complained bitterly and loudly about their increasing confinement within crowded, dilapidated neighborhoods, inhabited by people well below their social and economic status," say Massey and Denton.

The process continues today, as blacks, and to a lesser degree Hispanics, pay the ransom that breaks them out of the old ethnic ghetto, only to find that the ghetto follows them even after they paid a premium to get out of it. The battle lines are now hardening in inner-ring suburbs, where the aging middle- and working-class populations cannot use home prices to maintain the color line. Their small towns become the path of least resistance to minorities trying to escape the ghetto.

In their purposely lurid and titillating 1950 travel book *Chicago: Confidential!,* authors Lee Mortimer and Jack Lait take their breathless readers to the South Side as Stanley took his *New York Herald* readers down the Congo a century earlier. At first they marvel at the extensive "Bronzeville" of the late 1940s and early 1950s: "Negroes have taken over mile upon mile, lineally and laterally, whole public parks where no Caucasian is seen, entire business streets, churches of all faiths, synagogues, hotels, and what were the first of the big movie palaces, and perhaps a third of the twenty-six miles of lake shore." *Chicago: Confidential!* portrays this movement as a mark of black liberation, and a remarkable departure from many other places in the country. Then we leave postwar progress for the nineteenth-century Congo: "From the lousiest shanties and the lowest reaches of human existence, you gradually enter a seemingly endless city of fine homes and lawns, but overrun and overcrowded by a dusky multitude with its own ways and in many instances with its own laws."

That blacks should live separately from whites is implicit in the reporting of these two old newspapermen. So they cheer for black self-reliance, tut-tut over political corruption, sit on the edge of their seats for vice and nightlife, and seem relieved that it all happens "over there." Could they have imagined how prophetic their words in 1950 would be when seen nearly a half-century later? "Most of Chicago's blighted areas are occupied by Negroes. But most Negroes in Chicago do not live in blighted areas. In truth, an amazing American anti-climax emerges: instead of being hemmed in by whites, the Negroes are hemming in the whites."

Massey and Denton have the strength of the data behind them when they allege a rarely contradicted law about the use of space in American cities: "Whites continue to avoid neighborhoods located near the periphery of established black areas, and display considerable reluctance to enter neighborhoods containing black residents. Although the mere presence of blacks no longer guarantees automatic racial turnover, the probability of white loss still increases steadily as the percentage of blacks rises and the distance to the ghetto falls."

The very black families that the society condescendingly lectures about staying on the straight and narrow, about deferring gratification, about earning the "privilege" of living with whites are the ones most likely to have been thwarted in their aspirations to better things in the last few decades. The assumptions that created even the meager opportunities for desegregation and mobility for the black middle class are now under complete assault.

Professor William Julius Wilson of Harvard University made an unusual splash for a sociologist with his 1979 book, *The Declining Significance of Race*. Hoping to marry the theories of a noted black sociologist to their own, members of the Reagan administration heavily talked it up. "Which convinced me," jokes Wilson, "that they never got past the title page and actually read the book." Surveying urban America and racial attitudes in the late 1990s, he makes few upbeat conclusions about the intervening years.

"*The Declining Significance of Race* was a profoundly pessimistic book. What I was trying to get readers to understand was that there was a growing gap between the haves, and the have-nots, in the black community, and that class had become more important than race in determining life chances. For example, middle-class black families, beginning in the 1960s, were able to pass on class status, and the advantages of middle-class and upper-class status to their children in the way that white families had always been able to do. In the previous years, racism had always been so overwhelming, a middle-class black family was not sure what kind of outcomes their children would face.

"I wanted people to realize and understand that, and also see the need to develop different public policies toward the have-nots. To address their problems, you have to focus on issues like full employment and training, and education, and affirmative action programs are good, because they move blacks into positions that were previously unavailable to them, but really don't address the needs of what I call the truly disadvantaged. I just wanted us to broaden our vision, and understand that policies that benefited trained and educated blacks may not necessarily be of benefit to the black poor."

I asked Wilson about the decisions made by hundreds of thousands of black families to no longer take a chance on safety, the schools, and the meager lifestyle choices offered in the urban core.

"I don't blame the black middle class for leaving the inner city. Black middle-class families are human, just like other families. They seek the best education for their children, and the best neighborhoods for their children, and I think it would be unfair to criticize them for remaining in a neighborhood that's troubled. I don't disagree with that. I was just trying to describe the nature of the process. These families who left removed a very important social buffer in these neighborhoods, making it much more difficult for the remaining families to survive in the face of growing and persistent joblessness.

"People who grow up in an environment of persistent long-term joblessness behave differently from people who grow up in an environment of high employment—I tried to get people to understand that the opportunity structure shapes the way you behave over time. On the one hand, liberals have tended to ignore the behavioral aspects of chronic subordination; on the other hand conservatives have tended to ignore the structural aspects of chronic subordination. I want to talk about how these two things interact over time. If you're going to examine the problem of joblessness, you're also going to have to look at the response to persistent joblessness over time, and the association of joblessness to other problems. For example, we found in our studies that employed black males were far more likely to marry the mother of their first child than jobless black males. Employment increased the likelihood of a legitimization of a birth by eight times, for those fathers ages eighteen to thirty-one, in these inner-city neighborhoods."

With cities increasingly home to very wealthy and very poor residents, Wilson sees a desperate time ahead for places like New York and Cleveland, with large welfare caseloads. He told me welfare reform will move large numbers of recipients to low-wage work, and it has. But for those who cannot make the transition, he predicts great suffering, especially among children, which may result in a backlash.

"What we're going to see, over the next several years, is a significant increase in the number of kids who are represented in the homeless population. A lot of them won't have the resources previously available to them. A lot of them won't have SSI, and won't be receiving any form of welfare once the mothers reach the time limit. I think that's something we have to be very concerned about, but, you know something, I don't think the American public's going to tolerate it. I think once they begin to see scenes of whole families and children on the street, they're going to say, 'Hey, listen, enough is enough already. We can't tolerate this. We're a civilized society and we've got to do something.' There will be some states that will prevent this from happening, some states that will take the steps to be sure that these mothers are not left to sink or swim. Other states, unfortunately, will not."

However, this country already tolerates having a third of its children living in poverty, and joblessness among minority youth is approaching

50 percent in many neighborhoods. Why would such dismal effects of welfare reform suddenly prick the American conscience?

"These figures and their meaning are very abstract. People don't really visualize them in ways that they would if the TV cameras are out there depicting families and children living on the streets and struggling to survive and searching for food. No one knows how many children will be affected by this. No one knows what steps will be taken by states and the federal government when we have to face up to it. This is just one of many problems created by so-called welfare reform that we're going to live to regret.

"People in inner-city neighborhoods support the norms of the work ethic, the family, and the basic norms of society. And many of these people are concerned that it's going to be difficult for their children to reach the goals and aspirations that they have for them. Many of these families talk about how tough it is to raise kids in some of the neighborhoods that feature high rates of joblessness—joblessness that triggers other problems, such as gang formation, drug trafficking, violent crime.

"In some neighborhoods people are even afraid to walk the streets during the day. People on the South Side of Chicago talk about how great it was, in previous years, when they could sleep out on fire escapes and in parks on hot summer nights, and walk the streets at night, and not have to worry about muggings and crime, and all of this has changed in the face of high levels of joblessness that trigger other sorts of problems that have affected the social organizations of these neighborhoods. We do a disservice to these people if we suggest that these problems don't exist.

"We are not going to improve their lives, and improve conditions for the children in these neighborhoods, unless we recognize that some of these neighborhoods have reached levels of social disorganization that make it very difficult for the children growing up to achieve pro-social outcomes. What I'm trying to do is talk about neighborhoods that have reached such a high level of joblessness, it has triggered other social problems. That doesn't mean that the residents in these neighborhoods are not committed to work, not committed to the basic values of society. It means that they have a much harder time trying to survive in this society.

I get sick and tired of listening to conservatives talk about family values and people not living up to the expectations of society, without considering the incredible obstacles that these families have to overcome, just trying to live up to the basic values of American society.

"The disappearance of work is associated with some of the broader changes in American society. It's as if racism, having put a lot of inner-city minorities in their economic place, stepped aside to watch changes in technology, and changes in the global economy, destroy that place. And unless we appreciate the overwhelming, devastating effects of these broad social changes that are occurring, we aren't going to be in a position to address the problems, to deal with the dislocation I write about."

One of Wilson's central theses over the years has been to establish the high correlation between tight labor markets and reduced joblessness in chronic, high-unemployment areas. In the years since the publication of *The Declining Significance of Race,* the worldwide labor market has integrated in ways unimaginable twenty-five years ago. A lightly skilled industrial worker in an American city is not just in competition with similar workers in other American cities or regions but with more than a dozen other workers, in places like Hermosillo, Mexico; Bangalore, India; and Shanghai, China. Haven't the breathtaking changes in global capitalism made Wilson's suggestion of federal government intervention—to tighten labor markets using high-growth national policies—outdated?

"The ranks of the have-nots have grown, not only in the African-American community, but in other communities as well. The economic dislocation that I've described in the inner city represents a more extreme form of the dislocation and growing economic insecurity sweeping across the United States, and indeed, across the Western world. I think that it's important for people to recognize this, and not think that the problems of the inner city are unique. It's part of a broader trend that's going to have to be addressed at some point. People are going to become aware that the gap between the haves and have-nots will continue to grow; I think the have-nots are going to recognize, and join some sort of progressive political coalition to address these problems.

"There are a lot of demagogic messages out there that deflect attention from the real source of our problems—economic sources, political sources—

so we turn on each other. People should recognize that our problems are similar, we have a lot of things in common, and we should be working more closely together to solve our problems.

"It's not at all clear that low levels of unemployment are going to trigger the kind of inflation we associate with tight labor markets. It seems to me, from public opinion polls, that people are willing to put up with a certain level of inflation, if it means that we would put America back to work. The public job creation that I'm talking about would not create high rates of inflation. You've got to get people to recognize the trade-off: Do you want a society that's going to have record levels of joblessness that could trigger other social problems, or do you want to tolerate a little bit of inflation and minimize some of these other social dislocations associated with high levels of joblessness?"

It is a stunning and provocative analysis: the residents of black central-city neighborhoods as the economic canaries in the coal mine for the rest of us. Don't be satisfied with putting economic and social distance between yourself and the poorest members of our society, Wilson warns, because you may be next.

What makes people work hard? What makes them strive? Surely it must in part be a belief in an eventual payoff. It is a central part of the American creed that hard work pays off. Indeed, the constant refrain of Americans trying to defend their turf is "I've worked hard for everything I've got." What that declaration doesn't allow for is all the Americans who work hard, all the time, and never get anywhere. Whites are less likely than blacks to face years of hard work that is not rewarded with the possibility of improving their station and quality of life by moving to a neighborhood with better houses and better schools.

Regina Lind's own ideas about race, place, and fairness were shaped in the crucible of a changing Louisville, Kentucky, neighborhood in the 1960s. What today's free marketeers are loath to admit is that sometimes success and failure are not doled out in the free market in response to making "right" and "wrong" choices, as the American myth machine so often tells us. Lind's questions about America were reinforced by watching right and wrong turned upside down on the streets of Louisville.

"In 1956, we lived over my father's pharmacy. My father ran the pharmacy, a real pharmacy from the days when people knew their customers and their problems. We found a home several blocks away. It was the last street on the West End, right near the river. There were brick homes, a quiet street. It was a nice setting. We moved in just as I was going to be eleven years old.

"Let me explain what was happening in Louisville at the time. Urban renewal had come and torn down half of downtown, and blacks started moving west. The minute that happened you could hear people saying it, adults, children repeating what they had heard at home, 'The niggers are coming. The niggers are coming,' as if it was the plague or something. The questions people asked revolved around it: 'When are they going to get here? What does it mean for me?'

"We're Catholic. So that was a central part of our lives, where we went to school, where we went to church. There was a girls' high school and a boys' high school, Christ the King. Holy Cross was where my parents had been married. People checked each other out by asking which grade school you came from. It was very stable. Very safe. Eight years of grade school and four years of high school. It was a really nice time to be a kid.

"This all started to become real for me when the next-door neighbors started to make it an issue. Next door lived the Meek family. Peaches Meek was the mother. Rumor had it that a black family was going to move into the area. The house was half a mile away. Peaches tried to get the neighbors to buy the house. Can you imagine? As if nobody else was ever going to try and sell their house. What were we going to do, buy them all? We told them to get lost.

"We had a nice house. You have to remember that in those years everybody had big families. With four kids we had one of the smaller families on the block. The people on the block didn't change very much from year to year.

"Then came word that Peaches was going to sell. She was the first one to go. She sold the house to Bill Moses. He was a surgeon. An African American. They had two children, and one of them had cerebral palsy.

One of the reasons they were interested in the Meeks's house was that it had a pool, so their daughter could do her therapy. So, Peaches bailed out. The Moses's moved in.

"It didn't take long for the FOR SALE signs to come out. One Sunday some high school boys collected all the FOR SALE signs for blocks around and staked them in Dr. Moses's front yard. They did it in the middle of the night. So on Sunday morning when Dr. Moses came out his front door, that's what he saw, forty FOR SALE signs standing on his lawn.

"I was a young teenager, maybe not old enough to understand the full gravity of this, but not enough of a kid anymore to miss the fact that this was an emotional thing. I was watching through the curtains as he looked at the FOR SALE signs. He moved with such dignity. You couldn't tell what he was feeling. Very quietly, serenely, almost eerie in a way, he pulled the signs one by one out of the lawn, stacked them in his garage, and went back in the house.

"My mother physically restrained my sister from going out the front door to help him. For the next day or so people passed by to get their signs.

"As a pharmacist, my father recognized all the training and education that a person had to get to become a surgeon. He was thrilled there was a surgeon next door. When my father would run into Bill Moses and the two would chat, Dr. Moses would suggest they go in the backyard, and my father would say, 'No, no, we can talk out here!' I'm not sure if Dr. Moses was trying to spare my dad the neighbors watching them talk like buddies, but I don't think my dad would have even realized that was what was happening.

"At first, the cost of housing kept the change very gradual. The new people moving in were doctors, and teachers. The editor of the Louisville *Defender* still lives there. My mother still lives there. Her street is very nice. By the time I moved back to the area, between 1965 and 1967, it was all black. But the change was always gradual, and the real decline came much later on. It's pretty bad now.

"My father's drugstore was on Broadway and Forty-seventh Street. It was, how should I say it? Geographically unsuitable. Some of his customers had to go all the way through the central city to get to us, and after a while they didn't want to do that. I had to travel to have a social life. All of my sisters, all of us ended up with a firmly grounded sense of what is important in life. I think living where we lived was a part of that.

"Why did we move there in the first place? Why did we stay there? Want to know the truth? It's because my father wanted to look at the river. Turns out that one of the reasons he fell in love with the house right away is that it was at the end of a cul-de-sac that backed up onto the river. I can always remember him sitting at the water's edge, watching the river, smoking a cigarette. He loved that place. That's why he loved that house. I always used to think it was a moral stand. My sisters told me we didn't have the money to move, especially after the pharmacy wasn't doing as well. My father wrote a thesis about how small businesses could survive in changing neighborhoods.

"There was no question, it had a major impact on the family's financial situation. General Hospital was downtown. The main sources of medical care in our neighborhood were now Medicare and Medicaid. Finally, Dad had to start another business in the south end. The crunch had really started around 1968. He had wanted to keep the West End store, but he ended up opening a pharmacy in a doctor's building. It was because of that we stayed.

"I was recently talking to one of my sisters about those years, she was remembering a meeting outside the Moses's house, talking about what 'we' were going to do about the changing neighborhood. She was reminding me of who was at the meeting. Many of them were people we had looked up to, people we thought had a little bit of class.

"Friends were moving out week after week; I can remember feeling a little bit stuck."

I lay in my bed one summer night after a D.C. scorcher and channel-surfed, watching the rat-tat-tat parade of images and contextless environments which make up our video world and stopped when the Speaker of the House, Newt Gingrich, popped up. He was addressing the summer meeting of the Republican National Committee. The anxious acolytes of the Republican Revolution were settling in their seats for a dose of high-octane intellectual nourishment from the pol who kept reminding us he is a historian and a former professor.

Well, he made me sit up in my seat. As part of his address he riffed on the creation of public housing, improvising a solo on the massive housing projects along the Dan Ryan Expressway on the South Side. The Speaker used the gulag of Corbusier-brutalist apartment blocks as an illustration of the failures of liberalism. Using classically fallacious reasoning he (correctly) identified the liberal New Deal and Great Society origins of public housing, then (incorrectly) attached the origins to the particular execution along the Dan Ryan.

Public housing was built in profusion in places like Chicago's South Side because the private housing market would not build the thousands of units needed in the early postwar years. The private housing market would not build the units needed by renters who could not afford high rents. The much-celebrated private market had yielded thousands of substandard rental houses in the tightly enforced ghetto, where black families paid higher rents than white families at similar and even higher income levels.

At the outset, public housing moved into a breach created, not solved, by the marketplace. In the particular example of Chicago, freeing thousands of black families from the confines of the historic black belt to live with their white economic peers was simply unthinkable for the white political structure. The new ghetto, the one derided as liberal social engineering and a Democratic failure, was built on the foundation of the first, with thousands of units crammed into high-rises separated from large areas of white settlement by railroad viaducts, expressways, and industrial districts.

The worst, most isolated housing projects in America are economic dead zones. Even buying a quart of milk can be a complicated task (though buying a lottery ticket usually is not). In this arid economic landscape, say the urban fabulists of the Republican Party, it is drive and personal initiative that result in personal progress. These important personal qualities presumably take the place of savings and loans, employers, and businesses.

"Liberals" like Richard Daley père and black power broker William Dawson tried to keep the new ghetto within the historic boundaries of the first, so blacks moved up (in floor elevation) but never out. Dawson stayed relevant by remaining the conduit for all black patronage, and Daley continued to preside over a City Council where black political expression was channeled into a small number of black aldermen elected by virtually all-black wards.

With the projects lined up along the busy expressway, history delivers its ironies in profusion: the larger of the two enormous projects on South State Street is named for Robert Taylor, the first black director of the Chicago Housing Authority. He was an advocate of integration, defying his political patron William Dawson. He pleaded for new housing to spread out into different areas of the city. He was rebuffed, and now this monument to cynical segregation is called Robert Taylor Homes, and even worse, in common speech, is simply called Robert Taylor.

Did the historian Newt Gingrich care about the whole story? Did he know the facts while refusing to let the real story get in the way of a good partisan jab? It is hard to tell. That same year, columnist George Will also wrote about the "liberals" and the construction of Chicago's public housing. Perhaps George Wallace's battle cry of "Segregation forever!" would also qualify as a liberal mantra in the interesting world of Messrs. Will and Gingrich.

"I've always been at odds with the real estate industry over this. I've always been a supporter of public housing," said Ferdinand Kramer, ninety-five years old and a witness to arguments over public housing since they began in the 1930s. Such a rave seems strange coming from a developer and mortgage banker.

Kramer has seen it all: the experiments, the bright ideas, the white papers from blue-ribbon panels. His hard-earned common sense on race matters and housing is based on decades of experience in what works, and what doesn't. He built some of the earliest examples of publicly subsidized, integrated housing in the United States. But laws that ordered him to stop being race-conscious in leasing didn't encourage integration—it ended it.

"The Open Occupancy Law spreads the ghetto. It's as simple as that. We built a development, Prairie Estates, right next to Michael Reese [a major South Side hospital], and it was integrated, 70 percent white, 30 percent minority in a neighborhood that had been a terrible black ghetto. When the Open Occupancy Law came into effect, we had to take tenants in the order that they apply as long as they can pay the rent. That's what the law requires, and now that development is virtually all black."

I asked him if the law took all of his say out of screening decisions.

"There is no say left. We didn't have to take members of gangs or people with criminal records. We tried to be a little selective. But the choice we have to work with is primarily black, with a few Hispanics. From the standpoint of economics the project has not suffered, it's been a good investment, it's fully rented. But if you're looking for integration, there's no such thing there."

That is an important distinction for Ferd Kramer. During our talk he pointed out that for him, this was not a question of profit. He made his money on building and managing these developments that ended up segregating. His firm, Draper and Kramer, has been the largest developer of rental housing on the South Side, in neighborhoods many of his competitors avoid. He insists that black tenants want the same things his white tenants want, first and foremost a safe environment. Whites move first because it is easier for them to do so.

"A majority of people have fears of a criminal group getting into the neighborhood. In a place like Hyde Park, you may have a more intelligent group of people, but even there, it's a battle every day of the week to keep whites in there. Sure, the University [of Chicago] acts as a big anchor. But try to get more professors to live in the neighborhood and walk to work, you can't do it. Still, to this day, professors are moving to the North Side."

Keeping one of America's great universities anchored in a part of Chicago surrounded by decline has not just been a challenge in the 1990s. It's been an ongoing struggle since the end of World War II. By the 1960s, the university played its trump card, a threatened departure, and laid a heavy hand on Hyde Park. Today's neighborhood was molded by the university, from the street patterns, to the housing densities, to the physical barriers separating Hyde Park from the devastated ghetto of Woodlawn.

"I've been a trustee of the University of Chicago for many years. About forty years ago I got a call from Dr. Hutchins [then president of the university] to go see him. Now this is shortly after World War II. He says to me, 'We are hiring young instructors from Ivy League universities and they can't find any place to live, what do we do?' I answered, if you get the land, we'll build the building. They bought a church at the corner of Dorchester, sold it to us at reuse value, same thing as Prairie Shore but the government wasn't involved this time. . . . The subsidy involved was very little, maybe about twelve thousand dollars less than they paid for it when they sold it to us. We got drawings made and got ready to go to work on the building, and I get another call from Bob Hutchins. . . . He's got trustees there, and the treasurer, and he says, 'Mr. Kramer, my staff tells me we can't afford to build the building, and that if we build it no one will be able to afford to live in it.' Now Hutchins was a guy, we used to say, who had his feet planted firmly in the clouds.

"I asked him, how many are they saying could afford to rent here? It was a 120-unit building, and he tells me, twelve. So I ask him, 'What if I was to lock you in for twelve apartments at a thousand a month? Twelve apartments in perpetuity for a thousand a month?' He says, 'Let's do it.' In a few months it was 50 percent occupied by university staff and now probably about 80 percent, and it's a well-integrated building. We're still operating that building."

The champion of the Great Books curriculum, the man who pulled the University of Chicago out of the Big Ten and set its sights permanently on academic excellence, couldn't envision a world where apartments rented for $1,000 a month. If he had bought more units, there would be grateful staff today.

Ferd Kramer is still very much in the game, even in his nineties. He comes to the office every day, leaves at lunchtime for a squash game (though he mentions, sadly, that he is outliving many of his partners), and still has a keen interest in housing patterns, and what kind of developments help to rebuild blighted areas. One major building block in the effort to build residential neighborhoods at the south edge of the Loop came in the 1980s with Dearborn Park.

"Dearborn Park proved to builders that it was possible to build profitable rental housing on the South Side. We got involved with the project at the suggestion of Chicago 21 [a corporate group trying to redevelop

Chicago's downtown, a failure in many respects]. It was part of their Plan for South Side Housing. It's totally built out now, for the second phase the land has all been sold to the builders. There is one rental building, a building for the elderly. Again, before the Open Occupancy Law we had integration, now we have to take them as they come, and the building is 100 percent black." Again, Kramer endorses engineered integration over organic segregation.

"The sad part for Dearborn Park is the school down there. It was built there for Dearborn Park. Then the people came from the public housing south of there with demonstrations, and fighting. I thought there was going to be some kind of riot there. As a result of all that there are now 7 out of 350 students in that school who live in Dearborn Park, white or black. The families with young children in Dearborn Park send their children to private schools, parochial schools, or magnet schools, but they will not go to that school."

The elementary school battle was a textbook case of racially tinged battling over the pie when it hadn't been fairly dished out in the first place. The kids from the projects attended the Hilliard School, an aging building no longer suitable to many of their needs. Part of the draw for the new arrivals attracted to the South Loop by new yuppie housing was a brand-spanking-new school. In their residences towering over the cute row houses of Dearborn Park and several blocks to the south, the tenants of Dearborn Homes moved from a set-aside of seats at the new school to open enrollment. Now Carson Elementary, like virtually all South Side public schools, is virtually all black, and virtually all low income. For Ferd Kramer, these results were predictable.

"Now, with Dearborn Park families, when their children get to school age, if they can't afford private school, they leave. The city didn't cooperate. We bent over backwards. There was a library with no books in it, we donated some books. There was no landscaping when the school opened, it was a sea of mud. I went to the local School Council and offered, if they would agree to maintain it, to get a landscape architect to prepare a design, and I would pay for the installation of plants and grass, and an underground watering system. First, the local school council said they wouldn't accept it unless I also agreed to provide that for another school over in public housing and I told them to go to hell. Then they came back and told me they would accept it. So we did it.

"The school system is an important part of it. We have higher turnover because of it. Without good local schools it's hard to make developments like this work." Kramer remains a supporter of public housing, even as it has strayed far from his dreams of the 1930s and 1940s, when he was a member of the President's Committee on Equal Opportunity in Housing.

"I've always been at odds with the real estate industry on this. There is a need for housing for people who could not afford to pay an economic rent. I was very much concerned with the fact that public housing was starting to get a bad name because of the crime, and this is twenty-five years ago. There was a criminal element preying on the people who lived there.

"The deputy head of the CHA was a professor of sociology at the University of Chicago, and I had lunch with him. I told him the management of public housing is killing me. I told him you've got to get rid of the bad eggs in those buildings. He asked me, 'Where will they go?' I told him, 'That's not your problem. The Act requires you to provide decent, safe, sanitary housing for people who can't afford market rents. It's not your job to take care of those people who are criminally inclined.' At those early stages it wasn't so bad, it would have been easy to do."

Today the words of Ferd Kramer are echoed not in the conservative opinion journals, many of which want to end public support of housing entirely, but by recent secretaries of Housing and Urban Development.

I drove down the main street of Chicago's Roseland neighborhood, South Michigan Avenue, with Gregory Pitts, a forty-year-old man who as a teenager had been among the first blacks on his block. I said, "We tell the young men not to join gangs and sell drugs. We tell them to be straight and clean and to play by the rules. But, Greg, if you're sixteen, after you get out of your sophomore year of high school you're going to want a summer job. A young man could have walked down this street in 1965 and picked up twenty or thirty hours a week work, even more."

We drove past a shuttered JC Penney, a department store called Standard and People's, now home to a few retail and fast-food shops hanging by a thread. On one block one store remained, a furniture store that sells on time; on the next block, again, one store, a men's clothing store that looked as if the styles in the window were twenty years old.

"What is a young guy going to find here?"

"That's a good question," Pitts allowed, as we threaded our way through the streets of Roseland, "but these people have to keep trying. They can make it if they try."

Pitts's faith was encouraging. His daughter was home for the summer after a freshman year at the University of Arkansas. His son had moved to Galesburg in western Illinois to escape the traps and snares waiting for young black men on the streets of the South Side and finish high school. Pitts and his wife own a neat, snug, white clapboard home on a street of neat, snug, white clapboard homes near the southern city limit of Chicago.

Like many of the places he had lived in a lifetime in the city, this house was on an all-black street that had once been all white. Since Pitts had picked me up at the last subway stop, at Ninety-fifth Street and the Dan Ryan, we hadn't seen a single white person. We occasionally talked about them the way we might have discussed spotted owls or snail darters.

"They're not too far away. Over there at the end of the block is Calumet City, and there used to be no black people living there, but it looks like the white people are staying put." We got back in the car. "They're building new houses just on the other side of the city line, and a bank! I figure that's got to be good news. You don't see new banks going up too often." On our way over to the bank we saw them: the first whites we had come across in an hour.

In the face of everything he had seen in his forty years on the planet, Gregory Pitts remained convinced of the goodwill of most people. But he felt the people who had moved away from his father and mother, his brothers and sisters on their trek through the South Side had missed something important: him. "It's a hurting thing knowing that people are willing to sell their house and move and look for another place to live just because we moved in. It's a hurting thing all right.

"If they would have stayed they would have found out that we were a nice family." As demographers and social scientists have known for decades, the white families on Gregory Pitts's various home blocks would be less likely to hang around in Chicago than in any other city in America.

The urban experience of the 1950s and 1960s was repeated in the suburbs in the 1970s and 1980s, and the process continues to the century's end. Auguretto Batiste moved to Dolton, south of Chicago in Cook County. Like many in the growing black middle class, this native South Carolinian got a hostile reception from his blue-collar neighbors. Perhaps the small-scale vandals, casual haters, and neighborhood wise guys didn't know what they were getting in their tough, straight-backed, serious new neighbor. It didn't take them long to find out.

"Before I even moved in to Dolton in 1971, I had a ticket to appear in court, allegedly because I was littering my own property. After we closed on the house, but before we moved in, the good, red-blooded American neighbors gave me a welcoming party by taking thirty or forty cans of their garbage and dumping it on my front lawn. There is an ordinance on the books in Dolton that stipulates that if you litter your own property you are subject to being ticketed. So when I went to the home to move in, I found a ticket on my door to appear in court because I was littering my own property. Rather than getting the Welcome Wagon that's what I got.

"But the house was good. The location was good. And the school was good. That was one of my primary concerns. I was able to buy from the owner, and thus bypass the middle man. The middle man wouldn't have even shown me the house.

"Then one night I was taking things out of my car, and one of the good, red-blooded Americans walked up, someone who calls themselves a neighbor, walked up and asked the question, 'What do I mean moving into *his* neighborhood?' And I said, 'Son, this country is my neighborhood. I'm not the immigrant. You are.'" Batiste proudly claims his African roots and the American Indian heritage on his mother's side. "My people did not come through Ellis Island. My mother's people were already here twenty thousand years before Ellis Island was even thought of. This country is my neighborhood. I felt that way then, and I still feel that way. I'm sure that didn't convince him, but I'll tell you one thing. He got my message.

"I don't believe in turning the other cheek. My mother's people did and ended up losing the whole country. I don't bother anyone. I was taught that way. I'm not going to let anyone bother me, as long as there's breath in my body. I'm not a violent person. I don't believe in it. But I will take whatever measures are necessary to protect my family and that's what I had to do, at times with a gun in my hand.

"In the first years in Dolton I had Molotov cocktails thrown. I had bomb threats. I had fires set. I had bullets through the window. And when some of their lovely little red-blooded, flag-waving American kids came close to being shot, then they decided they better keep their little red-blooded American kids home. Off of my property. I've even had hand-to-hand combat with the police, on my own property. I have caught them going through my garage without my permission at four o'clock in the morning. My little dog woke me up. I hear this barking, I see these flashing lights, I jump into a pair of pants and that's all I had on with my gun. When I went out to my garage, there they are going through all my personal items in my garage. Being in the pharmaceutical industry, obviously I had medications designed for licensed physicians.

"I didn't know what they were trying to do but I asked them what they were doing in my garage. They said they had gotten a call from a neighbor saying they had seen someone breaking into my garage. This is at four o'clock in the morning. I asked them if it was true that at this time in the morning someone could see into my garage, and yet they could not give me the respect to ring my doorbell before they started poking around? They started telling me to put my gun down. I said, 'No, I'm not going to put my gun down. There are four of you. And each of you has a minimum of two guns, and you're telling me to put mine down? It doesn't work that way.'

"So when I refused, they decided that they would try to take it away from me. Four officers had to jump me before they got me to relinquish the weapon. I let them know that if they entered my property again, without giving me the proper courtesy, I would shoot first, and talk later. It's called basic respect. I am a law enforcement officer. I do lock people up. I do have at my side a .357 Magnum. I'm a state investigator, a sworn officer. If you're wrong, you're wrong. If I'm wrong, I'm wrong."

There's nothing subtle about Batiste's unwillingness to tolerate slights and disrespect. He had voluntarily enlisted in this struggle for evenhanded treatment in his new town. But what of his sons, who had to live with the consequences of their father's decision? "I had to get the principal of the elementary school straightened out, and I had to get the principal of the high school straightened out. Once I did that, no problem. There were incidents, especially with the young ones. Names were being called. Licks were passed, and my sons were taught to not let anyone walk over you. Don't start anything. But you are not going to turn the other cheek. So when they decided to defend themselves, that's when they were expelled from school."

Batiste says he didn't go in for calm negotiations. On one occasion he says he walked into the principal's office, locked the door behind him, and demanded the letters regarding fighting be removed from his son's files. The principal was told in an unequivocal way that his sons had to defend themselves because the school would not help protect them, and as long as the school would not do its job, his sons would fight. "I didn't move. My sons graduated from high school, and as a matter of fact the oldest one came close to helping his school win the state championship in speech for the first time. The other one was involved in forensics also, so was the third one. Mine was the second family in the state to have three sons inducted into the Forensics League, as well as the National Thespians Honor Society. And they got involved in the ACT-SO [an African American academic competition], and the middle one got involved in tennis, and in acting. The third one won the state championship for speech, and I'm not saying that just because he's my son. He is the one who put them over the top, and that's why today he's at the University of Illinois, as a sophomore, in the Shakespearean Festival."

It ended up not mattering to his white neighbors that Batiste was prepared to be as good a neighbor to them as they were willing to be to him. The pace of change in once almost all-white Dolton picked up in the 1980s. "It is not a hard thing to deal with and I'll tell you why. When you take a look at the new homeowners, you'll find that in intellectual background, their upbringing, their socioeconomic level, their stability, most of the neighbors who moved in . . . intellectually, financially, socially, are superior. Not that I base my relationship with human beings on that. But that's just the reality of things."

As in so many other changing areas around the country, there was at first a promise not to flee. "There was a movement for a time when many of the neighbors got these signs that said, 'I'm not moving.' 'I'm staying.' 'I'm not selling.' Most of them are the first to move. I was able to settle most of my problems after three years. I moved out there in October of '71. By 1974 things started dying down because people realized I was dead serious.

"Some of the neighbors had their picture windows broken so many times in a month, many of them were threatened by the insurance company to be canceled, because you had these broken one after the other. I started to try to organize other blacks who started to have similar problems. Many of them didn't want to admit it at first. Many of them didn't want to organize. Many of them wanted to deny they were having problems. Many of them raised the question, why should I get involved in any kind of an organization?

"I organized a group of men who I thought had the intestinal fortitude to stand up and protect their families, their neighbors' families, from whatever danger ensued. But many of them were afraid of a formal organization. My feeling was, unless it was a structured type of organization it would end up as a vigilante group. I felt it had to be chartered by the State of Illinois. We were meeting with Mayor McCabe, the mayor at that time, explaining to him the various problems the neighbors were having. The slow response from the Dolton Police Department, the attitude that the Dolton Police Department had, the lack of minority police officers on the force.

"We had situations with something they have in the suburbs called 'sod-busting,' I had never heard of it before, but I should have put it together. It's a process wherein these teenagers would drive up onto your beautifully manicured lawn, and gun their wheels, and tear up your lawn. That's very expensive. There was one lady by the name of Mrs. Perdue who in the first month she was there had thirty different incidents. While in the process of this organizing, I'm making additional contacts with other agencies, the FBI, the Justice Department, and we're explaining to them other things that are happening, to keep them abreast. Superimpose on that the fact that the police kept saying, we didn't see anything, the neighbors didn't see anything, and I told them that we were going to have to do as neighbors was make up our own police force, and that's what we did."

Batiste's group kept its own incident reports, and its own records of times, dates, and locations. When black residents in Dolton finally brought in federal authorities and began to threaten investigations into possible civil rights violations, change began. "After that we started getting some kind of real feedback. We presented a list of demands and concerns to the mayor with an eye toward eradicating many of the problems which we had been experiencing. We were concerned not only about our physical welfare, the welfare of our children, but we were also concerned with creating some representation on the police force, the board of education, the fire district, the park district, and so on. In all honesty, everything we asked for got a very positive response, with one exception. That was sensitivity training for the Dolton Police Department. Which we never got, not to this day.

"We had always said we don't want to start problems. We said we wanted to make Dolton a livable, viable community. We kept improving what we bought at inflated prices. We're a stabilizing force to the community. We don't want to happen in Dolton what happened in Harvey, what happened in Phoenix [nearby south suburban towns] where the whole community went down and the economic base fell out."

Now, almost thirty years since he bought his house, Batiste sees a different place from the one he helped integrate. "Dolton has changed tremendously. It is now about 65 percent black, 35 percent white. Might be more, could be less, but I think that's about right." Not everyone, he admits, could wait for the quiet stability he sees today. "Some families moved out. I think they were caught off guard. Many of them moved to South Holland [another south suburban town], and that area is changing now too."

Like many people in his position who've watched the moving trucks load up and drive away, he wonders how far people think they can move to flee black neighbors. "I don't see where it's going to stop. Situations change, but people don't. That attitude is not going to change. People have a tendency, even if you meet all their criteria, to come up with something else they don't like."

"The property values in my neighborhood are solid. I've been there, as I mentioned, since 1971, and I'm glad to see people taking good care of their property, hanging flower baskets, installing new patios. The area is decorated at Christmas time with lights and greens. For a time black families put up with having their Christmas lights stolen from the front of their houses. Black families also had to put up with the theft of their garbage cans. Sometimes the lids, sometimes the whole can."

"But didn't you at any point during all of this say to yourself, Life shouldn't have to be so hard?" I asked.

"I never said that," Batiste responded. "I can't say that. Certain other families said, after they had been in the area awhile, 'I never thought that I would be subjected to' this or that treatment. Please understand me. I'm proud of my mother and father. I am very proud of my heritage, which is a rich and deep one. I decided that I would not be run off.

"I don't defer to threats. I grew up in the South. In the town where my father grew up they knew they better not mess with him. My father also grew up in a white neighborhood, as a matter of fact it's *still* a white neighborhood. When people would ask him about that he would say, 'If they want to live with me too, that's fine.'

"Once I solved my problems in Dolton, people know not to stop by my address if they had trouble in mind. I am a light sleeper. I didn't bother anybody, but like I say I don't turn the other cheek either. If you want to come by my place and vandalize, you have to be ready to take whatever comes.

"The community still has a very good school system. You've got the same accelerated degree of problems you find in schools everywhere, but today the school board is advocating a levy they want passed to make sure the schools have the economic base, so they will not falter.

"Everybody can melt in the melting pot except so-called black people. Look at American history. The same people who came for the freedom they lacked at home are now suppressing other people's freedom. We had Haitians dying off our shores the same month we made eighteen thousand foreigners into citizens. We are hypocrites.

"After everything that's happened to me I could be the biggest racist there is. But there's an old saying, that where there's life there's hope. *'Whereof a man thinketh, so is he.'* If we became pessimists there'd no longer be anything to look forward to.

"This country is in denial. Four hundred years of free slave labor has made it possible for people of many ethnic persuasions to live rather comfortably in the United States. I have every right to be a racist. It's just not in my nature. Thank God for my mother and father, for teaching me a better way."

Clevelanders are working hard to create a postrace future for their city. A black mayor mingles easily with African-American homeowners, Eastern European elderly, and suburban investors. New housing is rare enough in Cleveland. Today it rises with the intention mixed into every trowel of mortar and bucket of paint that planned segregation is securely part of the city's past. Let's start with a quick tour of downtown.

Chapter 8

Gentle Decay? Staving Off the Future in Cleveland

Strolling through downtown Cleveland at night, you can hear the roar of another sellout crowd at Jacobs Field–home of the Cleveland Indians– and a few blocks later catch a glimpse of the floodlit Rock and Roll Hall of Fame and Museum, and the just completed Science Museum. The new arena has brought the Cleveland Cavaliers of the National Basketball Association back from the suburbs. A huge new theater complex and Public Square, the symbolic heart of the city, are circled by top-flight hotels and modern office towers. The mayor, Michael White, tells everyone he can about Cleveland's "revival," its "comeback," its "renaissance." I was leafing through a vacation issue of *Town and Country* recently and saw "comeback" Cleveland cheered in the same article as Taos and Aspen.

The makeover has certainly worked on one level. When you talk about comeback cities, people in other parts of the country say, "What about Cleveland?" There is no doubt that the city has done a very good job maximizing its strengths, and attracting investment and attention. Believing in "rebirth," however, requires the visitor to ignore too many of the city's present-day realities.

As you move around Cleveland, you are constantly reminded that about half the number of people who once lived here remain. The city of almost one million, now inhabited by barely five hundred thousand, looks empty. The school system is bankrupt. Major employers continue to leave. A tour of the Industrial Valley alternates between hopeful signs—new plants and new investment in old ones—and vast graveyards of industry. There is idle land, empty warehouses, decaying docks, and buckling streets crisscrossed by rails to nowhere. In the heart of downtown, as in many places in the neighborhoods, the sidewalks are empty. Big, broad streets carry little traffic. In poorer areas, where demolition was the preferred method for stabilizing the housing stock, huge chunks of vacant land sit permanently idle, occasionally covered in grass and skinny saplings for appearance's sake.

To get a little realism about the fundamentals undergirding a city where half the households live below the poverty line, you have to refer to documents like the city's petition for a new empowerment zone, an area where special incentives and tax abatements are offered to investors. In a plea like that, in which a brave face wouldn't do too much to strengthen the application, reality reigns. Another cold slap comes when selling a house. During an evening walk in the Warner-Turney neighborhood, I passed a house with a new SOLD sign on the front. I saw a man working in back and headed over to talk.

Ed Schoffstall is leaving for a rural area just outside the south suburban ring. How much did he get for his property? "That's kind of a sore subject. I wanted to list it for a hundred and my real estate agent said, 'No way.' He said around here nobody would even come look at it if I listed at a hundred. I ended up selling it for eighty-nine thousand dollars." My jaw dropped. *Two* two-car garages, three bedrooms, two baths, modern kitchen. Fifteen minutes from downtown. Big backyard. Big *front* yard. Eighty-nine thousand dollars.

"I'm tired of what's going on with the schools. The people in this town would rather donate so that millionaires have a new arena to play in, than for decent schools for the kids. We passed tax increases for a new football stadium and a new baseball stadium, but we won't invest in the streets or the schools.

"No one's done anything for the school system. You're busing kids so they *all* won't get an education. The Realtors are telling homeowners in the city of Cleveland it's all about education. No one with kids is going to buy your house. So where's the incentive to buy another house in Cleveland? Whatever I do to it, I can't get my money back. I just took a beating. I ended up selling to the first person who looked at the house."

Just across the street from Schoffstall's soon-to-be former home stands the sales model for an extensive new development. Attractive, well-built, reasonably priced homes will soon replace the vast lots that succeeded a state asylum. Will those houses make a difference to the future prospects of the neighborhood?

The new development didn't raise Schoffstall's mood. "I've seen the houses. I love the houses. And you know what? All those people over there are going to get tax abatements. So with the schools going bankrupt you'll have people moving into new houses and not even paying into the system."

Other departing Clevelanders echoed Schoffstall's sentiments. Boyce McGhee, forty-two, told the Cleveland *Plain Dealer,* "You can only stay on a sinking ship for so long. When you see that the politics in the school system isn't going to change, then you have to change." Another Cleveland native, thirty-six-year-old Jeff Richie, told the newspaper: "When we started looking at the money we'd have to spend for a private school, we figured, why not pay for a bigger house, in a good community, with good schools right now?" Property taxes will be higher than in Cleveland, "but for the difference in services you get, you don't mind paying.

"I bought into the whole get-into-Cleveland attitude to the old neighborhood. I felt bad about moving, but I just didn't feel I should be the Lone Ranger in this."

"There's so much land, so many empty buildings," said Dennis Keating, associate dean of the School of Urban Studies at Cleveland State University (CSU). Many of the middle-class homeowners still hanging on in the city are finally, reluctantly, planning to leave to avoid being burned twice. "A lot of the people who've chosen to stay had already experienced white flight in other neighborhoods, and really feared it was going to happen again, and it's hard to convince them otherwise. A lot of damage was done the first time."

As in so many cities, schools loom large in these calculations. "The moment of truth comes in the eighth grade. There are many parents who are willing to send their children to local elementary schools—public or Catholic. But people have misgivings about public high schools. And there are very few Catholic high schools, which are very competitive and very expensive."

Keating told me a lot of Clevelanders are so fond of their city they would even be willing to try and stay, with some hefty provisions in place. "If they were ready to get rid of busing, if the schools were stabilized, if there was a new superintendent, if they could get the dropout rate down. . . . There are too many ifs. Most just decide to go instead."

Recent research from Cleveland State University's School of Urban Studies found that, of almost eighteen thousand home sales in the greater Cleveland metropolitan area from 1987 to 1991, 71 percent of home sellers moved farther out from central Cleveland after the sale. In the city of Cleveland, 88 percent of home sellers moved out of the city altogether. In the inner-ring suburbs, the numbers were just as disturbing: 78 percent of the sellers there moved farther away from the urban core. Less than half of the sellers in the outer suburbs moved farther out. When CSU researchers did follow-up interviews with sellers, they cited three chief factors for moving: safety, schools, and a newer house.

The results were most dramatic in the old, inner-ring suburbs, which experienced the highest levels of racial change and saw huge rates of departure. Their homeowners seemed to see no point in looking for what they wanted closer to home, particularly in the small suburban communities to the east of Cleveland. In East Cleveland, 95 percent of sellers left the city, and 7 percent moved out of Cuyahoga County. In University Heights, 93 percent left the city; a little over 11 percent moved to the adjacent county. In Euclid, 79 percent of sellers left town; a whopping 59 percent left the county.

Tom Bier, a professor at Cleveland State, supervised the research. "All over the region, people are deciding to move. Overall, fully one-quarter of everyone who moves in Cleveland and the inner suburbs moves to the next county. It's really easy to move. It's easier to move than to fix your house. A sizable chunk of the economy depends on continued movement to survive. In the real estate industry alone, you've got agents, appraisers, banks, moving companies, title companies. That's a lot of people with an interest in getting people to move."

But in the specific case of Cleveland, there has to be a "push factor," not just the "pull factor" of suburban living. "You've got to look at price," said Bier. "In 80 percent of the transactions, the purchase price of the house goes up, and goes up by an average of 50 percent." That often means the place where the homeowner was living originally offered a very narrow range of housing opportunities. People who might otherwise have traded up in the same area leave instead. "If you look for a geographic pattern of home values, they generally increase as you go out from the center. If our cities are structured in a way that prices rise moving out from the center, then you are going to have a situation where in order to move up you have to move out. The market in the city of Cleveland does not offer an array of choices. Public policy never addresses the dynamics of capital and choice. How are things going to be any different in the center city if 98 percent of the investment goes to developing the edge of the metropolitan area?"

With this centrifugal attraction to the edges of the region, especially for higher-income families, two things can happen to the chances for downtown living, still in a very primitive state in Cleveland. The city and developers can either create further pressures for a residential "dead zone" at the center, by doing nothing, or increase the desirability of living in town with a mix of purchase options and tax and financing incentives. For middle- and upper-income buyers, center-city life can be more attractive when the other available "choice" means living farther and farther away from the region's commercial and governmental center. But worrying about the future of the downtown in Cleveland is nothing new. "If you look at the central area, you can see change in a place like 'The Flats.' Twenty years ago, 'The Flats' were empty. Now development is going forward there. At the same time, there are no rental apartments downtown, or almost none. The suburbs get subsidies for everything. In one way or another, water, roads, power—all are subsidized. But the state of Ohio won't subsidize in-town development. Columbus, for instance, won't subsidize a land cleanup that would make some of the parcels of land you see right in or near downtown open to development.

"There was a survey done in the last several years that showed thirteen thousand people would like to live downtown. That's a lot of people. Why don't we make it possible for them to live downtown?

"There is one sign that people are turning around. We're finally starting to get suburban decline. Outward movement is getting to the edge of its possibilities. Now these suburbs in the county are learning what the city has known for years about draining resources out from established places to finance more sprawl. It took quite a few years to get decline out there, but now that it is there, maybe it's time to create some inward momentum."

Bier and I talked about the new housing development sprouting up in the heart of an area devastated by the riots that followed the assassination of Martin Luther King Jr. Church Crossing—part of the Beacon Place project—offers sizable homes at bargain prices, and a grab bag of governmental and private subsidies. Bier said, "Beacon Place and other new redevelopment projects represent the first time black and white homeowners have chosen to live together. That's the great promise of doing things like this in Cleveland." Bier said a history of attempts at integration that forced established blacks into a defensive posture looms large in Hough. "To blacks, a development like Beacon Place is part of an offensive, part of a drive to retake parts of the city near downtown."

I attended the ribbon cutting for Beacon Place and liked what I saw. The houses are pretty and spacious. They are brick and frame, in several different styles, from row house to cottage, with small gardens (in keeping with people's deep yearning for a comfortable and familiar domestic icon, the lawn, but also recognizing the desire of busy white-collar workers not to have to mow too much). The garages, alleys, and streets do not abandon the Cleveland street grid. The overall effect is cozy and harmonious. The person on foot is neither cramped nor marooned on the street, but "just right." The builder said he wanted people on the street to be able to say hello to people on the front porches, or for people to hail each other from across the street without having to shout. These homes offer suburban comfort within a short bus ride of downtown, within an unquestionably urban setting.

Until recently, the Hough district looked as if its rebirth would be stillborn. It was once the neighborhood of white senior and middle managers, the petite bourgeoisie of Cleveland's heavy industry. They plied the side streets on weekdays and talked to God on Sundays from their pews in the magnificent churches erected by mainline denominations on Euclid Avenue. But by 1968, Cleveland was in economic decline, and Euclid Avenue had long since been abandoned by the carriage trade. The killing of Martin Luther King Jr. provided the spark for a flame that burned down much of Hough. And down it stayed. Like a patient with a compromised immune system, Cleveland simply wasn't strong enough in the other ways that mattered to fight the opportunistic infection of neighborhood degradation in the districts just east of downtown.

Today, there are vast stretches of Euclid Avenue with no buildings at all. It's land that has fallen from the peak of style to dereliction, pausing briefly at all the stops in between. If you have forgotten just how long some of these lots have been vacant, nature provides a clue. Almost three decades after rioting left so many vacant lots, some of the trees in the lots are large, mature, and shady. It's been a long time since 1968. Only the massive churches sitting like islands in a contextless sea of grass tell you that something big has happened here.

By the late 1990s, a few things could not be changed about Hough. It was all black. It was very close to downtown. There were vast pieces of empty land. Off the beaten track, less visible from main streets, the land had returned to an urban bush. The empty lots sported a thick growth of shrub-sized specimens of weeds usually nipped at a few inches by even the most laissez-faire gardener.

Today when you talk to Clevelanders about their city and its prospects, one of the first questions they ask is "Have you seen Hough?" There is a strong sense among a wide array of city and suburban residents that things are better there. For a long time the name Hough was used to stand for everything most degraded about city life. After the neighborhood bottomed out, it took a while to find people ready to buy in. At first, black middle-income workers were the only people interested in the first generation of new Hough properties. They found unbelievably cheap land, a city desperate to build, and banks suddenly very willing to play ball. Some of the Cleveland-based banks had looked on passively in earlier decades as their city declined. They were now energized by a new generation of senior managers who didn't want to preside over the death rattle of Cleveland, and who were focused by new federal regulations that watched very closely the amount of deposits held by banks in comparison with how much money they loaned in the community.

It's hard not to be encouraged by the new buildings in Hough. They are attractive, roomy, and appear well built. They simply affirm the not very revolutionary notion that neighborhoods that decline can be brought back if enough variables can be wrestled into line. But walk another two blocks after a cluster of new houses and you find yourself in the scary Hough talked of as the heart of darkness in the rest of the city.

While the signs of life in the middle of what had been a barren neighborhood, in the heart of a city that was once in free-fall, are exciting, be careful about overstatement. The poverty rate approaching 50 percent is bad enough, but keep in mind how low family income must go before the federal government considers you to be poor (some $16,500 in annual income for a family of four). Remember that perched perilously just above the official poverty line are thousands of families you might call the "struggling class."

Detractors can also point to more subtle things: the ratio of empty and demolished housing units to occupied and newly built ones; a school system taken over by the state and placed in receivership; and the continued abandonment of the city for the suburbs, which still affords access to all the cultural baubles without the perceived risk and heartache of actually living in the city.

So developments like Church Crossing, where Mayor White and the assembled luminaries lift a giant pair of scissors and cut a giant ribbon at the doorway of the first completed home, carry a heavy burden. They must work. Period. Or else, Game Over.

As passersby congratulated them and thumped them on the back, I spoke to Charles Piazza, Melissa Burrows, and Jose Hernandez, whose new homes were under construction.

For Piazza, coming to Church Crossing was coming home. "I grew up in the East Side, and my wife and I moved to the West Side and we just decided for a new housing opportunity in Cleveland, this is like the perfect opportunity. We want to stay in Cleveland. . . . She works in

Cleveland. . . . I work *for* Cleveland, so you know, we can stay in the community, with something close so my wife can take a bus to work.

"There are a lot of people who've asked me, 'Why would you want to build a brand-new home there?' And my opinion was, it's an opportunity. It's an opportunity to get in on the ground floor of something that will prosper. I look at it as part of the whole community developing. When I really saw it developing was when my wife had our second daughter, and she had her up in Mt. Sinai Hospital, and I did this drive, morning, noon, and night. I saw all these neighborhoods, with all these beautiful houses coming up, and then I knew this development was here, and it was perfect.

"I grew up in a neighborhood where everybody up and down the street knew each other, you still had the doors open, and kids still played without the fear of anything happening. And eventually, well, the times are different now than they were then, but you still want that community for your children." While Piazza seemed overjoyed about the future prospects for Church Crossing to become a comfortable neighborhood and a long-term home for his growing family, he was less enthusiastic about the local schools. His own children would attend Catholic schools in Cleveland.

"Part of the reason I chose to live here," said Melissa Burrows, "is the location, and proximity to downtown. The interest rates were low; I wanted to have a new home and live in the city of Cleveland. When you compare taxes in the city of Cleveland to the suburbs, they're lower, and lower taxes in the city of Cleveland is definitely an incentive for me.

"Integration is important to me. This particular street is a diverse street, in terms of the people who are buying homes. But, the people who are buying and moving into this area are more than likely professionals, and so if an African-American family decides to move into this area, chances are more than likely they are a professional family and can afford to be here. I don't think it's an issue so much of black and white.

"If the area is going to become all African American, or a certain race, chances are the people here can afford it. The important thing is whether the people who move in are going to keep up their property; if they are, it doesn't really matter to me.

"I don't feel as though I'm a pioneer. I don't feel as though we're the first people to decide to live here. If you go back to the other side, on Chester, there are other homes that are much more expensive than the ones being built here. There is a rebirth occurring. We can either be part of it, or not be part of it, and we've decided to be part of it. The money that we will save on taxes will allow us the opportunity to send our children to private schools. Whatever city I chose I would probably opt for private schools. But, given the problems the city of Cleveland has with its public schools I will probably send my children to private schools.

"Based on the number of families who are moving in, on the fact that it's a diverse community, and people of all races are moving into the area, and based on the fact that people are moving into areas next to this area, it's not a gamble."

Jose Hernandez, who was born and grew up in Puerto Rico, and came to the mainland as an adult, agrees: "You speak about risk, I think, like Melissa said, most of the risk has gone on in the past. At this point, it's proven itself as a big development area. In Cleveland, right now, it's probably the hottest area in the real estate market. It was very attractive to me and my wife, looking for a home. We also liked the fact that many young professionals, like ourselves, are moving here and it seemed like a great place to raise a family.

"I'm an engineer for the city of Cleveland, so, I have to live in the city. At first, when I started working for the city I wasn't very happy with the fact that I had to live in the city. However, there are many pluses. The city is on the way up, we're close to work, we don't have the long commute. I personally don't like driving on the highways. I am four minutes away from work. I am a product of private education, so is my wife; we had never even considered sending the kids to public education even before we moved to Cleveland, so it really didn't play a role, it wasn't something to consider when we moved here. The people that I've talked to are all going to send their kids to private school. I can't speak for everybody. It's a personal choice. But speaking for myself, you can't get away from the problem of education in Cleveland. I think it's probably the main factor that's keeping property values down. The deal that you're getting for the kind of house that you're getting, the size, the quality, the incentives they're giving you is something that you can't turn down very easily. You get fifteen-year tax abatement. That's just one of the incentives they're giving you. Low interest rates. Low down payment. And you're also getting the UDAG [Urban Development Assistance Grant] money which is an amount that goes toward your down payment. It's a grant, I suppose.

"I believe houses here start at one hundred fifty thousand dollars, and go up. Of course that's made more affordable by all of the incentives. Basically, you're able to get more home for less money.

"Our mortgage was 5.625 percent, and the down payment was 5 percent," said Melissa. "Add to that the fact that you probably will pay about ten dollars a month in taxes. If you can beat that anywhere else in the city . . . move there, I guess," said Jose.

Clearly, the prospect of having Piazza, Burrows, and Hernandez living in new houses just minutes from downtown is encouraging. But at the edges of the good news lies a hint of caution. The Cleveland public schools were in state receivership. The voters of the city were just about to refuse to tax themselves to rush badly needed cash to the school system. And here were three new Cleveland families, none of which had the least intention of using the public schools.

In the old days, a city planner might look at these families and feel a little relief mixed in with the regret that educated, professional-class parents would not lend their energies to the public school system. But the relief would come from the fact that there were now three more families contributing to the school system's bottom line, without using the schools.

Our optimistic young buyers are not only making all their future plans based on private schooling, but they are buying houses with fifteen-year property tax abatements. Cleveland, like many American school districts, gets the largest single piece of its annual school budget from property tax levies. The new residents of Church Crossing will not give a penny to the upkeep of the public system and, in a towering irony, perceive themselves as taking their tax saving and using that to pay their private school tuition.

Building houses like these is a big gamble for a city as poor as Cleveland. It's terrific to have bright, happy, educated, optimistic home buyers bringing new life to a blighted part of the city. But with the heavy subsidies built into their purchases, what is the city buying with their presence in these new houses? A feeling that will rub off on others? Tax receipts down the road? Sales tax from stores and restaurants? An illusion?

After the ribbon cutting I talked to Norman Krumholz, who teaches at Cleveland State University after years as the head planner for the city, about what was exciting, and worrying, about a development like Church Crossing at Beacon Place.

"This is land that was abandoned by the market. In the sixties, seventies, and eighties, residential and commercial real estate in many East Side neighborhoods was seen as having no value. So, at the beginning, the owners milked the property for everything they could get, then just walked away. It went into tax delinquency, and eventually is owned by the government. Many of the buildings were vandalized, torched. So the city assembled land into the land bank, got clear titles on these properties, and began to put together these parcels. In neighborhoods like Central, like Hough, the city owns 10 to 15 percent of all the land.

"In the seventies, when I was at city hall, you couldn't get banks or S&Ls to lend money in the city. You couldn't get a supermarket to locate in the city. Finally, some of the chains recognized that there was money to be made here. . . . The Finast chain, for one, has built maybe half a dozen stores, to anchor new shopping centers in the city. Before you had commercial streets that could not attract a single drugstore; now you have three fighting it out for a market; you've got Revco, Rite-Aid, and Walgreen's, three to a block.

"The Community Reinvestment Act, a Carter administration law, changed everything. It made it possible to open investigations into lending policies, the kind of probes that could block consideration of other matters by regulatory agencies. Just the threat works. A city, or a community development corporation, can hold up bank transactions pending investigations by the regulators. The city has said to the banks, 'That's fine, you want a merger? We'll file a CRA complaint unless you play ball.'

"So the city assembled the land and said, 'Come and get it, boys!' Investors found large parcels with no encumbrances on the title, multiple banks offering to lend money to get you the land you want. The city does capital improvement work, streets and sidewalks, and in partnership with the bank offers new homes at below-market interest rates, with modest down payments.

"The housing in Hough is being sold to people who can handle a mortgage, people for whom it's hard to generate a rationale for government assistance. But the city is faced with the necessity of creating a market for land. And housing is still being abandoned at the same time as new housing is being built. There at Beacon Place, the value of land will go up, and people will stop abandoning property.

"When the fifteen-year threshold is crossed, the residents there will start to pay taxes. They're hoping it doesn't stop there. They hope these middle-class people will start to run for office in these new neighborhoods, send their children to local schools, and demand—as middle-class people do—a higher quality of service." But subsidizing people who can afford market-rate housing to build a demonstration model of modern urban living has a basic contradiction imbedded in it.

"If you abate taxes, the taxes have to go up for other people or the quality of services goes down for everyone else. There's no way around it. The city's finances are heavily skewed toward the payroll tax, and hardly at all toward the property tax. Today the lifeblood of Cleveland is the payroll tax. If you live in Hunting Valley, and work in Cleveland, you pay a 2 percent payroll tax. That 2 percent has to be, oh, 60 to 70 percent of the city's budget right now." That tax base is of no help to one troubled institution in particular: "It's property tax that pays for schools."

Cleveland is no different from any other troubled metropolitan area in America. There comes a time when the good and the great of an area, its business leaders and philanthropists, finally sound the alarm and begin emergency surgery: overhauling municipal finance, blue-ribbon commissions, enormous "home run" style development projects. That's all been tried here and, Krumholz told me, it doesn't change one basic fact.

"Cleveland is becoming less and less important in the metropolitan area. But we've still got the major educational institutions, the major hospitals, and the entertainment network. We've got the world-respected institutions, the art museums, the symphony orchestra, and the upstarts like the Rock and Roll Hall of Fame. They are all in the city of Cleveland.

"This may sound terrible to say, but there are advantages to decline. There are more green spaces, less density. Did you notice, there are no traffic jams? There's plenty of capacity in the system. Ticket prices for the orchestra are low, and there's never a line. There are desirable aspects to decline. It basically makes life a little easier for those of us who live here."

That refreshing bit of candor from the city's onetime chief planner is rare from the kind of people who go to the symphony, write big checks to the public radio station, or have their names chiseled in the stone lobby of the Rock and Roll Hall of Fame and Museum.

"Tony Downs, at the Brookings Institution, did a study called 'Futures for a Declining City.' He assumed there would be interest in taking measures to advantage cities over the surrounding suburbs. He came up with improvement packages in housing, tax law, education, transportation. He bundled the improvements into an optimal package, and found that it would only slow, not stop, the decline. The best you could do is slow the decline. It was kind of sobering. Then the reaction came, castigating the report, denying its conclusions. People here knocked it, they had to.

"The mayor is a tireless booster, but occasionally he'll make an unguarded remark. In the recent fight over a new teacher's contract he said, 'If we approve that the inmates will be running the asylum.' He said to the teachers, 'You are living high on the hog. You should have to live in the pathetic hovels some of your students return to at 3 P.M. every day.'

"Still, we can't really say this place is not going to survive," Krumholz said. "You have to be optimistic. You can't say to people, 'Look, here are the trends. In ten years, you'll be the only white person left in your neighborhood, and the house you own will only be worth about one-fourth of what it's worth today,' even if it's true. It's not easy for a politician to make a negative prediction."

Politicians and planners often know well in advance when even the best combinations of good intentions, smart spending, and well-designed programs cannot do much to change the ultimate fate of an area. "Go to city planning offices. There are no city plans for the South Bronx, for North St. Louis, or parts of the South Side of Chicago. There are no plans because cities don't talk much about the places they aren't sure they can do anything for.

"The larger issues are concentrated poverty and racial segregation. Unless you can deal with these in an honest, upright manner—ease poverty and soften segregation—you're never going to come to grips with the crux of urban problems.

"The Fair Share Plan for Public Housing in Cuyahoga County attempted to disperse public housing a bit, since it was concentrated in Cleveland. The suburban communities went crazy; they wouldn't even come to the meeting."

Calling that kind of reaction "nimbyism" lets the "not in my backyard" crowd off the hook much too easily. People say they want to help, they want people in the region to live better, and they wish "someone" would do something about the decay of the central cities. When you identify the problem, frame a solution, and these same people stand in your way, it is nothing less than selfishness and hypocrisy of the highest order. Only we rarely call them on it. Instead they are allowed to hide behind the tried-and-true defenses of quality of life. Even "have-a-littles" can use their clout to keep "have-nots" away.

"We Americans have made a Faustian agreement with the cities: Agree to be the regional poorhouse, and government—the Feds, the states—will agree to bankroll that with programs and support. Now the governments are cutting back, in effect, saying, screw you, you're going to have to make it on your own." Krumholz sees welfare reform, and its attendant mass push into jobs that may not exist, making central-city life even worse. "If we had an activist federal government, *if* we ever have one of *those* again, it could pay the suburbs to play ball," Krumholz said. I wasn't sure which one was more unlikely, an activist federal government or suburbs that would play ball. Bill Clinton had just won another term, in part, because of his abandonment of federal activism—selling the voters a long list of pocket-size programs that do not fundamentally change the structure of a society that allows one-third of its children to live in poverty.

Cleveland is among the top ten in American metropolitan areas and cities in single-female-headed families, growth in single-female-headed families, children in poverty, and births to unwed parents. The city's infant mortality rate is one of the highest in the country. The statistics tell a disheartening story. Cleveland is lucky to have a small army of people who refuse to lose heart.

Bobbi Reichtell is a community organizer and housing activist whose formula for stabilizing her east Cleveland neighborhood has been so successful that her little band of organizers has "gone legit," moving from ringing doorbells to establishing an accomplished rehab business, and building a large housing development—Mill Creek—on the edge of the community that could play a big part in the area's future.

"I was less optimistic when I decided to get into this. I mean, sociologists say anywhere from 5 percent to 50 percent is the tipping point where it's not ever going to go back. I had to say, well, that's one perspective, but let's look at examples around the country, and at what people are doing to make that not true. The examples are few and far between.

"Our neighborhood is right on the border of the Industrial Valley. Our service area is North and South Broadway. Most people think of this as a West Side neighborhood because this is the only predominately white neighborhood on the East Side of Cleveland. Our neighborhood is surrounded by predominately African-American and low-income areas. The neighborhoods right around our community are low income. And some of the people here used to live in Corlette, Kinsman, Union Miles, and moved west when their neighborhoods became integrated.

"Part of the reason it's stayed so white is population loss. We took our biggest hit when the schools were desegregated. In 1978, I was doing a Summer Youth Program for kids to meet the new kids they would be going to school with. We got the school lists, the names of the kids, started going door to door, doing outreach to get kids to come to a summer day camp. It was fairly successful. We had about a hundred kids from this neighborhood, paired with about a hundred kids from the Central neighborhood, which was where they were being bused. In 1979, we went back to start door-knocking and going back to all the families we had worked with the previous summer. It seemed like half the families were gone. Not gone, like, moved to Garfield Heights. They were gone, like, moved to West Virginia. Some families stayed and they shipped their kids out to the suburbs to live with relatives and go to school there. It was probably the worst time in this neighborhood in terms of instability.

"Another thing that's kept this neighborhood so white is the Catholic schools. There's a preponderance of them. There were lots of families who weathered desegregation; it didn't matter to them. Their kids went to the Catholic school down the street, and it didn't really matter to them what was going on in the public schools. Those were predominately middle-income families. When I went to Catholic schools, it cost something like ten bucks a year for books and that was it and the parish paid for it. Now, in the last twenty years, you need a pretty decent income to afford a private education. So we didn't lose all the middle-class and working-class families, because they had their kids in private schools. In the last ten years, we have lost a significant number of middle-income families and what that's resulted in is not enough kids to go to the Catholic schools, so four out of eight in this area have closed.

"Since 1980, two more public grade schools have closed and that always takes a bunch of families with them. Since the late seventies our population has actually stabilized, with only a 7 percent lost from 1980 to 1990.

"We started a citizen's advocacy group, a grassroots group back in 1980, because of the insurance and bank redlining that had occurred; the neighborhood was deteriorating pretty rapidly, and the Citizens to Bring Broadway Back were active on both those issues, and won some victories with Nye Insurance—one of the worst insurers, which then made sweeping commitments. It was amazing the number of people who could only get the Ohio Fair Plan—fire insurance and nothing else—no other kind of regular commercial insurance. All of those things had contributed to the decline in housing stock and the stores closing up. So our organization was founded to rehab houses, and to provide affordable housing for low-income families, which is what we did for about ten years, exclusively. It was all geared to low-income residents in the neighborhood. The banks, who were getting hit by the Community Reinvestment Act, finally bellied up to the bar and contributed money for rehabs, and wrote insurance loans; insurance companies gave small grants for housing development activities but not in the size that banks did. We could get a house fully re-habbed and a family, making thirteen thousand dollars a year—a working family—into a house for twenty-two thousand dollars and we figured, great. A lot of families now have houses because they bought them from us.

"But when the ninety census came out, we had to ask ourselves, who is the population we're serving? It's getting poorer and poorer. We decided that, in addition to our focus on low-income housing, we really needed to try to tap into the other end of the market, or create a market for middle-income families. As there's lower and lower incomes in the neighborhoods, there are fewer and fewer places to shop, because businesses look at the demographics—and they don't even have to drive through a neighborhood, you know, they look at census information, they look at aerial photos, and say, 'OK, we're not going here, or we are going there.' We asked ourselves, are we really doing the neighborhood a service? In 1990–91, we wrote a three-year plan that targeted upper-income housing . . . and by that I don't mean Chicago or New York 'upper income'; upper income for Broadway would be families earning forty or fifty thousand dollars a year.

"So we started doing more upscale housing. It's still our bread and butter to buy vacant and abandoned housing, rehab it, then resell it, but what we added to the equation were things we hadn't done before—vinyl siding, decks, higher-quality carpeting. Then we started to advertise differently—in the *Free Times,* the weekly paper. From a housing perspective, we've adjusted our focus. We still do two-thirds of the houses for low-income families, and a third are for middle-income families. Our houses now, for that target market, are averaging around seventy or seventy-five thousand dollars. So what they can get for seventy-five thousand dollars is a house, fully renovated, all new mechanicals, new roof, new siding, they won't have to do a thing for twenty years on their house. They get more house in Cleveland than they could get in any suburb. Generally, they get a big lot, and a house in a part of the neighborhood that's pretty stable. We're building in areas where we're already pretty active as organizers, where community groups are doing things to support investment, dealing with slum landlords, dealing with crime. You can't really run away from crime anywhere. I deal with it all the time. I live on Franklin Boulevard, near West Sixty-fifth. My husband and I have two kids, school age, and so we say to ourselves, 'Are we crazy? How much crime can you take? Where do you draw the line? How bad do the schools get before you leave?'

"We were really fortunate to get our kids into a neighborhood school—

the Irving Community School, which is actually not a parish school. Its mission is to serve low-income families, so it's very diverse—economically, racially, culturally, but it's not part of the Cleveland public school system, which is what we were looking for. If it was not for that, even given the kind of work we do, we would have had to think really hard about leaving the city. Could we put our kid in a school system where one out of two kids doesn't finish high school?"

I told Reichtell I was intrigued by groups like hers that soldier on even though so much of the dynamism in Cleveland is on the decline; for every person who buys a house in Cleveland, two people probably leave for the suburbs. The people who buy in probably don't have children at all, or don't have children of elementary school age, or have the means to avoid the whole public school question. So many people simply won't put their kids in the public schools. They'd rather sit behind the wheel cursing for the entire length of the bumper-to-bumper ride from the suburbs muttering, I hate this. Once there's a critical mass of those people, the company moves its head office to the suburbs too.

So if you come in from the outside, as many people do—with the medical centers, the colleges, and the downtown office buildings—and you're deciding where to be, it's tough to decide to live in Cleveland, unless you are a confirmed cityphile and you are determined to move into the city, no matter what. Why not go to the western suburbs, so you could trumpet the good things about Cleveland, and your prospective employees wouldn't have to put up with any of the bad things?

Reichtell said, "We don't have delusions of grandeur that we're going to turn any part of Broadway into a neighborhood like West Lake. We have the people we have living here, and that's not going to change, nor would we in good conscience promote that. Look at other neighborhoods in Cleveland, like Ohio City, where, in a matter of two to three years low-income families were just displaced and families making one hundred thousand to one hundred fifty thousand dollars would move in, and renovate. There are parts of Ohio City that are totally different, night and day, from what they were twenty years ago.

"When people ask us about the schools, there's not much we can say. We're not trying to sell people a bill of goods. We do have a couple of bright spots in our neighborhood, with one elementary school that was just chosen to be a fast-track school for local autonomy. It happens to be, luckily, right across the bridge from our new two hundred–unit single-family housing development, and they've got a great principal who is very reform minded, so they're doing some joint projects with them. We point to the bright spots.

"Another issue for a neighborhood like Broadway, which is predominately white, is you not only have to have the mind-set that you're going to tough it out—deal with safety concerns and school concerns—but you also have to be an open-minded person who is not intimidated by knowing people who are different from you! For instance, due to the declining population, they've had to close the local elementary school and merge it with Miles Park. The good news is, it's just about the best elementary school on the southeast side of Cleveland. But people don't see it that way; and the image that people have of it as the heaviest drug area in the southeast side is unfortunate, and still persists.

"So we did a summer project where the kids—ten kids from Warner School, ten kids from Miles Park School—learned the neighborhood's history. These two neighborhoods were once joined, once both part of the same Newburgh Village. At the end, we had an art exhibit and invited residents from both sides of Broadway to come. And we had about 150 people. It was amazing! Old-timers who I never thought would come. There were people saying, 'I haven't been across Broadway Avenue in twenty, thirty years.' People saw inside the school. The outside looks like a fortress—they had to build it that way to keep it safe, but when you get inside, there's a vibrancy, it's full of happy kids. They have their share of troubled families—they take kids from the Selma George Shelter—a woman's shelter in Broadway. People saw this incredibly dynamic place, filled with great kids taking them around, showing them their art project, and it was one of the best things we've ever done as an organization.

"We've started organizing safety meetings together, because issues like safety are shared by people in Broadway and people on the other side of Broadway. We've done some cleanups together. There's a creek that divides the two neighborhoods, with a spectacular forty-five-foot waterfall, and we're working with Cleveland Metroparks to create a linear park that would bridge the two neighborhoods together—so we have people from Miles Park participating with that. We have a really good relationship with the community development corporation in the Miles Park area. We're making baby steps toward better race relations.

"Our other challenge is with the Mill Creek development, with the two hundred units. If you look at the map, one neighborhood is 98 percent white, the other is 3 percent white. The development is right in the middle of those two neighborhoods. It's right on the line. The problem is that the real estate community will peg a development as either a white development or a black development and they will then steer who they bring or who they tell about a development depending on the color of their skin. So we have a contract with the Cuyahoga Plan, which is the fair-housing organization in Cleveland, to monitor for any blockbusting, which is against the law, but companies still do it.

"What we've done is call all the real estate agents on the southeast side to a meeting, and basically shown them the stick of the Cuyahoga Plan, and offered them the carrot of cobrokering deals on Mill Creek. First, it was the Cuyahoga Plan saying, this is the law, and this is what happens when you break the law. We're going to monitor any illegal practices for the next five years. And then our partner, the developer, told them, you don't have to earn money by turning over the neighborhood. There's lots of money to be made by bringing buyers to the development. You don't have to do any work: bring them over, sign them in, and you get 3 percent of the sales price as your commission. The most effective tool we have in the Warner-Turney neighborhood for dealing with blockbusting is having a close relationship with people in the neighborhood. They have a number to call and say, 'I just got a phone call from Rybka Realty, or Haven Realty saying, "Gee, I just listed a house on your street. Do you want to sell?"' Which I know is legal, because they don't say, 'Hey, I just sold this house to a black person.' They don't have to say that. They don't have to say who bought it. It's just the fact that they're calling. A lot of people have lived through that, in moving from Corlette or Mount Pleasant. They had real estate agents calling them.

"We started the planning process for this development back in 1990. Everybody was convinced that this was going to be low-income housing, that it was going to bring in minorities, that it was going to have drug dealing and bluh-bluh-bluh-bluh. I think that through the whole process, we've done enough good things and communicated things in a clear enough way that people aren't leaving in droves because of this development.

"Like last summer? That was a bad summer. Right on Turney Road, across the street from the development there were three houses up for sale. Normally there would probably be three houses up anyway, but those three houses got people whispering, 'Oh, people are starting to leave!' I'd get all these phone calls from members of the committee saying, 'All these people are starting to leave!' But then we'd explore it further and we'd find, well, the husband died and the wife is going to move in with her sister, at another one the guy lost his job, and they lost the house so they're going to rent somewhere. It's not people saying, 'I'm not going to live across the street from black buyers.'

"The other evidence we're showing them is, we're building houses that are across the street, that are selling for $168,000 and $180,000 and $119,000. We have a community organization that took a vacant lot and turned it into this flower garden that's the focal point of one street. They have a group that maintains a tot lot, we're taking a vacant school and turning it into senior housing. They're working with Metroparks to create a hiking and biking trail to go over to the waterfall—most people in the neighborhood never even knew there was a waterfall! I think that they're seeing enough evidence that would tell them, this isn't exactly the same situation. And OK: so we have 10 percent, 5 percent—whatever the percentage is, more black residents than we had before. Let's look at who they are. For the most part, they're people who are buying houses—at least half. They work, they take good care of their kids. What's the problem?"

It's easy enough to imagine people saying to Bobbi Reichtell, "This is very nice of you to do this, but I really don't want to be part of your social experiment. I just want to be sure that my house is going to be worth something, that my kids aren't going to be jumped on the way home from school, that I'll still be able to shop. So, good luck, but I'm going." Does Reichtell take it personally when those people leave?

No. "I think, for a community development organization, we are really bending over backwards to deal with those nontangible issues, and those nonhousing issues. We're probably the first organization in Cleveland to try to get involved in community organizing, promoting integration and promoting diversity. So I feel like we've done the best we can do. I feel like I can sleep at night. We're not creating a bad situation by building that kind of housing, even though it is going to be an integrated development in a neighborhood that's 98 percent white."

One of the urban interest groups faced with little choice when deciding how and where to live is the elderly. Along the side streets of a thousand neighborhoods in cities large and small are people whose working lives are winding down or long over, who do not resemble the tanned oldsters in tennis clothes enjoying a quick lunch in the Arizona sun before another set. Far more older Americans are carefully playing out the string, gingerly balancing a pension and Social Security, Medicare and a little supplemental insurance, and trying to make a decent life out of what's left. In many cases their one big investment, their house, is a declining asset. The neighborhoods they call home today have changed a lot in the thirty years since they bought in. Some feel trapped. Others, like Lena Gannon, do not.

We sat and rocked on her porch one late-summer afternoon as kids jumped rope and played catch on the sidewalk across the street. A warm sun still floated above the horizon. Gannon's block in Warner-Turney was just a five-minute walk from an adjacent neighborhood that had gone from being all white to virtually all black in the space of a few years. Yet the same thing did not happen here.

"This place is not much different, really, from when I moved here. I came here from West Virginia and have lived here ever since. My husband first came here because he couldn't get work back home after the coal mine where he was working closed. He came here and went to work for White Motor Company on Seventy-ninth and St. Claire. It folded up about fifteen years ago. They beat 'em out of their severance pay. They cut their pension in half. Over half. He was supposed to get about eight hundred dollars a month and he's getting $236. He worked there twenty-five, twenty-six years. And the government took over the pension, so they said, and they cut his over half. Five hundred men los[t] their work when White went out. I don't know how the government lets 'em get by with that with the pension. . . . Well, they did step in and take over the pension but they cut it so much."

Gannon's block has fewer people than it did before the city's industrial collapse. Her own children have spread to other states and the far reaches of the Cleveland area. There may also be a willingness to try integration. "We have two black families living right up here, and there's another one that leases right up here. And on Tioga, the next street down, there's eight or nine houses. The people who moved here when I moved here are all still right here. The people next door bought their house the week before I bought this one. There's three, four families up here who were living here when I moved here. So you see, it has to be a nice neighborhood.

"This is a pretty nice area. Real handy for the bus line. It's nice. We're on the Homestead Act and they help us out with lower taxes for senior citizens. And we get a discount on the water. Sewage. Gas. I love Cleveland. I sure do."

Four hundred thousand of your neighbors decided to move! I told her.

"I didn't. I feel just the same as I did when I moved here. I've never had any problems. I tend to mind my own business, and so does everyone around here. Nobody bothers nobody. My husband is an invalid now, he can't move around after his stroke. He's got to be in a wheelchair or a walker or else he can't go anywhere.

"There was a black family that moved up here in the house before the corner. They had people shooting at them, and they ran 'em off. I don't know who it was, but they shot through the bedroom window. That family stayed there a week, I think. And they moved out. There was one other time there was a problem down the street. . . . I don't know exactly which house now, but they run 'em off too, I don't know exactly what they did. Nobody never said anything about it. Boom, it just happened and they were gone, and there wasn't any news about it.

"There was a family that moved in right over here, I'd say last year. A black man and his mother. There was no problem. Nobody bothered him. He went by every day and spoke. Then we had the police up there one night—his mother died. And once his mother died we didn't see him anymore. But there wasn't nothing said about it or anything, and now there's these three families here, and nobody's said anything's wrong. And nobody's bothering them. They haven't lived here that long—about six months. The younger people don't want them in the neighborhood. I don't know. At the time, we didn't say anything about it. I believe in live and let live, as long as they don't bother me, I'm not going to bother them. I've always been relaxed about it. I've never been around that many. But I started going to bingo, and you meet a lot of nice black people at bingo. And I don't see anything wrong with them. We've had two black mayors, and Mayor White is really nice. He's a good mayor. He's for the people too. And Carl Stokes was nice when he was in there."

On another porch, another senior, Lucille Holloway, watched her street on the other side of Cleveland, in the Collinwood neighborhood. This area, in Cleveland's East End, was built for and still houses many higher-income people. It shows in the orderly rows of comfy brick homes, each with a neat front lawn and a fringe of flower bed. Along these streets there is the occasional house that must have been truly spectacular when new, now held together with hard work and loving care. This particular part of Collinwood is now virtually all black. If Holloway was ever bitter about what happened here, she doesn't let on today.

It wasn't easy to get Lucille to talk to me. She was wearing a housedress and comes from that generation that still sees granting an interview as a formal act, for which a person must be properly dressed. She had that exaggerated modesty regular folks often have. They spend their lives watching stories on television of the wealthy, the powerful, and the connected and find it hard to believe that anyone wants to listen to them, or finds their stories interesting. She was born in Cleveland in the mid-1930s.

"My dad worked in the rail yard. You know there used to be rail yards right over that way in Collinwood. I was never made to feel that I was different living on our street. I didn't even know I was black until I went to school! I thought I was just like everybody else. We went everywhere we wanted to go . . . to the library, to the shops, and so on. I felt secure. We were the only black family on the block.

"When I was a little older my family moved away. We were the ones who were selling and moving out! We sold to my grandmother's cousins. Ten kids—they all grew up in that house and went to Collinwood High.

"My family came up from Georgia to work for the railroads. When they first came up here they lived in boxcars. The railroads were big in those days, and the word was passed from person to person that the railroad was one of the few places that hired blacks. Those first years, they lived in boxcars, then they built some project houses on Thanes Avenue off 152nd Street. Those houses are still standing; they're in back of Joe's Bar. They're still there. That's where I was born.

"We were good neighbors. We had our own little church. We didn't go to the big church on the Avenue, we had our own. Sometimes when we went to Euclid Beach Park people made remarks, but I didn't care. I was living free. I didn't hate nobody. And I never wanted to get even with nobody.

"The biggest change in my life came when I was born again, so I found my security in Christ. He takes care of you, and I find that you never want for friends if you show yourself to be friendly."

I reminded Holloway of all those big, fancy churches on Euclid Avenue. Cleveland's history murmurs to passersby in those beautiful old buildings put up by wealthy white congregations at the turn of the century. The people in the pews thought of themselves as good Christians. They were praying people. They listened to the Sunday sermon, heard what the preacher had to say, and went out into the world on Monday and many thought there was nothing terribly wrong with making sure that they never had to live with people like Lucille Holloway. Many of the people on both sides of the civil rights struggle thought they had it right with God, that they were living the kind of life they thought their religion told them to live. That included the people in Cleveland who wanted to keep neighborhoods strictly segregated.

"They were afraid. I don't blame them. They thought those black people were going to wreck everything. They thought their house values would go down and there'd be nothing for them to leave their children. When I'm around people I don't know I just try to find something we can be in common on, some common ground. I don't know if people are still being prejudiced, but the world is so small, and full of so many people, how can you keep it up? They have to be around people they want to be around. I don't hate them for that. You should run your life to be around the people it makes you happy to be with."

One constant in America's sporadic monitoring of rapid urban change has been the empathy for fleeing whites, while arriving blacks are ignored. Whites portray themselves, to themselves, as victims of wider forces beyond their control. Blacks are in many ways also driven by big forces in the society, but empathy has often been in short supply.

Like the Bubbles in the Wine was a documentary prepared by the then NBC owned and operated television station in Cleveland. It is remarkable for its detailed attention to the lives of the "tragic" white people who are watching their way of life disappear, while giving almost no attention to the black people on the other end of the equation.

Whites are detailed, nuanced people who live dense, valuable, interesting lives. The blacks who are moving into the neighborhood are people who walk up and down the street, and in and out of stores, but are rarely heard from in the documentary.

The local newsroom of the 1970s, a place where white people work and "observe" the world around them on behalf of the community at large, watches the changes in this one Cleveland neighborhood—Buckeye—from a point of view so deeply rooted in white middle-class life that the producer and narrator seem to have missed the fact that there are two sides to this story. This makes *Like the Bubbles in the Wine* more valuable as an artifact than as a thorough or accurate picture of what is happening in this part of east Cleveland.

The narrator begins: "Time, and the changes which have taken place in the larger community, have begun to make their mark on even the most tightly knit ethnic neighborhoods. The flight of the upper middle class out of the city and into the suburbs has left the ethnic community, and particularly the older generation, who are less prepared to meet the challenge, on the frontier of a social confrontation that threatens the future, not only of the neighborhood, but, in a larger sense, the entire country. . . ."

From the beginning the testimonies of white Buckeye residents give great weight to the idea of a community built by individual effort and sacrifice, a community that's now under great threat. A woman on the street said, "These people are hardworking people who have their savings invested in their house and in taking care of their house, and their property, and they've raised their children and they've done it more or less the hard way."

Seconds later, a woman drives home the point again, "The men work in the steel mills or in the factories, very hard."

A man on the street adds, "And all of a sudden in a changing neighborhood you've got people who didn't go to the same schools as you, and they don't go to the same church as you, they may not even go to church! This upsets people to a great extent, you know, and consequently what happens, there's this fear, this just mistrust, and I've seen this happen in other places and I think it's the saddest thing that can happen to a neighborhood."

If black people who are moving into the neighborhood work hard, or see their move to Buckeye as a product of their own dreams of a better life, we television viewers get little chance to find that out. The feeling of dread is exposed, but never explained; the "problem" is understood by all as the arrival of blacks in Hungarian Buckeye. A recent black arrival, Mrs. Leslie Gibson, provides the sole counterpoint to the man-in-the-street testimony and the narrator-reinforced idea that something terrible is about to happen. "The Democratic Club had talked about having more communication, more meetings, to meet with different areas, different neighborhoods, and this way you can learn how they live and they learn how we live. And they can still live in the area; they don't have to worry about moving, or being afraid because the area is changing. And this is what we all have to get used to. Here's what we can do to help, keep it from going down."

That narrow definition of television news "fairness," that is, accusation and rebuttal, is part of the program's story. City Council member Jane Muir Zborowski tells her story: " My office received many, many phone calls asking what so many real estate companies were doing in here, waging such a vigorous campaign to sell. Our office particularly needs help in deciding whether or not this is a form of blockbusting, and if it is, we need legal help in order to decide what to do to change that. Because there's nothing in an area that creates fear and panic quicker than twenty companies asking everybody in the entire neighborhood if they're not ready to sell."

Then James Hudak, the owner of Hudak Realty, says it simply isn't happening. "I truthfully couldn't tell you how other companies operate, but myself, I can tell you of my own company. We will not harass anybody, we will sell to anybody, we will obey the laws, and observe the law itself. I personally do not believe there is any blockbusting that is used.

And as far as harassment goes, it is possible that there is solicitation, of finding homes for sale through real estate agents. Now when they make a call, possibly different companies may call the same owner to sell, now they may consider it harassment, but personally I do not know of any company that is harassing or anything. It's just doing its job, that's what I'd consider it. I always feel that it's supply and demand."

Mrs. Barbara Nagy speaks for everyone from Boston to Los Angeles who has ever faced neighborhood change. "You can't keep running, you have to make a stand, and I think that's just what we have to do, we just have to be involved. You move, you look around, you'll have the same thing that you had before. You just can't keep running."

Men's clothing store owner Ralph Rosenbluth sat in his empty store for his interview. It sounded as if he wouldn't be there long. "When an area starts to deteriorate, everything will start to go at once. This has happened on the lower end of Buckeye, where it's completely gone because the city has not come in and done its job. The Negro population has been moving into the area, they've brought an economy into the area, although we have groups who are harassing the older generation who are still remaining here. We find we have a lack of police protection, and a lack of interest as far as the city is concerned in trying to maintain the area. I know, even for myself, if I see the area is starting to get real rough, I will not stay here either, I would leave. Because I think life is worth more than risking my life for something that isn't worth it."

Councilwoman Zborowski saw some hope for the future in redeveloping the neighborhood for cultural tourism, like German Village in Columbus, Ohio. Milwaukee's Third Street has more recently tried to capitalize on its Old World heritage. But back when people were calling Cleveland the "Mistake by the Lake," bringing tourism to Buckeye seemed a little farfetched.

As the documentary moves to its close, over Rob Ioschka's vibrant gypsy violin the narrator talks of the Hungarian-born restaurateur's despair, "that is both private and universal. Despair at the passing of a way of life, for which thousands left their native lands in search of peace and freedom from oppression. Despair that in a day and age when airplanes and satellites and television signals have made the world a vast global village, where geographical boundaries are meaningless, the one thing which continues to be stopped by borders is human understanding and trust."

Ioschka says, "My son, who came down here as a bus boy and wanted to learn the business that is our Gypsy Cellar business from the ground up, told me, 'Papa, we've got to go,' this was three years ago. I said, 'Son, you're silly, this is our home, this is our bread and butter. Here's how we bring happiness to the neighborhood, all the Hungarians and the Slovaks, and the Bohemians.' He said, 'Papa, you've got to sell, you've got to go,' and I refused. I was adamant not to. Two years ago he said the same thing and again I said no. Two months ago, he said, 'Pop, I've got to break now, I've got to leave. I'm going out on my own because if you can't see that the luster is gone, that the people are afraid to come across town and drive at night . . . don't you know they're even afraid to walk downtown, how do you expect them to come into the neighborhood that was once the proud Hungarian's. They say, Rob, we love your music, you still playing, we still love to hear it, but . . .'

"So, with a heavy heart, I am leaving my son go; as a matter of fact, he has gone away only a few short days ago, and I will not know what the future brings. Before you know it the snow will fall and I will still remain chained here, with the people afraid to come in. The most important thing for me now is to relocate, but where? You tell me where. Where can I open up a spot and make my dream complete? Where shall I turn? How will I know what to do? I'm in a tough situation, and I truly am. This is all I know. . . . How can I make music again at another location, start all over again? Was it a waste for me to be fifteen years here in business? Should I have started somewhere else? Why did I have faith in Cleveland? Why did I love my nationality group? Why did I come and give my music? I wanted to get gray here, I wanted to get old here in this neighborhood. Shall I forsake the neighborhood that's given me a fine living, that I've played my heart out for constantly?"

Buckeye today is a sadder place than the documentarians might have imagined more than twenty years ago. The Ioschkas and the Nagys are gone. The neighborhood is heavily depopulated, the housing stock heavily deteriorated. It is tempting to say that part of the decline of a place like this was a natural and very American process. Parents from older immigrant waves raise children with high expectations, who get better educations and are able to choose a life for themselves outside the ghetto. But visit any city that's experienced gentrification and you'll find former European immigrant neighborhoods that did not go the way of Buckeye.

It was a setback for this place not to have a natural constituency, its own young men and women, to stay and stabilize it. However, the way race informed individual decisions to stay or go can be seen only as having made Buckeye's already long odds even worse.

Since racial change and resegregation have been part of Cleveland neighborhood life for so long, the city has a rich store of community organizations, academic institutions, interfaith groups, and other entities organized around the principles of integration and neighborhood preservation. Some of the people who have made trying to save Cleveland one block at a time a big part of their lives showed me around the city and helped me understand what the place was up against.

Chapter 9

Washington, D.C.: "Will the last one out please turn off the lights?"

People can learn something relevant about one city by reading about other places. It could be housing, schools, crime, or politics—there are solutions in Chicago that might work in New York. There are parallels between Cleveland and St. Louis. Washington, D.C., is so odd in so many ways that it defies comparison with other places. Yet, as the capital of a wealthy and powerful country, it demands attention. For all the resentment focused on cities around the country, Washington may draw special scorn. Its government is overseen by the very politicians who come to the Capitol after successfully railing against "Washington."

It's 8:30 A.M. Another day is under way in the capital of that region of mind still called by some "the free world." The kids are off to school, so I make my way to the subway. My own street is now lined with parked cars with Maryland and Virginia plates, their drivers taking advantage of the permit-free, all-day parking and proximity to the Metro system, to head to their jobs in the District. I turn my corner onto River Road, which feeds traffic from Bethesda, Maryland, into the main arteries of Northwest D.C., to find choked, bumper-to-bumper traffic heading to Wisconsin Avenue.

I walk as my fellow commuters sit. They drive a wide range of swell vehicles—Lexuses, BMWs, Cadillacs—and an assortment of expensive four-wheel-drive, urban-assault machines so beloved by suburbanites. They need those chunky vehicles and monster tires to navigate their smooth streets and head to the Fresh Fields Whole Food Market for their weekly shopping. Walking alongside the tie-up for two, three, four blocks, I do an easy cost-benefit analysis: I get the cost, they get the benefit. I am a taxpayer and a homeowner in the District of Columbia, and provide my neighbors in Maryland and Virginia with vital services: They get a stage on which to play out the dramas of their Very Important Careers, an income free of local taxes to take home and spend back in the suburbs. The district also provides a permanent cause for complaint and the butt of jokes at their dinner parties and weekend golf games.

When you cross the Hudson River from New Jersey to earn a wage in Manhattan, the city and state of New York get a piece of the action. When you cross the Illinois-Indiana line from La Porte, Hammond, or East Chicago, heading for a job in a Loop office tower, the state of Illinois and the county of Cook dip into your check before you get it home on Friday night. However, when a resident of Bethesda is sitting in the traffic, passing me in the city on the way home, paycheck burning a hole in his pocket, it is untouched by the municipal government of the District of Columbia. The streets that worker strolled at lunchtime, the traffic lights that guided his drive home, the police who made a drug bust in the park near his office were all paid for from two sources: the shrinking number of people who live in Washington and all the American taxpayers from Presque Isle, Maine, to Chula Vista, California.

The city is also not allowed to impose a residency requirement on its employees, who have been rushing to the exits. Washington, D.C., performs the functions of city, county, and state government. My car sports the only American license plate issued by a municipal government, and I am authorized to drive it by a city-issued license in my wallet. There is an overcrowded prison in Virginia, operated for the city by the federal government, that gives us the highest percentage of our citizens behind bars of any prison system in the country. This city of just over half a million also has the highest ratio of public employees to citizens of any state or city, which, in turn, gives me and my neighbors one of the highest income tax bills in the United States. Which makes it all the more galling to watch that tax money head across the city line every Friday. Like everyone else bellying up to the District trough, most city employees don't pay District income tax.

The people sitting on River Road as I approach the train pay as little as they can get away with and find even this pittance buys them the privilege of endless bellyaching. It is a quick lesson in what money can do: When the poor complain, it is portrayed as quite unseemly; when the well-off complain, it is their *right*. When a previous mayor raised the taxes on parking spaces downtown, the moaning was almost hilarious in its excess. Few paused to consider that taxing the God-given right to park was one of the few revenue raisers not nixed by Congress. When a District politician dares to suggest a commuter tax, it is immediately dismissed as terribly unfair, and anyway, a political impossibility. Even suggestions that the District might *lower* its taxes are similarly dismissed by the surrounding jurisdictions as terribly unfair.

In recent years, Eleanor Holmes Norton, the city's delegate in the House of Representatives (whose committee vote was stripped as one of the first official acts of the new Republican Congress in 1995), suggested the creation of a federal tax haven in the District of Columbia. In return for the forfeiture of the federal contribution to the city's annual budget, the District would no longer pay into the federal tax system and would run itself out of local revenues. Delegate Norton knew that the promised relief of some 35 percent of their current tax burden could bring high earners flocking back to the District. As one commentator said, "There'd be houses on flatbed trucks backed up on Wisconsin Avenue, waiting to get in."

As it turned out the nation founded with the cry "No taxation without representation" was content to let the half-million citizens of the Federal City continue to pay some of the highest taxes in the country, with no hope of representation. The arguments went this way: Asking those who come in to work to pay taxes was unfair to outlying communities, *and* allowing the city to relieve its citizens of federal levies was unfair to those same suburban communities. The only thing that was fair to my daytime neighbors was to leave everything just the way it is.

Here's how it is: In the better-off elementary schools of the city, the PTA hires art and music teachers, school aides and math tutors, and buys library books and school supplies, knowing no such necessities will come from the central board. Some police officers buy their own tires for their squad cars, while others simply ride their unrepaired jalopies into the ground. Sitting in the midst of a metropolitan area, ringed with large and profitable computer consulting and software design firms, the city limps along with a totally outmoded filing, billing, and record-keeping system. But despite a Third World infant mortality rate, a bursting prison system, and a permanently desperate underclass, the per capita income of Washington, D.C., continues to be among the nation's highest, its privileged class floating above it all like an oil slick on a sea of despair.

As a ward of the Congress and a sensitively tuned meter of national opinion about it, Washington soars and dives with the national mood. When the federal government was tiny and a faint influence on life far away, the city remained small and a place that members sought to leave as soon as their business was done. The city sprinted ahead with the twentieth century to become a year-round residence for a larger and larger population. It was, very importantly, a magnet to blacks across the South, a place promising relief from Jim Crow and opportunity to the bright and ambitious. Today, with the black and white middle classes streaming over the city line, leaving behind a population of multiracial wealth and black urban despair, Washington has been laid low by something approaching a massive stroke: There is one mobile, workable side to the urban body after this terrible attack, a potent money spinner, a magnet to millions of tourists, a place of great scenic beauty with a vibrant economy and a treasure chest full of unique items.

The other side is shut down, paralyzed by crisis. A tragicomic mayor, adding gold braid to his epaulets like the fop in a Restoration farce, spent his days defending his cronies and shouting high-toned, near meaningless phrases into the pages of the local newspapers. In the Marion Barry universe, everything, it turns out, hinged on "race." After cutting his political teeth as a civil rights activist, Marion Barry has not been able to add much to his rhetorical tool kit in thirty years: Every slight, every lost battle, every setback rested on the endless struggle between black and white.

The District was hampered in its efforts to enlist the concern and support of other parts of the country, not because of white animus against black but from a national animus against one black man in particular . . . him. He was useless in any struggle to change a system of legal pillage, run in the interest of some of the wealthiest and best-educated suburbs in the country, while a pitiful municipal government stoked the fires of every antidemocratic impulse aroused by the endless litany of bad news. Maybe you support the principles of self-government, one person–one vote democracy, and taxing income at the source. Maybe you support them in the abstract and find your ardor cools when all those freedoms are demanded by this country's capital city.

During the building spree of the 1980s, Mayor Barry was a swaggering wheeler-dealer, feted and stroked by developers clamoring for project approval as massive office blocks filled the downtown. The money rolled in, and the mayor built his patronage army with low-skilled jobs for the truly disadvantaged workers, and cushy boards and commissions appointments for the white-collar cronies.

The mayor and a Greek chorus of toadies were laying the groundwork for eventual D.C. statehood, which had about as much chance of happening as a Marion Barry presidency. The city grandly awarded itself shadow members of the House of Representatives and Senate, who demanded the dignity of the office with none of the real functions. The chimera of statehood began to resemble Groucho Marx's Freedonia, or a comic Brigadoon, vanishing in the mists. Just a few technicalities needed to be dealt with before Governor in Waiting Barry could begin to hand out titles and fiefdoms from his bottomless bag of goodies. Even without the grainy video of His Honor taking a monster hit from a crack pipe and the years of fallout that followed, it had always been an illusion. To expect legislators who profited from the status quo to send two senators and a House member to Congress from a place they wouldn't even live in has always been folly.

Barry was reelected mayor in 1994, following his infamous arrest, trial, imprisonment, drug rehab, and election to the city council. The mayor-elect did not waste any time currying favor, mending political fences, or doing any of the other shabby tasks of contrition a chastened man might be obliged to perform. After picking up the support of 3 percent of white voters and a similar share of the votes of residents of the city's wealthiest and whitest district, Ward 3 (which alone pays half the real estate and income taxes in the city), the mayor told white voters disappointed by the election's outcome to "get over it," and shortly thereafter headed to West Africa to be named an honorary chief. When questioned by reporters about leaving the country for weeks at a time when budgetary and school crises were reaching their peak, he pointed out that a Jewish mayor who traveled to Israel wouldn't be asked the same questions. Way to go, Your Honor! When in doubt, don't explain, don't defend, just do a little Jew-baiting!

When the Congress established a financial control board to ride herd on his shambolic administration, he complained, then went along. When one of the few popularly elected bodies in the city, the school board, was stripped of its powers and superseded by an appointed body, the mayor was in China and South Korea, purportedly drumming up tourism for his city. While the schools remained troubled and a continued source of the exodus to the suburbs, the streets are yet to be crowded with package tours from Pusan or Seoul, Guangdong or Hunan.

In 1997 a panel of mayors testified in House-Senate hearings on the future of the District. Democrat Ed Rendell of Philadelphia said, "People are more willing to give aid if they see you taking the tough steps. If Mayor Barry and his people have done that, they certainly aren't getting any credit for it. You would find far greater support for the city if there was a sense he was making the tough decisions." That was a diplomatic statement from a fellow Democrat. Republican mayor Stephen Goldsmith of Indianapolis was far more blunt: "The national perception of Mayor Barry is that he is an obstacle to providing forceful leadership for change." Goldsmith cited his own, larger city's experiences with cost cutting and privatization, and made withering, unfavorable comparisons to the District of Columbia, "If D.C. is going to remain a high-cost, low-quality-of-service city, our taxpayers are going to be very reluctant to transfer money to the city." Just in case anyone had missed his point, Goldsmith added, "You can't change a city from the bottom."

Credit Mayor Goldsmith with prescience. Later that same year, the

Congress moved aggressively to strip Mayor Barry of large chunks of his remaining authority—in the realms of Medicare, public housing, and schools. The family silver can't be sold more than once to the same buyer. With each agreement to "help" the District of Columbia—from Congress and the White House—self-government was diminished. In response, the still-bankrupt city, struggling to maintain appearances, protested in ringing phrases, laced with the word "democracy."

Later in 1997, the Congress further stripped the mayor's power: He oversees little beyond cable television, tourism, and the appointees to various boards and commissions. Mayor Barry still insisted "this isn't about me," and that the key to the restoration of the District's fortunes would be the election of a Democratic majority to the 106th Congress, which opened for business in January 1999. What Barry failed to recognize, when a "recall" petition, begun in what was once his political stronghold, spread through the city, was that the Democrats were not very likely to help him either.

The District's fate should not hinge on one person. But it is now too late to judge the case on its merits. It got harder and harder for friends and foes of the District alike to look past that one man, the man who was mayor of Washington, D.C., for most of the last quarter of the century. After playing a coy game in public for months, Marion Barry announced that he would not run for mayor in 1998.

He provided comfort, in the form of a perpetual alibi, to the suburbs that want to continue to have it all their way and needed political cover for a very sweet deal. While the sizable black middle class pulls out, mostly headed for the next-door Maryland counties of Prince George's and Montgomery, a bedrock of the poorest citizens still praise and cheer their ex-mayor and honorary African chief. The split between haves and have-nots in the District on this issue is so deep that Barry even mused about another term as mayor, and it was taken as a formidable threat, rather than a joke. A new chief executive is now in his early months as mayor. Anthony Williams is serving in his first elective office after working as the financial manager imposed on Mayor Barry by the control board. Williams's election and transition were both marked by high hopes in the face of ugly realities.

A diverse and varied crowd of interests now sit down at the table to hack the body of Washington to pieces, fighting all the other diners for the choicest cuts, and once sated, faces covered in grease, bibs soaked in gravy, they lampoon the carcass for no longer being able to rise from the table and walk unaided. Given its permanent penury, deep debt, and bloated and antiquated local government, the District of Columbia can only lie back while the people in the traffic jams decide what's fair and what's not.

The feast goes on. . . . President Clinton and former Speaker Gingrich preened and postured over saving the District and did little. Poverty pimps filled up the managerial ranks of guilt-edged programs, extorted from a white power structure; local empire builders continued to prance and spend, asserting their shabby dignity in the face of imminent fiscal collapse, winking and telling themselves, "The Congress will never let us go under."

Marion Barry was a public relations problem, but he was not the real cause of the city's current woes. Even if Barry had been a talented administrator, a creative thinker, and a dynamic leader (and he was none of these), the basic structures that underpin the city's financing and governance would leave D.C. at a permanent, insurmountable disadvantage. The city is created by the Constitution and specified as a creature of Congress by Article 1, Section 8: "The Congress shall have power . . . To exercise exclusive Legislation in all Cases whatsoever, over such District (not exceeding ten miles square) as may, by Cession of particular states, and the acceptance of Congress, become the seat of the Government of the United States, and to exercise like Authority over all Places purchased by the Consent of the Legislature of the State in which the Same shall be, for the Erection of Forts, Magazines, Arsenals, Dock-Yards, and other needful buildings." Appointed commissioners ran the place on behalf of the Congress, which voted annual appropriations for the task.

As long as the city grew steadily, enjoyed the indulgence of Congress, and its residents didn't squawk too much about their inability to exercise the franchise, Washington moved on, genteel, segregated, and, for the most part, quiet. After the New Deal years, the federal presence grew and the permanent size of government kept rising to new plateaus. A vigorous black middle class, with strong networks built in historically black colleges, sororities, fraternities, social organizations, and the church, developed into a parallel universe and provided the petri dish for the coming generations of social and political activists. Perhaps you had no idea that the national seat of power still had segregated schools until the 1960s, and a de facto segregated housing market for decades after that. The citizens of the District of Columbia could not vote in presidential elections until the 1960s, and had an appointed mayor until the 1970s.

Washington's story is so different from those of all the other cities covered in this book. The federal role in the city distorts everything: formation of a political class, municipal governance, policy setting. When compared with places like Cleveland and Philadelphia, which remain, even amid their troubles, formidable political players in the lives of their states, the District is an orphan. Chicago has a sometimes contentious but ultimately workable relationship with its suburbs, because both sides in the transaction know that Chicago cannot fail without devastating consequences to the region. In contrast the suburbs of Washington, D.C., know they can continue to ride the one-way street of their relationship with the city without apology. They have representation in Congress, while the District does not, and no matter what devastation the one-way street eventually brings, Washington has a rich relative always waiting in the wings: Uncle Sam.

In the mid- and late 1990s, the outcry concerning the quality of the D.C. public schools could be heard all the way to the White House. Major national figures, like Newt Gingrich and Hillary Rodham Clinton, had their pictures taken during visits to D.C. schools. Everyone needed to be seen being concerned. Reading to children, giving them pep talks, and promising to see whether something could be done was the order of the day.

That "something" came in the form of stripping the authority from the elected school board, for decades the only public officers elected by the people of the District. To augment the Emergency Financial Control Board put in place by the Congress to gradually strip the authority of the mayor and city council, in came an appointed emergency school board, with wide powers to replace the elected board members.

In keeping with the new enthusiasm for having retired generals bring a little butt-kicking discipline to our civic life (witness the desire to have Colin Powell do almost *anything,* and the appointment of General Barry McCaffrey as the head of national drug control policy), retired general Julius Becton was installed as the head of the sagging school system in November 1996. The man on the white horse came riding into town and the peasants rejoiced: When General Becton visited the schools, tut-tutting over the lack of repairs, encouraging young children, and meeting with PTAs, he was often greeted with enthusiasm and relief. But the schools were neither as bad as people generally say they are nor as easily fixed as people hoped. Before his first year in office was up, the bloom was off the general's rose, at least somewhat. Cleaning the Augean stables may have been just a matter of diverting some river water for old Hercules. But cleaning up a system of encrusted cronyism, widely tolerated mediocrity, and enduring public scorn involved more than hosing it down. The general was caught in a public relations trap; he had to fix multivariant problems decades in the making, while politicians demanded immediate results, and parents of seventy-eight thousand District schoolchildren didn't have years to wait for solutions to problems their children faced every day. When Julius Becton arrived, many schools were crumbling from lack of maintenance; no one was sure exactly how many students were in the system; large, antiquated buildings were kept open for shrinking numbers of students; grant money had disappeared after not being spent; and many of the ten thousand system employees did not work at the jobs to which they were assigned. Little by little, the appointed emergency board, which included one member of the formerly elected board, chipped away at the problem and tried to replace chaos with order and predictability. General Becton had made news earlier in the year with his unveiling of new, tougher standards for promotion; hundreds of new teachers would be ready to greet the incoming students.

Then came the summer of 1997. Under orders from Federal District Court judge Kay Christian, who oversees the District of Columbia schools, repairs were under way to scores of school buildings that did not meet fire codes and had leaky roofs and aged electrical systems. In the old days, contracts for such work would have been let to cronies or the repairs would not have got done at all, at which time another extension would have been granted.

But by early August, Judge Christian was informed that at least forty schools would not be ready to open the day after Labor Day. The normally even-tempered judge began to let her impatience show in court. When required at both a congressional hearing and for a statement in court, General Becton headed to the Hill. The judge gaveled the scheduled court hearing into recess and issued an order: "You go up to the Hill," she told a Becton deputy, "and you bring General Williams [another senior administrator] or General Becton back."

Faced with the unhappy choice of letting 130 schools open on time while forty others remained closed, or keeping everyone home, Judge Christian went with the latter and kept D.C. schools closed. But opening schools late would not keep them open in June; no, the three-week deficit would be closed by a longer school day within a shorter school year.

Shortly after the missed opening day, Judge Christian levied a thousand-dollar-a-day fine for each school not finished by September 11; then word reached her of botched repairs, unmade inspections, and different departments of the District government proving unable to work together. When faced with the looming deadline and persistent difficulties in meeting the fire code, General Becton petitioned a Senate subcommittee for changes in the definition of a code violation, so that schools could remain open while repairs continued.

For all the optimism that greeted his appointment, General Becton's problems with parents and the D.C. City Council deepened, while his support remained strong in Congress, which appointed him in the first place. Increased parental backlash may be around the corner with the end of social promotions—the widespread practice of moving children up to the next grade even when their performance is short of grade level. In a system where so many of the schools are underperforming, where so many high-needs children are watching as their funding dollars are burned up by an enormous school bureaucracy, and where so many kids are poor, it is not unreasonable to expect that large numbers of children will be held back. For all students performing below grade level, summer school was not advised but required. A third of the entire enrollment spent the summer of 1998 in class. It will be interesting to see what happens when public sentiment collides with sound educational principles.

General Becton will not be at the helm to see whether his early changes really work over the long term. His chief of academic standards, Arlene Ackerman, is now in charge. In many ways, Ackerman is no different from her boss. Her superior political skills, however, may help her succeed where General Becton could not: in restoring faith in the improvement of the system, one family at a time.

Seizure of the power over public schooling in the face of plummeting public confidence has gone better in other big-city systems. In 1996, less than a year after the Illinois State Legislature voted to give the mayor day-to-day management of Chicago public schools, the country's third largest, Mayor Richard M. Daley told me, "People get on me about streets, and jobs, and stadiums. But if I don't fix this one thing, I'm wasting my time. If I keep the neighborhoods looking nice, and safe, and the school on the corner is no good, what am I doing? Those people are going to move out, and I can't stop them."

Daley appointed schools chief Paul Vallas, to fix a system racked by biannual labor battles, flirting daily with bankruptcy, and called "the worst in the nation" by former secretary of education William Bennett. He has begun to take bold chances. The worst fifth of the city's schools were placed under academic probation, which opened them to a variety of outside help and internal reorganization. For eighth graders seeking promotion to the city's high schools came the news that those not reaching seventh-grade level in math and science, summer school and retesting would be required. If that was not enough, eighth grade would be repeated.

Vallas has repeatedly called social promotion "educational malpractice," and wonders why it is so important to move children on when they are so desperately in need of an education. When looking at the kids who are routinely passed up and out by hundreds of big-city schools, he asks, "How many became members of street gangs or public aid recipients? What's wrong with having children spend another year or two in elementary schools? What's wrong with taking five or six years to finish high school if that's what it takes to get them prepared?"

It was often assumed, when the new "back-to-basics" plans were announced, that when faced with widespread failure or parental backlash, the schools would back down. In Chicago, they did not. A quarter of the system's eighth graders were sent to summer school in the first year of the new standards, and in the second year, students short of the mark were not allowed to march in cap and gown with their graduating class. If you are reading about that unremarkable fact while sitting in a comfy chair somewhere in the world where everyone finishes high school, keep in mind how large the prospect of that eighth-grade graduation ceremony looms in neighborhoods where most children are not going to walk in any other graduation procession.

The medicine administrators intend to minister in Washington appears to be working in Chicago. Of 473 elementary schools, 393 have better math results in standardized tests, and 271 have raised their reading scores. In New York, Rudolph Giuliani has also wrestled greater political control of the school system into the office of the mayor. During an interview, I pointed out to the mayor that the firewalls between the political structures of the elected city government and the school systems existed to remove the abuses of cronyism, corruption, patronage hiring, and favoritism. He agreed with my history but pointed out that urban America had changed during the decades since the reform and good-government crusades in New York and other cities. "I was elected mayor of this city and the people of this city hold me responsible for what happens in it, and that's appropriate. There is a problem with holding me accountable for the problems of the schools if I am prevented from doing anything to change them."

But when mayors survey their policy options regarding the public schools, they are hemmed in by far more than whether the thousands trooping off to class each morning are learning the Three R's. Middle-, and especially upper-middle-class parents have expectations of the public schools, in facilities and in educational enrichment more in keeping with their station in life. Thus the families paying the highest property taxes, still the single-largest source of public school funding and voting at the highest rates, have a beef about the schools that reverberates to the highest levels. Gifted and talented programs, magnet schools, programs in science, computers, and the arts are all bait for upper-income families to stay in the system. Woe betide the school system manager or elected official who tries to move, or close, such amenities, aiming to make systemwide improvements. In the past few years, New York City has faced repeated battles with parents over the distribution and size of gifted and talented programs.

In the District of Columbia schools, the parent's groups in the wealthiest areas head into battle each spring to raise tens of thousands of dollars to provide the kinds of staff and programs that are provided in the poorest neighborhoods by means-tested U.S. Department of Education funds. Amid this ad hockery the students who finish last in the big, urban school systems are in the middle-class and working-poor neighborhoods, neither rich enough to raise the money necessary to compensate for the school district's condition nor poor enough to qualify for federal largesse.

In a lower Manhattan school, the mayor and his schools chancellor, the widely praised Rudy Crew, have had to square off with public school parents over their desire to retain a popular teacher after budget cuts brought about a layoff. On the one hand you might applaud the commitment and effort necessary to raise more than forty thousand dollars. Move the scenario to less affluent neighborhoods and the fund-raising covers a good-bye party for the laid-off teacher, not his or her salary and benefits for the year.

In the biggest school districts, higher-income parents can have the brownie points from supporting public schools and sending their children to them, while working hard to insulate themselves from the worst effects of chronic underfunding and central administration shenanigans. These families also use the neighborhood schools in a different way—just for kindergarten through third grade, or for elementary school, or as a last resort—out by high school and then into the private academies to prepare their kids for college.

When critics of public schooling point to the high per-pupil expenditures and the low-level results achieved in many inner-city districts, they use these variables as proof of how muscular teachers' unions and over-populated bureaucracies have destroyed urban education. Granted, the District schools do have more supervisory personnel per one thousand pupils than most school systems in America and, in the main, show scant results for the nearly eight thousand dollars per student it spends each year. But this pat answer fails to recognize just how expensive it can be to educate a student body plagued with all the ills and challenges of modern urban life: family dissolution, inadequate or nonexistent health care, homes with no books or any educational stimulation, dangerous streets, parents who are ill-educated or speak no English, poverty, and, in many areas, the siren song of the drug trade. What the critics who point out how much systems like Washington's, Chicago's, and New York's spend per student in comparison with more successful suburban systems don't acknowledge is the added cost of teaching and caring for children burdened by the accumulation of effects of urban pathology, sitting in classrooms that are often eighty to one hundred years old.

One look at the percentage of dollars applied to classroom instruction in the newer, smaller, higher-income school districts and those dollars actually making it to the classroom in the big urban systems reveals that in wealthier districts, as much as seventy-five cents on the dollar actually goes to classroom instruction; in the older and poorer systems, the provision of health care, emotional counseling, bilingual education, nutrition, security, and maintenance siphons off more than half of every dollar. Hence the "high cost" of education provided to urban public school children.

The problems of urban public schooling are profound and long-standing. Parent patience is tempered by the knowledge that one's kid gets only one childhood, and only one shot at primary education's preparation for later life. This is the urgency driving thousands of families out of the eastern, heavily black neighborhoods of Washington, D.C., into next-door Prince George's County, Maryland. This is the impatience that drives the fear of a high-stakes gamble with children's lives in struggling neighborhoods, and drains off the children of many of the most concerned, motivated, and energized parents, into urban Catholic schools—whether they're Catholic or not.

This also may explain the growing support in the poorest neighborhoods for school voucher systems. The theory is that vouchers—which represent a fixed cash value when presented to a school—open up school choice for families stuck in the worst schools. Moving into the breach created by a leadership vacuum at the top of the District of Columbia government and declining support for the schools, the Congress is making good use of its extensive power over the lives of the people of the District. A pilot voucher program has been framed as a bill to make two thousand vouchers available to children in the five poorest schools in the district. Their families can use them in public, nonsectarian private, or parochial schools.

For their supporters, vouchers are an easier answer to the intractable questions about raising the quality of public schooling. They put added power into the hands of often highly motivated but immobile parents to choose better schools for their children. They also take the kind of parents who become the "vanguard class," fighting for improvement of local public schools, out of the equation. What liberals obsess over, and conservatives won't admit, is that those vouchers and the market forces of "school choice" will continue to leave neighborhood schools unimproved in some of the worst neighborhoods.

What conservatives have insisted all along, and liberals won't admit, is that many inner-city schools are worse than they have to be. These schools have not been held to high standards, have not replaced faculty and administration who are not up to the job, and have been allowed to meet the abysmally low expectations set for them. To a greater degree than anyone wants to admit, parents set the tone for a neighborhood school. No poor kid with a voucher will be able to turn one in for new parents.

The children of the middle and upper-middle class taking their seats in a public school classroom have arrived, from the very first morning, with a set of advantages over their poorer peers. They travel. They visit museums. They have books, magazines, and, increasingly, personal computers. They have parents who are heavily invested in their educational attainment. They have families who hire tutors when they struggle and are in the faces of principals when they suspect a teacher is incompetent and poorly serving their children. All these factors may also be true for kids from poorer families but statistically decline at every step down the income ladder. Individual educational attainment correlates with family educational attainment. Children of high school dropouts can and do go on to earn four-year college degrees and graduate degrees. But any given child of high school dropouts is many times less likely to earn a master's degree than the child of a mother and a father with two framed master's on the wall, and is many times more likely to drop out of high school himself. What public schools seek to do is open the opportunity structure for the poorest students. What they do too often, instead, is simply reproduce the opportunity structure their parents face all day, at work, back in the schools. Washington, D.C., plays out this drama on its streets every day.

From my window at National Public Radio, I can see the contrasts on the city streets. Traffic from Virginia pours into the area from an interstate exit ramp just a few blocks away. As drivers wait for the light on our corner, homeless men weave their shopping carts through traffic, pulling up stakes for their nomadic ramble after a few hours' encampment from the park across the street. The park forms the grounds for the beautiful Carnegie library, one of hundreds that dot the country's landscape from the fortune the richest American of his time squeezed from the bodies of his Pennsylvania workers. The shadow men, economically irrelevant throwaways in the modern economy that has richly rewarded those driving by, are part of the neighborhood for the time being, but may soon be hustled on, like birds looking to roost in a shrinking habitat.

I can see the degraded skyline of the Shaw neighborhood, home to large working-poor and welfare-dependent populations. This part of D.C. is shot through with vacant land, some lots covered with trailers that serve as nighttime shelter for the local homeless, and others having sprouted meters and a guard's shack for cheap daytime parking. Much of this land may soon be covered in a new Washington Convention Center. Out my left window stands the topped-out silhouette of the new MCI Arena, the new home of the Washington Bullets of the NBA and the Washington Capitals of the NHL. When this new north-south axis of middle-class destinations is built, the people of Shaw, if the model holds, will simply be priced out, and moved on. They will not share in the millions being spent before their eyes. The good jobs, and the season tickets, will go to the people in the cars. The low-paying jobs—hawking popcorn and beer at hockey games and parking cars—would offer little better than the bleak future that already stretches before them without these new baubles in Washington's already heavily jeweled crown.

The split personality of gracious, conspicuous consumption and desperate poverty and urban misery is *not* seen as the shame of the United States, a distinction that makes this country unique and surprises foreign visitors. The curious, searching for parallels in other countries, can only look to a small number of collapsing capitals, and none of the comparisons are flattering. The Thais are shamed by Bangkok's squalor and set national priorities to address the ills of the burgeoning capital. In the capitals of many other developing countries, the old "first" city has become a national embarrassment, and replacing it becomes part of the task of nation building. In orgies of patronage spending and modernizing zest, many countries tried purpose-built capitals to show the rest of the country a better side of itself. Brasilia, Dodoma (Tanzania), and New Delhi all tried to turn the nation's and the world's gaze away from the old, corrupt, historic chief city by trying something new.

It is useful to remember that Washington was also conceived in that same spirit some two hundred years ago. It was meant to build a new political order out of the old regional rivalries and parochial obsessions of Boston, New York, and Philadelphia. Its location would unite the urbanizing North to the agrarian South. The new city was in the very heart of the string of settlements huddled against the Atlantic seaboard, not withering at the edge of a continent-sized nation, as it is today.

Conspiracy theorists see combinations of dark forces in the modern story of Washington, D.C. You can sometimes hear black residents simply refer to it as "The Plan," a white plot to trash a black majority city, retake it, and rebuild it as a newly revived possession of white capital. But those who are behind The Plan are surely taking their sweet time, as the capital city continues to live from hand-to-mouth and to empty out. What is missing from this tale of white avarice is the degree to which the transformation is occurring without any resistance. The Plan, if you will, does not make the national capital the prize in a racial wrestling match but merely beside the point, irrelevant.

The city is gradually meaning less and less to the operation of this major metropolitan area, the country's sixth largest with more than four and a half million people. With just 12 percent of the area's population, a percentage that is dropping, the fate of the District has a declining impact on the lives of the increasingly smaller share of the people who live here. Most of the area's residents can continue to react with bland detachment or angry resentment when asked about the city's future. The suburbs have won, if by default. Allowing the city to descend further into decay will not be, as in some other metropolitan areas, a case of killing the goose that lays the golden eggs. Bethesda, Chevy Chase, Reston, McLean, Potomac, and other well-heeled suburban municipalities have raised their own geese. In the meantime, they can force every last egg from the big goose, keep all the eggs, and don't even have to chip in for the funeral when it dies.

In the near suburbs, opulent shopping areas, theme restaurants, and high-end auto dealers cluster, reinforce themselves, and continue to concentrate, increasing in density. Along the strip of Rockville Pike, just a few miles from the District line, all the signposts promising gracious, upper-income consumption follow one after the other for miles: there's a new Barnes & Noble Superstore, a Nordstrom, computer retailers, Fresh Fields, and a Land Rover dealership.

In other parts of the country, the logical assumption is: "The place can't go down. The government's there." Tourists see the Capitol, the headquarters buildings for major federal departments, and the White House, and figure, "This will always be here." Maybe the buildings that grace the backs of the five-, ten-, and twenty-dollar bills will stay right where they are, but where is the Atomic Energy Commission? Where is the National Oceanic and Atmospheric Agency's headquarters? The National Institutes of Health? Quietly lurking on the Federal Page section of the *Washington Post* is news of one federal facility after another mimicking the corporate retreat of a previous generation, moving not from antiquated Washington facilities to newer digs in town but to "corporate campus"–style buildings in the suburbs–farther and farther away from the historic federal core.

Just as the needs and desires of middle and upper management, already removed to the suburbs, gradually peeled away office buildings from the cities' downtowns, the needs and desires of a privileged class are now taking federal facilities from the only city in the United States established for the sole purpose of being the home of the national government.

What will this city be, after the syndromes all under way complete their march through this exquisite corpse?

One by one, middle-class homeowners are abandoning Northeast neighborhoods along the border with Prince George's County. In the city, their incomes offer them the choice of housing in lower-end, near-slum conditions in some neighborhoods, or block after block of untouchable housing selling for more than twice the median price of housing in the United States. Many make the only rational economic decision: they leave. In the four years from 1990 to 1994 there was an almost 7 percent decline in the city's population, and there is no indication yet that the rate of departure is declining.

Vast tracts of underdeveloped land sit in the lower Northeast and Southeast sections of the city, as new federal offices, annexes, and storage structures head for the suburbs. Painful, large-scale cuts lie ahead, as the massive city government Mayor Barry built in the 1980s is dismantled by an appointed board of baby-sitters, smashing to bits any illusions the city had about self-government.

As the clearinghouse for billions in tax dollars, the nerve center of national legislation and resource-hungry federal departments, Washington, D.C., spun off its riches with centrifugal force into the once-sleepy communities of northern Virginia and central Maryland. The corridor along the Dulles Toll Road, connecting the infamous Beltway with Dulles International Airport, has spawned U.S. headquarters for major European multinationals, regional bases for the big, high-tech firms, luxury retail, and the movie-set downtown of Reston Town Center. Afraid of going to Georgetown? Think your car radio will get stolen in Adams-Morgan? Instead of heading for authentic urban street life, why not go to Reston Town Center, where you can walk on the sidewalk, lick an ice cream cone, shop for clothes, take in a movie—all without the risky, random, noisy hubbub of a *real* city?

Reston Town Center is more than a little scary. It is what a very smart planner realizes is just enough urbanity to be attractive, while lacking the reality that makes suburbanites jittery. There is no litter. No noise. No aggressive panhandling. It reduces the essentials of urban life to a consumer experience. Reston says, "All that makes one place different from another is how and what you consume." The designers who have built an ersatz Key West on mainland Florida so you don't have to schlep down to the real one should have their hearts gladdened by Reston. So should developers who are bringing knockoff environments to places like Midtown Manhattan.

In their slavish desire to reassure middle- and upper-middle-class customers, cities are straining to turn the urban landscape into a live-in theme park. Take the real thing, make it sanitized and orderly, and wait for the tourists, even residents-turned-tourists. Dipping your cones, sweeping up the cigarette butts, and busing your tables are the residents of the other city, the one that exists behind the Potemkin facade of Urbanism Lite.

For all its political paralysis and its bizarre institutions, the District of Columbia at century's end is a cautionary tale, applicable even to the "normal" American cities. The real suffering of tens of thousands of its people mired in permanent poverty, its construction of parasitic suburbs that get to make the rules and benefit handsomely from them, the extreme inequality that ranks D.C. among the top places in America in per capita and family income *and* incarceration, household poverty, and syphilis, the crumbling streets and world-famous monuments, the best and the worst schools in America, the Starbucks and the methadone clinics, the metro area with the highest percentage of master's degrees in America *and* the lowest SAT scores should all send a shudder through the mayors of New York, Philadelphia, Chicago, Miami, and Los Angeles.

Cut through the fog of high-toned political speeches and the handwringing over crime and drugs, schools and streets. Let's call the country's capital what it really is: America's Magnificent Orphan.

Chapter 10

Still a Stranger: Latinos and the American City

We were among the first Americans. Why are we still strangers? The people you call Latinos, Hispanics, Spanish, wetbacks, illegals, and so on drew their first breath when an infant was yanked, wet and screaming, from his mother's womb nine months after Christopher Columbus and his hungry men alighted from their ships and walked ashore on the out-islands of the hemisphere.

Five hundred years later, we bus your tables, make your television tubes, watch your kids after school, pick your strawberries, trim your hedges, lay your sod, tape your drywall, entertain you at Disney World, and frighten you on darkened streets. Weak of mind and strong of back, we populate your dreams of fabulous sex and immigrant invasion. We fill up your jails and fight in your wars. We live here for years and never learn your language, so you've got to pass "official" English and English-only laws. We veer between reckless bravado and donkeylike deference. Our men can't hold their liquor, but they can sure carry a tune. They beat their wives and anyone who dares insult them. Their wives turn to lard after a couple of babies, and remain sweetly compliant as they take care of yours.

You know us so well, it seems. Why are we still strangers?

That endless wrestling match between black and white—a struggle over everything, real and symbolic—needed some fresh blood. They enter, from stage South. So you leave a Miami drugstore angry and resentful when a counter girl doesn't understand a perfectly simple question. Elderly homeowners who are frightened, but can't afford to move, mutter about noise and cooking smells, and every Sunday Catholic churches turn into a stage for the social drama playing itself out on the streets the other six days of the week.

Writers like Linda Chavez say Hispanic Americans are like any other immigrants, and their lives will follow the same generational trajectory as those of the Italians, Irish, and Poles. Others, particularly in civil rights organizations like the Mexican-American Legal Defense and Education Fund (MALDEF) and the National Council of La Raza, say something different is happening this time. Having the Old Country two hours away by jet, instead of on the other side of a hard-to-cross ocean, means these new Americans don't have to slam the door on their place of origin, the way so many other immigrants have done.

In the popular mind, there is a close association between the arrival of Spanish-speaking immigrants and neighborhood decay. Reality is more subtle: neighborhoods sag in some places, spruce up in others with the arrival of these newcomers. Despite the wildly different outcomes, there's a kind of reductionism at work—a tendency to regard these "arrivals," of Dominicans in Upper Manhattan, of Mexicans in Chicago, of Central Americans in Los Angeles, as an undifferentiated meta-event.

They'll move too many people into too-small houses. Their gang's emblems will start showing up in spray paint on garages. There'll be trouble at the local school. You won't be able to talk to your neighbors. (They may smile amiably enough, but they won't understand a word you say.) It's all true. It's all false.

A new generation of nativist critics wring their hands over their nightmare scenario of millions of unassimilated residents forming a fifth column and bringing Quebec to our door. They want the old-style "total immersion"—that is, throwing immigrants in at the deep end of the American pool. Their opponents, I'll call them the ethnicists, want it both ways:

When foreign-language services from government are threatened, they plead necessity for their long-term continuation. However, when Latino acquisition of English is criticized as too slow, they insist that these immigrants are learning English as quickly as other Americans did. That's *Nuestra Raza,* able to learn English quickly and not learning English, at the same time.

Latinos are settling in urban enclaves, yes, but it remains an open question whether they are bound to the ghetto the same way black families of similar income have been. Inner-ring suburbs in Los Angeles, Miami, Chicago, and New York have all become a popular second stop on Latino family journeys. At the same time, Latinos' lack of political and economic clout has persisted in many cities, where they have been moved out to make room for civic projects, or simply priced out of the housing market in the path of gentrification. Though people of all colors have been gradually displaced from time to time by gentrification, blacks and Latinos, more often renters than their white counterparts, are less likely to exert any influence on the process. Low- and moderate-income renters must leave the neighborhood in the face of rising values, while owners can derive tremendous benefits from the rising fortunes of a neighborhood, whether they personally contribute to that change or not. Year after year, in Labor Department surveys Latinos post the highest levels of overall workplace participation of any Americans. Yet they remain disproportionately poor, and drop out of high school at stubbornly high rates.

To the extent that residential segregation contributes to school segregation, Latinos suffer acutely from social isolation. Gary Orfield of Harvard University has tracked urban school populations for decades and has concluded that Latino students are even more likely than black students to attend schools that are mostly or entirely populated by people like themselves.

Most of the metropolitan areas with a significant Latino presence are clustered in the South and West: Miami, San Antonio, Los Angeles, San Diego, Houston, and Austin all have populations that are 20 percent Latino or higher. Some of these places were once in the Spanish empire and are more used to having these New World men and women around. In places like Chicago, New York, Boston, and Philadelphia, their presence is more recent and has contributed both to the urban underclass and to economic vitality. The main shopping street of Chicago's Little Village—Twenty-sixth Street—is one of the most extensive and economically potent Latino commercial districts in America, and it hardly existed twenty years ago.

One million Latinos in Chicago and its suburbs, and more than two million each in Los Angeles and New York, force you away from a binary black-white view of the struggles over the city. The new math means that standing between white and black is a new brown interest group waiting to be courted, often holding the balance of power in municipal elections. When Latino voters backed Harold Washington, he won. When they favored Richard Daley after Washington's death, he won. David Dinkins became mayor of New York with heavily Democratic Latino support. When Rudolph Giuliani pried away chunks of the Latino vote from the Democratic candidates in both 1993 and 1997, he won, too. In Miami, San Antonio, and, increasingly, Dallas, you can't win without Latino support.

The Immigration Reform and Control Act of 1986 brought hundreds of thousands of Latino immigrants out of the shadows, giving them legal status, citizenship, and voting rights. As Latinos enter the political arena in bigger numbers, fueled by voting rights suits, federal mandates, and consent decrees, the equation is altered and takes some of the spotlight away from the perennial black struggle for political empowerment. Stopping in court on the way to the voting booth has forced cities to end the gerrymandering of large Latino residential areas and made city councils reconfigure their districts, moving away from at-large municipal and county seats that have often made it difficult for minority candidates to win any seats.

The rapid growth of Chicago's Latino population has come at a time of significant overall population loss. The steady increase of New York's already enormous Latino population has come at a time of relative stability in the number of people living there. Population stasis or decline while the Latino population grows means large areas of the city are experiencing Latino settlement for the first time. In Chicago, Los Angeles, and parts of New York, graying neighborhoods, where white homeowners are retiring with no white buyers interested in their properties, are "browning." Gage Park in Chicago counted 24,445 residents in 1980 and 26,957 in 1990, making it one of the few communities in the city to experience an increase in population. Hidden by that overall number is the tremendous change in Gage Park in those same ten years. The number of black residents has grown from 154 to 1,292, still less than 5 percent. The white population has declined from 21,292 to 14,819, and the number of Latinos has jumped from 2,701 to 10,574. The numbers in the year 2000 are expected to show strong Latino increases again, and may find whites in a minority for the first time ever, in a community where it was never expected to happen.

In Manhattan and the Bronx, immigrants from the Dominican Republic have moved from tiny numbers to neighborhood majorities within the past twenty years. The census counted a little over 125,000 Dominicans in the city in 1980, more than 330,000 in 1990, and about half a million by mid-decade; projections call for 700,000 by the year 2000—or about the number of people in the entire city of San Francisco. With nearly half that population living below the poverty line, Dominican household income is only half the New York City average, which is itself only two-thirds of the national average. This large, young, unskilled, and poor population leaves New York City, already wrestling with persistently high unemployment in an era of robust job growth nationwide, with ever greater challenges to meet.

In many older cities, Latino residential patterns show an interesting trend: For example, as elderly white homeowners sell and leave (and their children are already in the suburbs), Latinos on Chicago's South Side—almost all Mexicans—are becoming a buffer group between the huge black communities in the south and the white neighborhoods huddling closer and closer to the city's western limit. The pattern is a little different on the North Side, where Latinos have lived for decades, but in constantly re-configuring neighborhoods. On the North Side, Puerto Ricans have been the largest Latino group and, since their arrival in large numbers, have moved or been pushed away from the lakefront, farther west and farther north. Predominantly renters, Puerto Ricans have seen their neighborhoods shaped by the needs of landlords rather than residents, and rising rents have opened up areas just north of the city for gentrification. Once run-down Lincoln Park and Lake View, formerly home to large numbers of Puerto Ricans, are now picture postcards of gentrified splendor. Neighborhoods just west of the lake,

Bucktown, Wicker Park, and Logan Square, have undergone significant change in recent years, as young white homeowners have moved in and rebuilt block after block of worker's cottages, originally erected in the nineteenth century to serve European workers and artisans of the factory district on the Chicago River. Puerto Ricans have had to move or face rapidly rising housing costs.

After a lifetime in apartments, I bought my first house in the Logan Square neighborhood, on a side street off the more expensive boulevards. Built by Germans and Swedes during World War I and in later decades the home to Ukrainians and Poles, by the 1970s Logan Square had become a growing center of Puerto Rican life in Chicago. By the mid-1980s, the area's well-built graystones, picturesque boulevards, and good transit links to downtown had those white buyers priced out of the lakefront market taking a look.

I was a straddler. My block club included Puerto Rican homeowners—mostly city employees, blue-collar workers, young white-collar whites, and me with a foot in each camp: Puerto Rican and, recently, a refugee from tony Lincoln Park. Longtime Latino residents of the block had fought long and hard to bring safety and stability. The block club had worked closely with the local police district, the city's Department of Streets and Sanitation, and other agencies. Their hard work was evidenced by the young white buyers, who wouldn't even have driven down this street a few years before.

My house had once been a major sales and distribution point for cocaine, through a network run by a father and his sons. That meant young armed men coming and going from the street at all times of the day and night. The block club had taken real risks, and struggled to get the police to watch the street and bust the pushers.

The Latino owners knew what the bad old days on the street had been like, but the young whites, unused to the idea that they could be ignored by the city and its agencies, missed the full import of what had changed. People who had once been in real danger were now feeling safer. Their home values were rising too, but this was not uppermost in their minds. Their new young neighbors seemed to monitor house prices day by day, and saw life here as a step toward something else. To that degree, I wasn't that different. When my small house promised to be a tight fit for my growing family, I moved too. I didn't leave the city, or even the neighborhood, but found that by moving some three hundred yards, my world changed.

Palmer Square, my new neighborhood, had been laid out and developed in the early years of the century, along the lines of an old carriage-racing oval. Today it is lined by beautiful old homes and apartment buildings, with ornamental stone and terra-cotta facades. From the living room of my new house, I could see my old house but, in fact, I had crossed from Striver's Row into Yuppieland. My Latino friends would laugh when they heard I lived on Palmer. "You're over there with the yuppies? I'm proud of you, man! We're taking over!" Many assumed when I told them where I lived that I really meant the "Palmer Square area," since the square itself was simply a place Puerto Ricans did not live, a place they could not live.

In the years I lived on Palmer Square, I soaked up the neighborhood lore and got an earful from both sides in a fascinating tug-of-war over the park that formed the square's centerpiece. In the years since white-collar homeowners returned to Palmer Square, much of their concern had focused on that park, which greeted them each morning when they looked out their windows. It had been the dividing line between two major gang territories, and thus had become the scene for pitched battles with baseball bats and guns. The north side of the park was home to Orquesta Albany; the south side was part of the turf of GBO/YBO—the Ghetto Boys Organization and the Young Brothers Organization.

Longtime residents of the area have told me that fear of the gangs emptied the park of all conventional users after dark, and the neighborhood retreat became a self-fulfilling prophecy. Public drinking was common there, as were fistfights and joyrides across the grass in speeding cars. Many nights were punctuated by the sounds of gunfire. This remained the situation even as the buildings facing the park, which had once been the homes of families in the Chicago Blue Book, the city's social register, were now being restored to their former elegance.

One of my neighbors, a man named Steve, had been among the first of the new generation of owners. The concerns of the new young families were many, and restoring the park took a backseat to more immediate threats. "We already had the home for the mentally retarded kids down at 3118 [Palmer], and now the Gateway Foundation wanted to buy 3116 for a drug halfway house, and the Safer Foundation wanted to house ex-cons around the block on Kedzie."

Several new owners joined Steve to form a group that would later be incorporated as the Homeowners Association of Palmer Square (HAPS). They had figured out what many residents of poorer neighborhoods already know: The lack of competition for housing in marginal areas often leads to a clustering of institutional users, like shelters and clinics, and that such clustering later precludes more desirable future development. In the early 1980s, the newly organized residents enlisted the help of their neighbors to fight the location of several treatment centers and group homes in the area. The HAPS also successfully resisted zoning changes in its struggle to maintain the residential character of the boulevards, which were now up for landmark designation.

The HAPS then turned its attention to the park. The new homeowners knew how to push buttons, rile politicians, and use "squeaky wheel" activism to get the police on their side. Through phone calls and neighborhood watch tactics, calling for immediate police response to the slightest infractions, the gangs were gradually moved off the square. The public drinking, fighting, and late-night sex in parked cars was nearly eliminated during the early 1980s. Occasional low-level vandalism, couples "parking," and the use of the park as a late-night beer garden would persist into the 1990s, but on a level that appeared to be bearable to the residents. But there was one piece of land, and two visions of what it was for. These twin visions followed class lines and ethnic ones.

The new homeowners around the square, already hard at work restoring their houses to their original condition, wanted to make the park what it once had been: a pretty place, a walking place. The HAPS members knew whom to call for donations of sapling trees to begin replanting what had once been a woodsy glade in the heart of the city. In earlier years, police, park authorities, and neighbors had thinned out the park's vegetation to lower maintenance requirements and to make what had become a dangerous area easier to police. Muggers can't hide in an acre of flat grass. But the crowded side streets and big apartment buildings of the neighborhood spilled their people onto Palmer Square too, making it a different place: a place for cookouts, bicycle riding, and ball games. Even after Palmer Square became a "demilitarized zone" for warring gangs, its fortunes were hostage to gang violence. Teenagers were reluctant to traverse the invisible lines that divided neighborhoods into warring clans to reach Humboldt Park, three-fourths of a mile to the south, one of the great jewels of the Chicago park system. It was a full-service park, with ball fields, playgrounds, a field house, even a boating lagoon. On the most beautiful weekends of the summer, Humboldt Park still looked empty.

Organized ball clubs had taken over Palmer Square for years, putting pressure on the land. The barren, blasted spaces, stripped of grass by constant heavy use, turned to mud after a rain. The occasional pedestrian had to dodge caroming softballs or watch out for the simmering contents of dumped outdoor grills. For the Palmer Square homeowners, ball fields and mud damaged a splendid setting for their houses. For a land-hungry, crowded community short on safe parks, here was grass and open space. They needed grass and open space. Simple.

The Palmer Square homeowners knew how to read statutes and pull the levers of government, and the young Latins playing softball didn't. Like an endangered species that never knew what hit them, softball teams had their habitat taken away. NO BALLPLAYING signs blossomed from the lampposts, and then follow-up calls to the police kept the heat on. The homeowners also bought trees and planted them throughout the park. The HAPS figured it's tough to play ball in a forest, even a forest of saplings.

The first installation of trees did not go well. Whenever they interfered with the geography of the playing field, the ballplayers simply uprooted them and continued playing.

"We realized that was not going to work," said Steve. "The trees alone would not stop the ball playing." The homeowners group approached the nearby Chicago-Minneapolis-St. Paul Railroad, whose tracks run just south of Palmer Square, and obtained a truckload of railroad ties as a donation. The ties were sunk several feet into the ground to stop the ballplayers and the joyriders who tore across the square in cars. Steve recalled, "We would plant two or three of them around each tree, and it didn't make any sense to pull up the trees anymore, because you couldn't pull up the ties."

The baseball was gone. The gang shootings were over. The park was no longer edged by used condoms and beer bottles. The homeowners had tamed Palmer Square but were rarely seen in it themselves. "I would call it 'substantially improved' since the new owners got together to work on it," says Bob, who had lived on Palmer for ten years. "It's moved from barely tolerable to good, but not excellent. When the big soccer games would go on the weekends, twenty-five-year-old guys would arrive in cars to play; maybe they lived within a mile or two but not right around here. And everyone else had to leave! Now I see a younger bunch. The people in the park are still not for the most part people who live facing the park, but they're younger, they come from closer by, and they often come as families."

Carlos, a neighborhood activist, attaches no such benign motives to the changes in the park. "Look, the yuppies who live on Palmer don't want young guys to have a place to play. They want someplace to walk their dogs." It must be noted, however, that Carlos himself travels half a mile to walk his own dog on Palmer Square. "They planted all those trees so young Hispanic guys wouldn't have any place to play ball, that's all."

Jose, a high-ranking officer at the nearby Chicago Police Department district headquarters just a few blocks away from Palmer Square, said neighborhood boys who came to his station for an Explorer Scouting program asked him why "*los blancos*"—the whites who live on the square—planted so many new trees in their most recent wave of improvements. "They ask me, 'Why don't they want us to have a place to play?' I don't know what to tell them." For many Latinos in the neighborhood, even those climbing the ladders of American status and economic clout, it is easy to see that change in Palmer Square—from a disputed gang turf to a "quiet" urban park—meant keeping young Hispanics out. Though people on the side streets and on the square may all root for the Bears, vote Democratic, eat fast food, watch similar prime-time television shows, drink Old Style beer, and wear jeans and running shoes, Latin American origin is used as a slide rule to calculate who is "them" and who is "us."

Yet the young men and boys who can be found playing in the park on a recent Saturday seemed to carry none of these implied resentments. Volleyball players said the only contacts they have had with Palmer residents were the few times they were asked not to use trees as supports for their nets. They have since complied and now routinely use poles. Otherwise, "they don't bother us, and we don't bother them," said one player. Asked what they know about the residents, they most often said they are "not Hispanics" and "have money." Both these attributes were identified matter-of-factly, without setting up an "us versus them" confrontation. Pressed on the question of wealth, one ballplayer used empirical evidence, "*oye, muchacho* [listen buddy], just look at those houses!" The changes in the square are seen as part of the ebb and flow of clout: who's got it and who does not.

Luis came to Chicago in 1953 from Puerto Rico. He has spent most of his working life in factories on the north and west sides. A back injury now forces him to wear a brace and plan a return to Puerto Rico to escape Chicago's ferocious winters. He has lived on the corner of Palmer Square and Kedzie Boulevard for seventeen years, and has terrible memories of the days when he first moved in with his three young sons. "They [gang members] used to come from Albany Avenue shooting at each other, and shooting at people who were just there. People they don't know!" Luis's oldest son, now in his thirties, was the victim of a gang attack as a teenager. "They stab him three times in the head. . . . He is not the same anymore, but the doctor told me he was going to die, so I guess I thank God for his life." Luis called his decision to come to Palmer Square from Humboldt Park a good one, and said the neighborhood is "now getting real nice," and contrasting his first years in his apartment as "very bad."

Luis does not see the "whitening" of Palmer Square as any kind of threat, or part of some wider conspiracy to relocate Puerto Ricans from an established barrio. Luis assumed that these white people—his new, unknown neighbors—naturally brought better police protection, garbage pickup, and the power to get the city to fix up the park with them. It was the flip side of his assumption that the city would not do much of anything to help people like him.

One of the most recent additions to the park is a running track, filled with gravel and covered in wood chips. Carrie, who has owned a home on the park since 1984, says she thinks the track was the least desirable improvement, and that viewed from outside the homeowner's association, the running track was the part of the project most likely seen as being for "them," and not "us."

Carrie also realized there was a class dimension to the park conflict. "I know that neighbors who do not front the park feel that rich people moved in and took their park away. They're just wrong. When it came up before the group—whether to prohibit ball playing altogether—that proposal was defeated. We just didn't want organized ball playing, the leagues. The park just can't take it."

In the early 1990s, El Rincon, a not-for-profit agency that treats heroin addicts with methadone, announced its intention to move its clinic into a storefront a quarter-mile south of Palmer Square. Nine hundred signatures were gathered by local people, and several urgent meetings were called with then Alderman, now U.S. Representative, Luis Gutierrez. But the meetings, petition drive, and political pressure were not spearheaded or organized by Palmer Square residents or the homeowners' group. The prime movers in the effort were the residents of the blocks south of Palmer Square.

The attitudes of "white" and Hispanic opponents of the clinic speak volumes about the understanding of how ethnic politics are played in Chicago. The HAPS leaders were in regular contact with Luis Sepulveda, a leader in the local effort against the clinic. Both groups agreed that HAPS itself would not take a high-profile role in the opposition to the drug treatment center. The area's Latino residents, now well schooled in the ways of local politics after years of successful organizing and independent Democratic politics, showed themselves fully capable of pushing all the pressure points in this battle without the assistance of HAPS. HAPS did not want to give El Rincon, the directors of which are all Latinos, the chance to play the ethnicity or class card, reducing the struggle to "white people not wanting a treatment center for Hispanics near their houses, in the middle of a Hispanic neighborhood."

As it turned out, that did not stop El Rincon leaders from making pointed remarks about yuppies, whites, and those "who did not want to help the Latino community" at public meetings and smaller encounters with politicians and community leaders. Nonetheless, anticlinic flyers were distributed on the boulevards and side streets, in English and Spanish, and Alderman Gutierrez faced a large, integrated, united crowd at a public meeting with the board of El Rincon on March 10, 1992.

A year later, the largely Puerto Rican executive board of El Rincon tried again to use ethnicity to forge common cause with the opponents of the clinic by citing shared Latino roots. This attempt to split the Hispanics from their "Palmer Square yuppie" allies did not work, and again the opposition was led from the modest frame two-flats near the clinic site.

The implication that they were incapable of opposing the clinic on their own enraged some of the leaders of the petition drive. After all, during the neighborhood's worst days, many young men and women were lost to drugs. The clinic's Latino opponents knew far better than their allies on Palmer Square what junkies were really like, and what having them coming and going in large numbers from the clinic was going to mean. At the public meetings, El Rincon leaders used soft, reassuring, twelve-steppy vocabulary to explain the eventual role of the clinic in the life of the neighborhood. What they found was that after years of getting dumped on by the city and everyone else, the Latino homeowners near Palmer Square now felt they had something worth fighting for, and did not believe that having heroin addicts within a radius of a few miles, making their way through the streets to El Rincon, fit in with their renewed hopes for the neighborhood.

In the struggle that followed, Hispanic political leaders first tried to make peace between the two Latino factions but later left El Rincon to its fate, which was sealed when a large delegation of the petition signers testified before the zoning committee of the city council, without needing the aid of the local aldermen in their corner. In the days when the first rehabbers banded together, they worked among a Puerto Rican majority, gerrymandered into five different wards and unlikely to have its voice heard on the public stage.

It took a voting rights lawsuit and a victory in federal court to get a map of the fifty wards that allowed for the possibility of a representative council in a city now 60 percent black and Latino. In 1986, federally ordered special elections created a series of new wards. The Twenty-sixth Ward put Latino and black neighborhoods that had once been in five different wards into one, and the last white ethnic alderman headed into retirement. More than a decade later, the "empowered" population of the blocks around Palmer Square appear ready to meet their "rich" neighbors on equal footing and work with them toward common goals.

Today there is a new generation of Hispanic homeowners. Their level of education, earnings, and consumption patterns makes them resemble their gentrifying neighbors more than their Hispanic working-class *hermanos*.

I sat and talked with a dozen Latin strivers with household incomes in excess of fifty thousand dollars living in my old neighborhood, Logan Square. They ranged in education from associates degrees to M.D.'s; all were bilingual, roughly thirty to forty years of age, and came from a variety of Latin American national groups. In many ways they were representative of Latin baby boomers: largely the products of public education, they were the first or among the first in their families to experience post-secondary education, they had grown up in largely Hispanic communities, and they were a mix of those born in Latin America and those born in the United States. None had lived at his or her current residence for more than five years.

Yet they knew that the mixture of their ethnic backgrounds, income levels, and personal histories in the city (growing up largely low-income or working class) put them in an unusual position among their neighbors. "I'm an urbanite," says Jerry, a thirty-three-year-old "Mex-o-Rican" (his own term—his father is Mexican, his mother Puerto Rican) who owns a single-family graystone home just north of Palmer Square. A high-income skilled tradesman whose wife also works, Jerry acknowledges that he had his pick of places to live in the city and suburbs. "But I feel it's important for the majority of low-income Hispanic kids in Logan Square to have someone as an example—to show that people like them can live comfortably, own a nice home. It's important for kids to see me going to work in a shirt and tie rather than head to a construction site with a lunch bucket." Jerry is a rough Hispanic equivalent of the "Race Man" talked about by black intellectuals in the 1950s and 1960s. He speaks Spanish at home, watches Spanish television, though not exclusively, and is learning to play the quatro, a small, twelve-string guitar as central to Puerto Rican traditional music as a banjo is to bluegrass. For all that, Jerry concluded, as did virtually every other Latino homeowner I interviewed, that he had more in common with his white neighbors of European origin than with his Hispanic neighbors.

The respondents are split in their view of whether the neighborhood would be able to satisfy their rising expectations and growing families. In the mid-1990s, three of the four neighborhood public schools serving the gentrifying areas of Logan Square were in the bottom third of all Chicago public schools when measured by standardized tests in reading and mathematics. Only the fourth, Brentano, was above the fiftieth percentile citywide, and is located in the most heavily white census tract in the area.

Patricia was born and spent her early childhood in Ecuador. She is in her forties and until recently was the executive director for an established citywide agency serving Hispanics. She and her husband bought a three-flat on Humboldt Boulevard in 1986 and had used the rapid appreciation of that building to buy other investment properties throughout the city. Patricia has left Logan Square for a new home in Wilmette. "I'm representative of a group of friends who moved here as young marrieds, as childless couples. At the time it seemed *we* would stabilize the neighborhood. But then our concerns about education and safety started to take over when we had kids, and this close-knit group of people who lived nearby is slowly eroding, and I didn't feel like I had any reason to stay around here anyway."

All those I interviewed said education was an important consideration for their families, and those with children at or approaching school age were the most likely to cite local schools as an impediment to their future residence in Logan Square.

Gustavo, also in his forties, is a senior department manager in Chicago city government. By law, he must reside in Chicago. He concludes that there is "no way" he would be living in Logan Square in five or ten years. It would be more likely, he says, to find him living in Colombia, where he grew up. "This is not a neighborhood I consider appropriate for my daughter Veronica." Having said that, however, Gustavo still has found much to like about Logan Square. He says he believes the neighborhood has become a magnet for upper-income Latinos, which has contributed to the sense of comfort he feels living there: "No one wants to feel isolated living in a neighborhood."

No matter the extent to which they socialize with other Latinos who live in Logan Square, the respondents report that their comfort level has been enhanced by the presence of large numbers of Hispanics in the neighborhood. They lack a context in which to place themselves at work (where many are the only, or one of few, Latinos), they have materially risen far beyond the circumstances in which they grew up (in Chicago or in Latin America), yet they still feel culturally and emotionally tied to "their" culture. The response is Logan Square, where one can both live a material life celebrated in the wider culture (as rehabbers, yuppies, or "Urban Pioneers") and readily acquire or consume the cultural markers (food, CDs from Puerto Rico, Afro-Cuban music at neighborhood nightspots, saints medallions at Milwaukee Avenue jewelers) that help them define themselves as part of a larger whole.

"It's good to have Spanish restaurants or Latin music nearby," said Harry, a forty-two-year-old real estate broker who grew up in a Chicago lakefront neighborhood. "I would hate to see those businesses leave, though I would probably stay in the neighborhood. But I don't want to live in an all-Anglo neighborhood." When Harry was growing up as part of a large Puerto Rican family in Lake View, there were many families like his in the area, though it was still majority "Anglo." His home on the east end of Logan Boulevard creates a similar social setting. His block is heavily gentrified, but there are still many Puerto Rican families nearby. Harry points out that another attraction of Logan Square today is the fact that many of his brothers and sisters also settled in the area after college. "It's good to be close to family," he says, a sentiment echoed by many respondents, whose families live in a string of North Side neighborhoods from Logan Square to Humboldt Park, Bucktown, Wicker Park, and Westtown.

One woman with a unique vantage point is Vilma, in her late forties, a Puerto Rican who grew up in Humboldt Park and is now a member of the city council. She and her husband, a Chicago firefighter, were likely the only people in Logan Square who were active members of both the Logan Square Neighborhood Association and Logan Square Preservation (LSP).

The Logan Square Neighborhood Association (LSNA) has been a "grassroots" community organization seeking to guarantee its largely Latino, working-class membership an opportunity to remain in Logan Square as gentrification works its market-driven "magic," especially in the northeast and north-central portions of the area. The group's publications and organized activities are frankly hostile to developers and major North Side real estate firms, which have shown great interest in Logan Square. Virtually everything the neighborhood association is, Logan Square Preservation is not. Many of its members are real estate brokers and agents. Its activities include boulevard beautification programs, organizing walking tours of houses that are prime examples of historic restoration, and communicating with city and county agencies about sanitation, trees, law enforcement, and other concerns.

The two organizations look across a divide of class, education, and ethnicity: both see a group of people trying to destroy "their" neighborhood, said Vilma. LSNA sees LSP as making the neighborhood more expensive. LSP sees LSNA as too "sixties," not in tune with the reality of the area.

"No one will say so, but LSP's goal means fewer working-class residents in Logan Square. But I don't think it's a racial thing, necessarily. They feel they've invested so much time and energy and money. I do sympathize with LSNA. They're saying the neighborhood is for the people, and that you need to give people the opportunity to stay." The two competing sets of ideas about the same piece of land make Vilma pessimistic about the future.

Middle-class Hispanics are inevitably class straddlers, especially when they are owners. They perceive the value of their property as tied to the future of "Anglo" investment in the area. They are thus economically tethered to whites of European ancestry, while they maintain strong emotional bonds to Hispanics in Logan Square. When the interests of one group conflict with the interests of another, must the straddlers make a choice?

The strong, stated desires of the respondents to teach their children Spanish, to live in an area in which Spanish is still an important language of commerce, to live near family, and to remain in Logan Square may demonstrate a late-twentieth-century attitude toward assimilation into the American Dream far different from that which opened the century. They appear not to be worrying over their class straddling, just living it.

At the other end of the social and economic continuum, yet living near these young, ambitious, and successful people, are young Latinos—boys in particular—who are convinced that America will never provide for them.

Over the years I got to know some of them well: They were street gang members, sentinels watching their territory, a decaying patch of urban streetscape, and waiting to die. One cold March day, I stood with members of the Spanish Cobras street gang, watching the cars coming and going. "We're all just niggaz out here. All we got to do is be out here, protect what's ours, and protect our families." They were the worst nightmare of the people busily scraping their oak parquet floors and shining up the brass on their antique light fixtures just a mile or so away. The boys, ranging in age from fifteen to nineteen years, said they had to resist frequent threats to their street. "Gangbangers from other 'nations' [gang alliances] can't just come through here disrespecting us. If they do, we might have to show them what's up. We might have to cruise through their territory and take somebody down."

The formalized language of disrespect and offense, colors and symbols, family and block and honor gives the scene a touch of unreality. Several of these boys are armed. They talk of being ready to face bullets, or unleash them on others, provoked by the ritual of packing into a car and flashing hand signs out a window. It is sad, even silly, but in no way a game.

I have watched too many times as a shopkeeper or homeowner sprays down the sidewalk, hoping to wash away the congealed blood that's stained the concrete, while police evidence technicians begin building the elaborate blind alleys their investigation will soon walk down. I have walked with homicide detectives as they've tried to work their way, door to door, as a block full of families develops amnesia.

The world of American Latinos, brought to you courtesy of your late local news, is populated by the hard and tragic young men who believe in little except their need to enforce their code on their block. They live among shuttered factories and empty warehouses. School becomes an irrelevant inconvenience before they are in their teens. I could have told the boys they weren't "niggaz" and tried to convince them that getting low-wage jobs was better than the life they were living. I doubt they'd have bought it. So we stood in a cold wind, talking about their futures, their enemies and rivals. They were having better luck convincing me of their bleak prospects than I was transmitting ideas about a better way to live. Amid the sagging tenements, broken water mains, double-digit joblessness, and occasional violent rage, their lives made sense to them.

America is going to have to see these young men and reach them somehow. With America's zest for imprisonment and "juvenile predator laws," the Spanish Cobras watch their own frontiers shrinking, but new recruits always seem ready to take up the empty spots on the corner opened up by death, imprisonment, or drift from the gang life into low-wage work. These boys know their country does not know them, even if they spray their names in ten-foot letters on train stations and office buildings. "We're all just niggaz out here." One nervously touches the gun in his pocket for reassurance, scanning the faces in the passing car, waiting.

Still strangers, they are products of the lead-poisoned soil of the American city. We ignore them at our own peril.

Chapter 11

Side Trip–Miami

For those not yet so numb as to be incapable of rage, the contrasts visible from the highways heading into downtown Miami from the airport are brought into high relief by its pool table–flat topography. You can sit *this close* and still be far away, watching others make money or having the fun that money buys. A homeless man can sit by the waterfront and look straight ahead at pleasure craft and cruise ships, and turn to the right and see the gleaming bank towers built in the days when drug money and flight capital were pouring into the city.

From a Miami sidewalk at the edge of downtown, in a city where few people walk, a pedestrian can watch the new arena for the Miami Heat rise from a flat patch of land at the water's edge. There's activity all around. A train takes a lazy curve, heading north out of downtown. Traffic backs up, waiting to speed across the MacArthur Causeway to the frantically gentrifying Art Deco gulch of South Beach. At one edge of the neighborhood, trucks load up to start delivering the Miami *Herald* and the Spanish-language *El Nuevo Herald* across South Florida. The metallic-iced wedding cake of the NationsBank tower is flanked by the fanciful and postmodern landmarks of its skyline. Hardworking single-engine planes drag ad banners over the beaches to the east, hawking suntan oil and a new Bacardi rum drink. Private jets swing low over the neighborhood, heading for a landing just south of downtown. Tour buses swoop down from the expressways and skirt the edge of the neighborhood, heading directly for the causeways that carry tourists to Miami Beach. Miami is unique in many ways, but it is also one possible future for many cities. From the old neighborhood of the oldest cities, I have come on this side trip to consider the future.

The light-rail system on rubber wheels quietly loops toward downtown. The Omni Mall stands just past the neighborhood's edge, and shoppers alighting from public transit to enter the mall pick their way past men and women sleeping on the sidewalk, curled into the fetal position on the heat-shimmering sidewalks in the middle of the afternoon. The distant ocean-view towers loom in full view of the perpetually low-rise and low-rent world of Overtown.

Overtown and nearby Liberty City have been the scene of riots in recent decades. Tempers boiled over in 1980, after an all-white jury acquitted four white Miami police officers in the beating death of a black insurance executive. Eighteen died and four hundred were injured in the riots that followed. Again in 1989, after marinating in economic resentment, simmering in concrete apartment blocks with no air-conditioning, and then flash-frying with the final perceived outrage over being victimized at the hands of an increasingly Latino police force, riots began in Overtown when a black motorcyclist was shot in the back by a Latino police officer.

In early 1997 Overtown made its way into the public mind again when an armored truck had an accident on the expressway that arches above the neighborhood. Cash and coin spilled out onto the streets below, setting off a frantic chase for the gently falling booty. Newscasts, forever on the lookout for thirty-second morality plays, got maximum mileage out of this one. The story gave rock-jawed anchormen an opportunity to raise an eyebrow, tut-tut over the paupers who did not turn in their windfalls, and celebrate the plucky Ragged Dick who brought back eighty-five cents and won his class a trip to Disney World. The difference with today's honest lad is that Horatio Alger's Dick had a chance to have his honesty recognized by a benevolent stranger who becomes a mentor. Miami's lad had his life portrayed in condescending detail by a media horde that swooped down for a day, then disappeared to let our hero melt into the unknowable masses of Overtown once again.

There's something positively Caribbean about Overtown, even if it's only the stereotyped Caribbean from a novel or a network newscast. The sun blasts down on near-empty streets, poorly shod children play in abandoned lots, and stray dogs and scarecrow men stagger from one shady spot to another as the sun slowly arcs through the sky. For block after block, there's no place to buy lunch, or a Coke, or a newspaper.

I was on foot, curious to see the neighborhood I had zoomed over several times in an automobile, a place so close to the action, and so profoundly separate from it. I finally found a place to buy a Coke. A woman sharing a laugh with the old man behind the counter turned to me and asked, "Do you know your way 'round here?" When I said I did not I was told, "If someone come up to you with some conversatin' don't say nothin'. Just keep on walkin'."

Nearby, the sidewalk overhang of an old commercial building became a refuge from the sun for a dozen sleeping men who occasionally took turns getting up from their makeshift beds for a piss in a nearby lot. The swirling odor of urine, *lots* of urine, rose up from the bushes like waves of heat. The men walked back to their spots with the loose-limbed gait of the perpetually stoned, all skinny limbs and makeshift clothes, callused ankles and unlaced shoes. As they approach, they might at first appear belligerent, as if walking right at you. They're really tacking down the sidewalk, swinging to port, correcting to starboard, and brushing a shoulder as they pass by.

Originally, I was going to keep on following the Metro line north, on foot, until I got tired. Then I would get on the train. It suddenly seemed the wise thing to get off the deserted streets. The place hadn't seemed threatening until just that moment.

There are a few carpet stores in view, taking advantage of the large square footage and low rent in the midst of nonstop "going out of business sales." The cardboard signs promise "genuine bukharas, dhurries, Chinese rugs." A few tackle-and-boat–gear shops remind you of Overtown's proximity to the booming harbor and pleasure boat industry nearby. This appears to be the total legitimate economic activity, just a few hundred yards from the Miami skyline, beloved by politicians and the real estate developers who buy both buildings and politicians. At the neighborhood's edge are sand-colored condominium towers, with terraces facing the sea. The "old" Miami downtown peters out just before Overtown, the fantasies of its Beaux Arts facades and opulent rococo doorways beckoning absent people from an empty street to come inside.

Plenty has been written about the international Miami of the late twentieth century, a pastel-colored entrepôt gathering newcomers from throughout the Caribbean basin into America's New World City, the Capital of Latin America. I don't want to add to that cliché-ridden pile. There *is* plenty that's modern and future-looking about Miami, but the future it promises, in some places, draws more information from *Blade Runner* and *RoboCop* than it does from the latest star-studded opening of yet another celebrity-owned restaurant in Miami Beach.

What is very up-to-date about Miami is the way urban life has finally transcended place, in its allocation of resources, space, and investment, and slipped the surly bonds of Earth. Even in downtown Los Angeles, the supposed epitome of auto-enslaved urban life, there is the occasional street not in full view of a freeway. In downtown Miami, the expressways are everywhere, curling and swooping through and leaping over the narrow waterways, dominating the metropolitan landscape with the giant footprint of their interchanges. The streets of downtown are full of highway signs, guiding the motorist to the nearest ramp, promising an escape from streetlights, stop signs, and the mundane world the driver is briefly forced to watch at thirty miles an hour.

Once upon a time, a place like Overtown would have gotten the attention of the downtown worthies who made decisions about such things at their weekday lunches at private clubs or discussing business over a round of golf. So much land, right next to the core of downtown, would have been too important, too valuable, simply to write off. Overtown would have been considered a blemish on the face of the city, a place to be transformed by infusions of capital and, eventually, wholesale removal of its current inhabitants.

Even without a "commission" or a "downtown revival district," places like Overtown might have gotten some economic attention in the old, accidental way, as in many other cities: Restaurateurs seeking cheaper space adjacent to downtown, institutional users, and businesspeople who like the proximity but don't need to be in the thick of things might have overcome their distaste for Overtown's residents and begun an economic incursion.

But Miami's downtown sent no such shoots into this section. Here downtown just ends. A cordon sanitaire of parking lots covers its exposed flank. Neither the impulse to transform, which has marked so much of modern urban capitalism, nor the fear that the blight will be contagious has pushed capital to take action. That kind of intensive care is no longer necessary. Overtown is now just a small piece of necrotic tissue on the urban body. Toughened. Insensate. Sealed off. Past help. One now must take care only that the tissue death doesn't spread . . . but what if it does? No matter. Like the lizard that drops its tail when seized by it, Miami can simply continue to grow in a new direction.

The life this kind of city creates makes it possible to stop looking at the urban landscape as a tightly integrated group of zones that are in a constant state of interaction, according to function. Now, from behind the wheel of a car, your day can easily consist of experiencing little pieces of desirable consumption, pleasure, or commerce. Then zip off to the next little piece of life waiting for you somewhere else.

The men who were making these calculations about Overtown have decided to turn Miami itself into Overtown writ large. The city that launched the creation of a wealthy metropolitan area has now been left by metropolitan Miami to fend for itself. Though residents, journalists, chamber of commerce types, and visitors from around the world use the shorthand "Miami," the actual city of Miami has become a small and shrinking share of the metro population. Miami University isn't in Miami; it's in Coral Gables. Miami Beach isn't in Miami; it's a separate municipality of one hundred thousand people across Biscayne Bay. Planes descending into Miami International Airport don't land in Miami, and the Miami Dolphins don't play in Miami.

Capitalizing on the name, and the associations with sun and fun, the money-spinning capital goods of "Miami" are safely outside the city; and just over three hundred thousand people try to keep the place going, after municipal greed and corruption have pushed it to the edge of bankruptcy.

Miami is the fourth-poorest city in the country. Now just over one hundred years old, it recently survived a referendum on its dissolution. A dissolved Miami could see its poorest districts, like Overtown, become unincorporated portions of wealthy Dade County, while its most success-ful neighborhoods reincorporated into new municipalities. During the campaign for a dissolution referendum, it became clear that the best-off Miamians, living in enclaves like Coconut Grove, were the most likely to want out. That demographic reality may not provide enough votes to put up a CLOSED sign on Miami's city hall, but it does make it very unlikely that those citizens who wanted out will be willing to dig very deep to help shore up Miami's sagging tax base, even after the city held on to life after the plebiscite.

When I interviewed the mayor of Miami, Joe Carrollo, in late 1996, he was working hard to discourage the referendum supporters and talk up Miami's continued existence.

"Miami's going to be back real soon. We're going to be out of this fi-nancial mess a lot quicker than anyone expects," Carrollo said. "We're go-ing to be able to lay the financial foundation strong enough to make sure that Miami is around another hundred years."

His optimism was touching, if not altogether warranted. When we spoke, the city manager and the finance director had just been arrested, and the mayor had found that with an annual budget of just $275 million, he was short by almost a quarter—$68 million—of what he needed. He had to cut back on garbage collection and other services. Miami's bonds had just been dropped to junk status, and borrowing the city's way out of that hole had never really been one of Carrollo's viable options. Higher taxes could not be paid by the poorest citizens, who make the city expen-sive to run, and would encourage further flight by the "haves," who knew that lower taxes, better schools, and more people like themselves were waiting just over the city line. But "safer streets" were not prominently featured on the list of attractions in the suburbs, either; the city of Miami crime rate is just over twice that of the outlying Dade County metropolitan area, but that's the lowest crime differential between an urban core and its suburbs of any city in America.

Mayor Carrollo was turned out of office by former mayor Xavier Suarez, whose unpredictable antics, public temper tantrums, and dictatorial management style became a daily soap opera in the local press. Miami never got to see where a new Suarez era at the helm would lead. A judge overturned the election results after gross irregularities were found, returning Carrollo to office.

Now that Pandora's-Box-on-the–Gulf Stream has opened, it shows no sign of swinging shut. Miami's city commissioner, Humberto Hernandez, was fighting legal action for mortgage fraud at the same time he asked a judge to be named interim mayor until the Carrollo-Suarez race was finally settled. Hernandez won reelection, retaking the seat he lost after his earlier legal battles. While he still maintains his innocence of any wrongdoing, the late Governor Lawton Chiles removed him from office by executive order.

Port of Miami Director Carmen Lunetta was indicted in mid-1998 on federal charges of embezzlement. Investigators say Lunetta used the port as a personal bank, siphoning off $1.5 million in public funds for golf, maintaining his yacht, and making contributions to the Democratic National Committee. Also in 1998, County Commissioner Bruce Kaplan had to resign after a no-contest plea to filing false financial statements. Part of his settlement was a promise not to seek reelection. According to the state's attorney's office of Miami-Dade, 263 public officials have been hit with criminal charges, and 171 have been convicted.

The chamber of commerce is planning an "ethics summit," while the recently reorganized Miami-Dade County government has appointed a new "ethics czar." All of which is pretty discouraging for the men and women who hold the metropolitan purse strings, since voters appear very unlikely to approve the kind of tax increases that might be requested to put the city and the county on stronger financial footing. It all makes the decision not to end Miami's existence an even more audacious one.

Not letting Miami dissolve has taken on the distinct whiff of ethnic politics. The Cubans are the dominant ethnic group in Dade County and in the city of Miami. Dade's growth and Miami's decline have both come as

Cubans have ascended to economic, social, and political clout after more than three hundred thousand arrived in South Florida in the years after the Cuban revolution. Miami is the largest municipality in the county and carries almost mystical importance for Cubans as their safe haven after leaving Castro's Cuba. It is where they succeeded, grasped the American Dream, and showed the rest of the country their economic prowess. The loss of Miami is a loss to Cubans, in the view of Milan Dluhy, an economics professor at Florida International University. "The Cubans have just got power. They will say, 'Now you want to take it away from us?'" Cubans can't let Miami fall while they're in charge, while blacks could benefit from a change. Blacks are better represented in the Dade employment rolls than those of Miami.

In 1996 local elections, the last black city commissioner lost to Cuban-American Humberto Hernandez, who hit the airwaves when the bankruptcy talk and dissolution petitions began, visiting the influential Spanish-language radio stations to appeal to Spanish-speaking voters against the abolition of Miami government. American-born blacks in Miami are now facing challenges from Haitian émigrés, who are also gaining political strength in South Florida.

Miami's current problems are partly of its own making, and partly a result of the structural relationship between the city and its surrounding areas. Each added mile of sprawl weakens the link between each outlying citizen and the historic urban core. Miami might have been the engine that pushed the development of the vast South Florida metropolitan area. But like the boys with progeria—the aging disease—the city of Miami has grown up, out, and into redundancy in just a century. Ft. Lauderdale, Hialeah, Miami Beach, and Coral Gables may still need a healthy Miami (the new mayor of Dade County also dismisses talk of the city's dissolution), but something important happens when the people in these places *believe* they no longer need the historic urban core.

"This is the northernmost banana republic in the hemisphere," says Jerry Haar, of the University of Miami's North-South Center. "The city has failed to attract business that could create jobs. The schools stink, the roads stink. Whether you live in Coconut Grove or Liberty City, you're going to be unhappy."

The city is a victim of the centerlessness it helped pioneer for Sun Belt America. The once tight and vital relationship between space and place has been demolished. It doesn't matter where Overtown is. Freeways create a simple bypass, and this part of Miami's body is permanently starved of the invigorating blood of commerce. The people there can also be written off, as long as citizens are willing to pay the benefits that sustain the poor at subsistence level and put up with the occasional explosion of riots. The riots in Overtown and Liberty City are meaningless to the people who zoom from the house to the health club, from the strip malls to the beach, and from the gleaming towers of the nearby downtown to faraway suburban homes.

In spite of this, Miami has done some things right. Unusual for a Sun Belt city, it has built three interlinked transit systems connecting the vast, far-flung suburbs to the central city: there's the Metromover, a "people mover," which loops around the downtown and is perfect for the "on-and-off" running of errands or meeting with business people at only twenty-five cents a ride; there's Metrorail, a conventional, urban rapid-transit system, running north and west from downtown; and there's Tri-Rail, a commuter rail system connecting the three metropolitan South Florida counties—Dade, Broward, and Palm Beach.

When trying to go from the downtown to the far north of the city one weekend afternoon, I was at first puzzled by the odd ways the rail systems connected, and where they went. Then I noticed that on all three conveyances, my fellow passengers were poor, foreign, old, or all three. My partners on the railcars, weaving in and out of expressway rights-of-way, were the people left behind by the go-go lifestyles of the new Miamians. The Miami generation that built businesses and fortunes on the rapid growth of the metropolitan area has decamped to the suburbs; they now talk about how nice particular neighborhoods used to be, the parks they can no longer walk in, and the schools they can no longer allow their children to attend. The ambitious and successful people who have poured into Miami since the 1970s have outgrown the charming but small houses of their scuffling youth, and no longer have any use for the vast, landlocked empire rolling out from the northern outskirts of downtown and marching west until the Everglades make them stop.

Out my window I could see people zipping to their next appointment at seventy-five miles per hour and the trailer parks, the tiny homes of poured concrete and corrugated tin—the sprawling, steaming neighborhoods where live the women who make the beds in the hotels, the men who bus tables in the South Beach restaurants, and the smiling twenty-somethings in the McDonald's hats.

The white, the middle-aged, and the middle class don't make much use of the public ways of getting around, and the suspicion of public transport and the perceived danger lurking in urban Miami keeps their kids out of the Metro systems, too. The deep penetration of high-speed vehicular traffic into every necessary environment has made the car a vital fifth limb and dictated patterns of development almost unbelievably inconvenient for everyone else.

I was on a fool's errand to Joe Robbie Stadium—now called ProPlayer Park—home to the baseball Marlins and the football Dolphins—for a baseball game. I reached the end of the line—"Golden Glades"—the ultimate in Sun Belt public transportation. It was a place that was no place. There was no residential area in sight, no commercial area visible beyond a "rent-a-space" place just beyond the highway. The Tri-Rail station stands at the edge of an enormous interchange, with soaring ramps swapping altitude and autos. I knew I was still some distance from the ballpark, but this was the closest I was going to get without private conveyance. The rail station offered intermodal transport, with transfers to four bus lines, none of which went near the park, and free weekend parking for private cars, neither of which helped the carless.

No wonder I got such odd looks when I asked a passerby, "Can I walk out of here?" The first answer was "To where?"—as if the possibility of walking anywhere was an idea that had never occurred to him. When I got to the edge of the bus station and the parking lot, I realized there really was no way to "walk" out of here. I could see the lights of ProPlayer Park in the distance. A bus driver confirmed my suspicion. "It's way too far to walk. You got to take a cab." I had ridden three different rail systems to get as far as Golden Glades, and was still far from my destination.

Granted, the option of renting a car to go to the ball game had been there all along. Earlier that day, the concierge in my downtown hotel had told me that going to the game by bus would take me two hours. He told me going by train was too complicated (and I was now in the midst of finding out he was right). And he'd also told me that a cab to the game was going to run about thirty dollars. "Why don't you rent a car?" He was trying to be helpful and hadn't counted on the notion that deep in the soul of an urbanite lurks a resistance to the idea of renting a car for a single, short round-trip. By the time I had learned for myself just how difficult it was to get around Miami without a car, traversing the city on foot all day to learn about how thoroughly engineered the place was to four-wheel travel, it was too late. By 3:10 P.M., I stood before the concierge a beaten man, in effect crying uncle. Where was the nearest rental place?

"If you had come just a little earlier, I could have gotten you a car. But the last place open in the city closes at three o'clock."

"What? In the entire city of Miami, at three o'clock on a Saturday afternoon, there's nowhere to rent any automobile at all?"

"Nope. You can get one at the airport."

There was no bus to the airport for another hour. I then reviewed my choices. (1) Continue, bull-headed, to go to the Marlins game by public transportation. (2) Wait fifty minutes for a one-hour ride to the airport to rent a car to go to the game. (3) Take a thirty-dollar cab ride to rent a car in order to *save* thirty dollars on a cab (and spend fifty dollars for the car once you add the one-day fee, gas, and endless tiny taxes).

I had chosen (1) and was a better man for it.

Throughout the game, a less-than-classic Marlins contest in the cavernous football stadium—Charo led the audience through several seventh-inning versions of the Macarena—I checked my watch. Half an hour . . . fifteen minutes . . . then no time at all until the last train from Golden Glades, back toward the city. The numbers didn't work. Fifteen-dollar cab ride to the train, to avoid a thirty-dollar cab ride to the hotel? Relax. Enjoy the game. Have another beer.

A happy crowd made its way through the exits and out to the oceans of parking lots that separated the stadium from the nearest main street. Apart from the comfortable use of Spanish all around me, this was like countless other stadiums around the country in its placelessness. After you left the anywhere ballpark, you hit the wide boulevards of

Nowheresville . . . franchise food, franchise retail, billboards for the local morning radio wild man—increasingly, even *he* is franchised.

The next day, the noise from a tremendous commotion drew me to my twenty-first-story hotel window. I looked down from my terrace at nine squad cars, canine units, cops everywhere, and an enormous crowd spilling from the next-door convention center, as another crowd tried to surge in from the sidewalk. Once downstairs, I exchanged pleasantries with the concierge and asked, "What's up?"

"It's a citizenship ceremony."

"Really? All these people for a citizenship ceremony?"

"There are three of them every Sunday."

Stunning. I wandered through the crowd as expectant families in their best outfits and every hair in place jockeyed for room by the entrance, and happily chatting clusters made their way to waiting cars (citizens for five minutes and they were way ahead of me on the need for a car) as they showed off their certificates. They were Ethiopians in traditional garb, with their high foreheads and almond eyes; Central Americans with the unmistakable mark of the Maya on their features and build; Russians of two generations; Pakistanis, Indians, Chinese, Nigerians—breaking from Gujarati or Bengali, Mandarin and Amharic to say "excuse me" in their new lingua franca.

For many, especially those with an education and aspirations, the American road will not lead from the city into the sunny promised land of the suburbs. Increasingly, immigrant journeys are starting in the suburbs and staying there. The Cuban doctors who drove cabs and college professors who washed dishes belong to history now. They changed the course of Miami history. They may find themselves at the helm, as the ship breaks apart in the heavy seas at the end of the twentieth century.

Chapter 12

Looking Ahead to the Next City

The city has stumbled through half a century, buffeted by a conspiracy without a plan, ganged up on by diverse cultural and economic forces, and in too many cases making its own problems worse. In 1950 the old-time American city looked down on the rest of America from near-Olympian heights, at the zenith of its political and economic power. Where does it stand now?

As we've seen, in the contemporary challenges and the recent past of many American cities, the diagnostic report would be mixed. Cities continue to decline in population, yes, but at a much slower rate than in the twenty-five years after the war. Some of the cities, like Philadelphia, may yet lose a couple of hundred thousand more residents before reaching a rough equilibrium, at which income and obligations are in better balance.

Public school leaders like Rudy Crew in New York, Arlene Ackerman in Washington, D.C., and Paul Vallas in Chicago have begun the long, slow march back to the kind of public credibility their systems need to survive. Make no mistake, the knives are out for public education. As the broad future of public schooling is fought over in the measured cadences and formal English of the federal courts, hundreds of thousands of families are making fight-or-flight decisions based on the quality of the schools in their communities.

Public housing is trying to become what it always should have been—smaller, less isolated, more economically diverse. For every demolition of old high-rises the current secretary of Housing and Urban Development, Andrew Cuomo, attends, he also heads to a ribbon cutting for a new low-rise, town house, or scattered-site housing.

Crime is down. Job creation is up. Some of the most glaring problems of urban America are finally being addressed, just as some cities come dangerously close to the point of no return. A few new downtown employers, a downtown people mover, or a fancy new atrium hotel can't hide an increasingly obvious trend: suburban America is growing more and more comfortable using the city—for employment, entertainment, education—but will not move in.

Many of the cities covered in this book are so desperate for economic activity that they can't be too fussy about that difficult truth. For now, the thinking goes, let's get them in here and spending money for as many hours as we can manage, before they head home over the city line. But hungry cities acting as the entertainer for suburban America just don't go far enough. A resident, in a thousand little ways, spins off economic activity unmatched by the casual visitor who visits your attraction, buys a T-shirt and a frozen yogurt, and heads home.

In an ideal city, a chief executive would have the luxury of working with private business to answer all a city's needs—for downtown development and neighborhood projects, for balanced development featuring jobs in manufacturing, services, and high-end "knowledge work"—but many cities will enter the new century with only a weak hand to play. With few offers on the table and too many other cities chasing the same investments, some cities may find themselves ready to fall for almost anything. As many of the cities in this book have found, beggars can't be choosers.

That neediness—the problems created by decades of abandonment and decline—tears away the veil draped by press agents and travel writers and optimistic mayors. A run of good news makes it easy to concentrate heavily on the positive (just take a look at a pile of recent press clippings about New York's "comeback"), and make believe the negative isn't there. When things are going badly, the cities are seen more for what they are: big, hungry monsters. Billions are spent getting food, water, apparel, and other manufactured items into cities, and what they spin off is garbage, sewage, and smog. When times are good, and the cities are spinning off jobs and pumping an electric jolt into the culture, less time is spent dwelling on the dreary.

The good news is that the current crop of big-city mayors includes some of the most talented and skillful chief executives ever to serve at the same time: New York's Rudolph Giuliani; Philadelphia's Ed Rendell; Cleveland's Michael White; Chicago's Rich Daley; Kansas City's Emmanuel Cleaver; Milwaukee's John Norquist; San Francisco's Willie Brown; Detroit's Dennis Archer; and Los Angeles's Richard Riordan. Even Oakland, the poor relation in the Bay Area, left behind in the economic boom gold-plating San Francisco and San Jose, has attracted no less a national name than Jerry Brown, the two-term governor of California. The bad news is that this remarkable class of mayors has less and less to work with, in the way of an industrial base, a tax base, transportation networks, and private investment.

Mayors still delight in posing with vast plaster models that show a large swath of the city remade by massive redevelopment projects. The difference now is that with much-degraded corporate bases, a less-interested federal government, and better-organized community groups, getting that plaster into brick, mortar, and glass is a lot tougher. And by the way, that's probably a good thing. No longer being able to rebuild acres of downtown real estate with a wave of your mayoral wand forces the projects to be better designed and their boosters to line up more and more diverse interests before they move ahead.

In other words, a mayor can do almost everything right and still not restore his or her city's fortunes.

One of the brightest spots in the urban scene is the lower level of violent crime . . . at least at first glance. There has been an unquestionable, generalized decline in crime nationwide and in some of the metropolitan areas that have contributed heavily to the statistics in years past. The star performer is New York, where violent crime dropped 77 percent in the five years from 1991 to 1996. In those same years the numbers were down by 54 percent in Dallas, 47 percent in Los Angeles, and 38 percent in Boston, the city with the lowest violent crime rate among major American cities to begin with.

But the good news hasn't been felt everywhere: In Washington, D.C., the crime rate actually rose, if only a tiny 0.4 percent in those same five years. Even in those places where the drops have been dramatic, the new stats play to a tough audience. Urbanites and suburbanites alike often say they don't believe the numbers are real.

By the late 1990s, the national murder rate was down to late-1960s levels, declining right along with other serious crimes. The murder rate for 1996 was 7.4 incidences for every 100,000 people, 17 percent lower than in 1992, and yielding fewer than 20,000 killings for the first time in the 1990s. It turns out the answers you get from smart people about why this is so are as politically divided as the experts themselves. The "get tough" school talks of the need for more "SuperMax" (a higher form of maximum-security prison) construction, trying more juveniles as adults, and eliminating a new urban class of "superpredator." They warn that we are experiencing a demographic accident that should not lead to comfort or complacency. It is pointed out that a new, larger cohort of teenagers is now percolating in America's elementary and middle schools. The teens will enter their high-crime years at the beginning of the new century, when the nonstop good news about violent crime, it is predicted, will inevitably slow down.

This school gives almost no credit to a different policing philosophy, more patrol officers on the street, or a lower social tolerance for low-level deviance that leads city residents to work more closely with police departments to rein in street life. Demography is destiny, they say, without explaining why crime rates did not soar through the roof the last time a big new stream of teenagers started heading for adulthood, in the early 1960s.

This is not to say an aging population has no effect on crime rates. A smaller overall fraction of the population in peak crime years plays a part in your risk of being a crime victim, as well as the incarceration of more and more people in this age group, for longer periods of time. The exaggerated feelings of vulnerability to crime among the white middle class has helped remake the urban landscape in the last fifty years. But that feeling of vulnerability does not square with who really suffers from crime. In a country in which 70 percent of the people call themselves white, only 49 percent of crime victims are actually white. The black population of the United States floats around 12 to 13 percent; crime victims are black 49 percent of the time.

Thanks to American television (and especially the news), with its unquenchable thirst for norming random, freaky crime, citizens in all kinds of communities feel their chances of becoming a victim of crime are far higher than they actually are. The conviction that something terrible is about to happen drives the scare talk of crime, dangerous urban youth, and dangerous communities. In all categories of violent crime, more than 50 percent of victims knew their assailants, and 30 percent of the women victims were killed by their husbands or boyfriends.

There is nothing inconsistent in the real world of the United States, in reading headline after headline about safer cities, and still working off the imaginary realm built in your head over a much longer time: a world of muggings and rapes, drive-by shootings, and wild-wired freebasers who need to kill you to earn their next hit.

And after all the successful reductions in violent crime, there's another thing to keep in mind. Violent crime is still 13 percent higher than it was in 1987.

The modern American city is a sumo ring, with heavy players stamping the floor, looking fierce, and pushing other fat boys around. In the last twenty years one wrestler, municipal government, has been on a diet. For every pound municipal governments lose, big corporations bulk up. When the government is weak and the corporate players have more options, when community groups are silenced by chronic need and there is no line outside the mayor's office with developers holding blueprints, then the city finds it less and less possible to say no. When the city knows it has a lot to offer investors, it can hold out for a better deal, look for a higher bid. But underneath some of the negotiations going on in late-twentieth-century urban America is a nagging insecurity: "If we don't say yes, they'll just go someplace else." Remember that relationship the next time you watch an ill-advised blockbuster project rising on a surprising piece of land, or poor people's housing falls to make room for rich people's cars.

One city that looked at that model and said, "no thanks" is Pittsburgh. Once the country's smoking foundry, Pittsburgh has shrunk to 360,000 people from 676,000 in 1950. Unlike many other older cities, Pittsburgh today is not losing urban-core residents to thriving suburbs. The metropolitan population is still declining, down to 1.33 million from 1.45 million in 1980. Enter the Regional Renaissance Initiative, a plan to build two downtown stadiums, for the National Football League's Steelers and major league baseball's Pirates. The plan also included a comprehensive convention center expansion and completion of a long-promised cultural district, including theaters and rehearsal space for performing arts groups.

All the voters had to do was agree to a 0.5 percent sales tax for seven years, which the initiative's backers said would raise seven hundred million dollars, and cost just thirty-five to forty-five dollars per family. Pittsburgh's mayor, Tom Murphy, called the vote a critical one. "This would put us in a position to compete with many other cities. Tangibly, it could lead to several billion dollars of investment commitments." Seeking to head off those critics who assured voters that a better plan would be proposed if this one failed, Rick Stafford, the executive director of the Allegheny Conference on Community Development, was grave: "There is no Plan B. Those who say there is don't know what they're talking about."

Yet the vote failed two to one, even losing in the city, where the biggest share of the new construction was planned. The Pirates and the Steelers still play in Pittsburgh, and as of this writing there is no plan for new stadiums or a franchise move.

Few cities seem prepared to say no. Don't look for a lot of Pittsburghs in your newspapers. Whatever tomorrow's cities look like, one thing is certain: the skyline will include fabulously expensive sports facilities, paid for, whenever possible, by the taxpayers of the area for wealthy team owners. Now that a diverse crop of downtowns has been hollowed out by the urban decay of the last generation, mayors and city councils are less and less able to tell owners to look for their own money and to assemble their own parcels of land, for fear the beckoning suburbs will win. As you walk out of Orioles' Park at Camden Yards, one of the most celebrated of the new generation of downtown ballparks, you will see the new football stadium of the Baltimore Ravens. In Cleveland, a massive park for football is on its way, getting ready for a new NFL franchise (if you want to watch the Browns, you have to visit Baltimore's new football field).

Georgia Frontiere, owner of the Los Angeles Rams, got struggling St. Louis off the hook after it built a new domed stadium by moving in with her nomadic team. Michael McCaskey of the Chicago Bears has regular, showy meetings with suburban mayors to remind Rich Daley that he is ready to move his legendary franchise and doesn't want to pay to build his own stadium. Maps of neighborhoods south and west of the Loop appear in the local papers every few months, the multiblock shadow of a domed stadium laid here and there the way a shopper may hold up a garment to her chin and say, "What do you think?"

Bostonians in Southie went to war with Mayor Michael Menino over a new park for the Red Sox, while Mayor Giuliani seems to get a map a week proposing a billion-dollar-plus stadium and infrastructure plan for the West Side of Manhattan as New Jersey governor Christine Todd Whitman beckons. New Jersey has already waved new stadium sites under the nose of Yankees principal owner George Steinbrenner. Baseball parks are planned for northern Virginia (hoping to woo the unprofitable Montreal Expos or the struggling Pirates) and blighted land near Capitol Hill in Washington, D.C.

Jane Jacobs, the author of the landmark of modern urban theory, *The Death and Life of Great American Cities,* the woman who told Americans to remember the city and all that was good about urban life—"cities are not disposable"—is right: Land cannot be destroyed or created. When Sears moves the back office out of Chicago's West Side and the front office out of the country's tallest skyscraper to a faraway suburb, and Westinghouse, now renamed CBS Inc., leaves Pittsburgh after more than a century there, and when the Cleveland Browns leave Cleveland, and a million

New Yorkers move to Long Island, the places they once did business in, or called home, do not disappear. The land remains, either degraded by earlier use or as a constant reminder of sagging fortunes.

As cities worry about the land inside their borders, Americans restlessly move on, developing new land elsewhere and searching for "solitude." The author of *The Rating Guide to Life in America's Small Cities,* Scott Thomas, told me, "There are Gallup polls going all the way back to the forties, in which people in cities were asked, 'Who do you think has it better, the people in the city or the people on the farm?' And the answer was always, three to one, that the people on the farm had it better. Before the situation of urban stress in this country, people idealized the countryside. Modern technology is making it easier for people to follow through on that feeling."

But Henry Cisneros, secretary of Housing and Urban Development in the first Clinton administration, seems genuinely upbeat about the prospects of many cities, even some of those that have become synonymous with blight and decline. When I suggested that lack of demand for emptied urban land and the shifting of the economic orbit away from older cities sent some past the point of no return, he made a case for urban renewal, 1990s style. "My theory is that the crisis of the American city was not really a crisis of urban function, as much as it was a crisis of the American economy. What happened was that the cities, as recently as the 1950s, were home to American manufacturing.

"It was not unusual, if you look at the employment numbers for cities in the 1950s, even early sixties, to have 30, 35, 25 percent of the jobs in manufacturing–I mean, clearly the importer of capital, the engine that drove the whole urban economy.

"As America lost its manufacturing base, it went offshore. It went to the suburbs. It went to the South. Some industries went out of existence. No entity in American life was harder hit by the loss of our manufacturing base and economic preeminence than the cities. Because, you see, the capital was mobile. The jobs were mobile. The plants were mobile. The companies were mobile. But the cities were not. They're fixed stock.

"And the cities were not only left without the economic life, but they were left with the residues–the empty sites, the toxically impeded land, et cetera.

"Now, over the last twenty-five years, we've seen a dramatic transformation of the American economy. Most observers would today say the American economy is back on its way to healthiness—the automobile industry, technology, telecommunications, new forms of manufacturing, global exports. But it's not happening in the cities. The city of Detroit is a basket case, but *metropolitan* Detroit, still the world headquarters for automobile engineering, is sending 747 aircrafts full of automotive engineers around the world.

"Detroit once had two million people in the city limits. It now has one million. It once had fifteen automobile plants. It now has three. Detroit is not once again going to be a city of two million people with fifteen automobile plants. But as the American economy has re-rationalized itself, Detroit has now had time, twenty years or so, to re-rationalize itself in the context of these new economic realities. And so, in the last year, General Motors has moved its world headquarters to downtown Detroit, to the Renaissance Center. It's decided to build a new stadium for the Tigers. The Empowerment Zone has attracted two billion dollars worth of investment. There are new home-ownership neighborhoods—two hundred fifty suburban-looking houses going up in those neighborhoods that you describe as vacant. Detroit can be a very livable city. The worst is over. It's coming back.

"I've seen this in Newark. I've seen the same dynamic in the South Bronx, where literally five hundred homes have been built on what was Charlotte Street, the picture postcard of urban despair among cities, in East Brooklyn, in Youngstown, in Cleveland. Evidence is piling up that the cities have been to the bottom of the well and are clawing their way back up. I am absolutely convinced of this. All of our efforts have to be sustained, unabated, intensified, or we will have a flare-up like the one in Los Angeles, or in St. Petersburg, or in Indianapolis. The little sparks that happen every year can grow into a larger conflagration. There's still too much isolation where there are no jobs. There's still too much youth unemployment. There's still too many drugs destroying whole families' lives and creating a disconnection of people from any moorings. There's still too many youth gangs and violence, too many guns. And welfare reform is going to pose some very difficult problems. We must keep our eye on this ball. We are, by no stretch, out of the woods."

The former HUD secretary sees good policy and good economic times working in tandem. "I do think that the base conditions—a strong economy, lower interest rates, which means more investment, growing jobs in the national economy at large, CDCs—community development corporations—have found their sea legs, a breed of mayors who are very capable of doing things, a partnership-oriented federal government, led by the president, the vice president, empowerment zones—exist to help the cities continue to climb back."

For Americans who don't want to watch the final chapters in urban decline written in their lifetimes, Cisneros's words are a balm for sore hearts. But out there in the marketplace, people's individual choices are aggregating into a clear message about the near future for the Urban American Dream. When middle-class Americans—the people who fuel the massive shifts of national life, who stubbornly dictate the style of life by their sheer force of numbers—make their choice, it is for new-style cities, like San Jose and Houston, not for the old, dense cities of Baltimore, Newark, and St. Louis.

The fact that San Jose has risen to eclipse San Francisco in wealth and population is a sign of where things are going. The most mobile members of the professional white-collar class, with jobs that can go anywhere and the skills to produce goods sent over a phone line with a keyboard stroke, are voting for San Jose. They're bidding up bungalows to half a million dollars, filling the bike stores with $2,500 handmade two-wheelers, and creating land hunger that is revving up the natural life cycles of capitalism. Chip making has long since migrated to cheaper pastures, where a factory can languidly spread out without driving development costs through the roof. Writing and debugging software code goes on in Bangalore, India, while Silicon Valley executives sleep, and back-office operations are spreading out to Utah and Texas. The San Jose airport is rebuilding to be ready for another ten million annual passengers by 2010. All this while other cities, even cities with large, well-educated populations, struggle to hold white-collar jobs and enter fierce bidding wars to entice employers, whatever color collar comes with the jobs.

When Americans conjure up what a city will look like in 2050, it may be marked by open spaces, downtown highways, plazas, and malls. San Diego ain't Boston, and Seattle ain't Brooklyn. The emerging taste for a subset of urban lifestyles is clear. Smaller is better. Even the biggest cities are resisting the inertia of history, which made them big and then saw them stay big out of habit. The San Fernando Valley is actively trying to secede from the city of Los Angeles. Canvassers are swarming parking lots, movie theaters, and shopping malls looking for the 120,000 signatures that will force a commission into being to study the breakup. The Valley would become, in its own right, a major American city—its 1.3 million people spread out over a vast 275 square miles, with billions of dollars of taxable property making a formidable base. Leaders of the secession movement think the city on the other side of the mountains takes too much of the Valley's money to subsidize the poverty and high-cost social services of the central city.

A spokesman for Los Angeles Mayor Richard Riordan uses the argument of urban administrations since the turn of the last century, when five counties were cobbled together to make Greater New York. "One of the things that makes L.A. so powerful in the nation is its size, and that demands a lot of respect in Washington," said Noelia Rodriguez. The Valley, after it secedes from Los Angeles, is hardly little old Mayberry. It would be the sixth-largest city in the country. But the San Fernando secession movement, along with Staten Island's request for a divorce from New York, and the refusal of suburban communities across the country to incorporate with their big-city neighbors, sends a clear message: the American suspicion of urban gigantism as a virtue is still running strong.

When Scott Thomas talked to people moving to the country's smaller cities, he found common attributes that linked the communities at or near the top of the list. "The place that ranked highest in the nation was San Luis Obispo, California, which is a university town, and you'll find lots of university towns near the tops of my rankings, largely for the solidity of their educational systems, partially because they're economically strong, and you know they aren't going to be packing up and moving out of town the next day, as you'll see with so many factories in smaller communities. So they have a solid economic base.

"San Luis Obispo is also economically well situated between San Francisco and Los Angeles, not too close, yet close enough to benefit from proximity to both. The others that were at the top were Corvallis, Oregon—again, a university town—Fredericksburg, Virginia, which is about fifty miles south of Washington, D.C., but really on the outer fringe of the urban development of Washington, a quaint historic town still within commuting distance of D.C., and number four kind of nonplussed people, Fairbanks, Alaska, which did exceptionally well as far as education. It has the highest ratio of high school graduates of any small city in the country, for example. Weenatchie, Washington, which is a couple of hours inland from Seattle, was number five."

I t is my impression that color still trumps commonality of interests, professional status, or educational background when gathering the first, quick impressions about where to live. In 1997, *NBC News* did an hourlong documentary about racial change in the suburbs by looking at one town, Matteson, Illinois, in Chicago's far southwestern suburbs. In recent years, the black population had quadrupled but still represented little more than 10 percent of the entire population. The familiar signs of white flight were beginning to show, with an accelerating number of FOR SALE signs on Matteson lawns.

When NBC correspondents interviewed white residents, whether they contemplated staying or moving, they had remarkably similar impressions of what was happening to their town. They felt the schools were beginning to decline. They reported that crime had risen. And they said with some assurance that real estate prices would begin to decline as a result. Not coincidentally, these are all variables classically associated with an increased black presence in a community. The opinions of white Matteson residents did not seem to correct for the fact that their new black neighbors often had higher incomes than they themselves and in most cases were paying more than they did for their houses.

In fact real estate prices had been rising all along and continued to rise. Crime in various categories had dropped. Standardized testing scores had risen in the past five years.

In the end, there may be no "unified field theory" of urban America on the edge of a new century. Different cities will try the same things—downtown housing, new cultural centers, light rail—and yield spectacularly different results. Some cities simply have too little going for them, and while they may not end up with tumbleweed rolling down Main Street, an easily identifiable entropy has set in, an accumulation of too many holes in the canoe and too few passengers to help bail.

Many of those who love the cities are already in them. Luring a large number of people in for a first taste, or to return, may remain a vain hope, as billions in new infrastructure investment continue to pour into suburbs. Many suburbs recognize their problems—poorly designed street patterns, isolating patterns of commercial zoning—but their robust tax bases leave them more able than many of the cities they surround to redesign themselves. Even with all the demolition going on inside the city limits, the physical skeleton of urban street patterns and existing structures prove too rigid in many places, compared with the permanently soft clay of the suburbs. Investment drifts, almost by default, to the "easier," beckoning suburbs.

The federal government has largely gotten out of the business of supporting cities, and if the prevailing political winds continue to blow from the right beyond the 1990s, that trend will continue. For all the complaints about ongoing subsidies, urban America is more and more on its own. This sink-or-swim challenge to the cities continues as suburbs go on enjoying tremendous visible and invisible subsidy—putting a house on a soybean field at the end of a new highway is far more expensive than building a house closer in, but that cost differential is not apparent in the purchase price of the new suburban house.

There is a good life to be had in cities large and small, but Americans are going to have to mean what they say, and say what they mean, in the coming years, for the sickest places to stabilize and the healthy members of the litter to remain the social and cultural engines of their regions. The code and the cant are going to have to be stripped from the things we say to each other. We have to look each other square in the face and be ready to talk about race, schools, and housing, and where jobs go, and where they don't. The essential ingredient to a sane and coherent life–honesty–has been in drastically short supply, while the cities burned and the new siding was hammered into place just over the line.

The American city is a stubborn club fighter, fat lip and all. After a long pounding, the crowd was looking for wobbly knees and a glassy stare. But this pug knows the fight is just half over.

Index